W9-AYR-699

INDEX YOUR WAY TO INVESTMENT SUCCESS

About the Authors

Walter R. Good, CFA, planned and organized this book and created the text. **Roy W. Hermansen, CFA,** conducted the analysis required for the many tables and other quantitative references, created the extensive graphic displays, and contributed importantly to the editorial content.

Walter R. Good has managed institutional investments both as plan sponsor and external investment manager. As a consultant to large institutional investors, he has worked with both private and public retirement funds as well as philanthropic organizations. He has served as managing partner of Capital Market Systems, president and director of the Mellon Universe Management Group, chairman of the pension investment committee of The Continental Group, Inc., and, earlier, as chief investment officer and director of research at major investment firms. Consulting arrangements have included membership on the Investment Advisory Panel of the Pension Benefit Guarantee Corporation and the Advisory Council to the New York City pension funds. A member of the editorial board of the *Financial Analysts Journal,* Good is also coauthor of two recent books that address investment issues: Walter R. Good, Roy W. Hermansen, and Jack R. Meyer, *Active Asset Allocation: Gaining Advantage in a Highly Efficient Stock Market,* McGraw-Hill, New York, 1993; Walter R. Good and Douglas A. Love, *Managing Pension Assets: Pension Finance & Corporate Financial Goals,* McGraw-Hill, New York, 1990. Memberships in affiliates of the Association for Investment Management and Research (AIMR) include The Institute of Chartered Financial Analysts (ICFA), The New York Society of Security Analysts, and the Stamford Chapter of the Hartford Society of Financial Analysts. Good holds undergraduate and MBA degrees from the University of Chicago.

Roy W. Hermansen has been responsible for institutional assets as a plan sponsor, external manager, and consultant. He has served as a partner in Capital Market Systems, executive vice president of Mellon Universe Management Group, director of portfolio development at The Continental Group, Inc. and as a security analyst specializing in technology stocks at a major investment counseling firm. He is coauthor of *Active Asset Allocation: Gaining Advantage in a Highly Efficient Stock Market,* as indicated above. Memberships in affiliates of the Association for Investment Management and Research (AIMR) include The Institute of Chartered Financial Analysts (ICFA) and The New York Society of Security Analysts. Hermansen is also a member of The Institute of Electrical and Electronics Engineers, Inc. He holds degrees in electrical engineering and engineering physics from Lehigh University and an MBA from Columbia University.

INDEX YOUR WAY
TO INVESTMENT SUCCESS

Walter R. Good
Roy W. Hermansen

NEW YORK INSTITUTE OF FINANCE

NEW YORK • TORONTO • SYDNEY • TOKYO • SINGAPORE

121108916

Library of Congress Cataloging-in-Publication Data

Good, Walter R.
   Index your way to investment success / Walter R. Good and Roy W.
   Hermansen.
      p.   cm.
   Includes index.
   ISBN 0-13-254020-7 (cloth)
      1. Mutual funds.   I. Hermansen, Roy W.   II. Title.
   HG4530.G66   1997
   332.63'27—DC21   97-39556
                                                            CIP

© 2000 by Prentice Hall
Paramus, NJ 07652

All rights reserved. No part of this book may be reproduced in any form or by any means,
without permission in writing from the publisher.

NYIF and New York Institute of Finance are trademarks of Executive Tax Reports , Inc.
used under license by Prentice Hall Direct, Inc.

This publication is designed to provide accurate and authoritative information in regard to
the subject matter covered. It is sold with the understanding that the publisher is not engaged
in rendering legal, accounting, or other professional service. If legal advice or other expert as-
sistance is required, the services of a competent professional person should be sought.

From a Declaration of Principles Jointly Adapted by a Committee of the American Bar Association
and a Committee of Publishers and Associations

Printed in the United States of America

10 9 8 7 6 5 4 3 2 1   10 9 8 7 6 5 4 3 2 1

ISBN 0-13-254020-7(c)   ISBN 0-7352-0135-8 (p)

ATTENTION: CORPORATIONS AND SCHOOLS
NYIF books are available at quantity discounts with bulk purchase for educational, business, or sales promotional use. For information, please write to: Prentice Hall Special
Sales, 240 Frisch Court, Paramus, NJ 07652. Please supply: title of book, ISBN, quantity,
how the book will be used, date needed.

NEW YORK INSTITUTE OF FINANCE
An Imprint of Prentice Hall Press

Paramus, NJ 07652

On the World Wide Webb at http://www.phdirect.com

To the next generation of investors,
Elizabeth Good Christopherson, Deborah J. Good,
William W. Good, Eric W. Hermansen, and Susan E. Hermansen

With much appreciation for the encouragement of spouses
Jean S. Good and Marilyn Y. Hermansen

CONTENTS

FOREWORD

Way back in 1951, in my Princeton University senior thesis entitled "The Economic Role of the Investment Company," I was bold enough to forecast great growth potential for mutual funds, then a $2-billion cottage industry. Today they have become a national force with assets at *$4 trillion,* and my optimism has surely been affirmed. In my thesis I called for a reduction in management fees, cautioned against the expectation of miracles from management, and warned against claiming superiority over the market averages.

Whether these three ideas were just the idealistic musings of a callow undergraduate or the prescient harbingers of the coming of the market index mutual fund, I leave to wiser heads. But I surely never dreamed that within 50 years, the index fund: (1) would be recognized as a truly superior performer during the 1980s and 1990s; (2) would come to represent the most rapidly growing sector of the mutual fund industry; and (3) would be the subject of a major book, *Index Your Way to Investment Success* by Walter Good and Roy Hermansen.

Both principle and pride demand that I acknowledge that The Vanguard Group—the mutual fund complex I founded in 1974—formed the first index mutual fund just two years later, and is today universally regarded as the major force among index mutual funds. Principle, certainly, as a matter of full disclosure: I am not a dispassionate observer, but an advocate, indeed a missionary, of the concept of indexing. But pride, too, as our pioneering index fund, at first the subject of amusement and sarcasm (Bogle's Folly), gradually came into its own, confirming in practice the validity of the simple theory that underlies indexing. With $45 billion of assets as I write these words, that first index fund has grown to become the second largest among the 3000 equity funds that now exist in the United States. Moreover, it has been joined by 20 other Vanguard index funds, plus 4 asset allocation funds using index funds as their investments, bringing the firm's total index fund assets to $100 billion.

The theory of indexing, in its simplest form, comes down to this syllogism: (1) the *gross* returns of all investors and managers, *as a group*, must equal the aggregate *gross* returns of the financial markets in which they invest; (2) the *net* returns of those investors must fall short of the market returns by the amount of their costs of participation in the market—advisory fees, other investment expenses, and portfolio transaction costs. Since those costs can be estimated with some confidence—about 2% of assets per year for investors in equity mutual funds, for example—it should follow that in a market providing a 10% annual return, the typical mutual fund should provide a return of about 8%. In Chapter 3 of *Index Your Way to Investment Success*, Good and Hermansen, using much more detailed analysis, arrive at a similar figure in their striking "sticker shock" examples.

The performance records of mutual funds have provided practical confirmation of this elementary theory. Over the past 15 years, clearly a halcyon era for equity investments, a low-cost, passively managed index fund based on the Standard & Poor's 500 Stock Index provided an average annual return of 16%. Morningstar Mutual Funds reports that the average common stock mutual fund provided an average annual return of 14% during the same span. Result: the 2% differential in practice confirms the 2% difference suggested by theory.

And this 2% differential matters. A 16% return over 15 years turns $10,000 into $92,700; a 14% return produces $71,400. The difference: an astonishing $21,300, a value added that itself is more than twice the amount of the initial stake of $10,000. And bear in mind that 15 years is only a fraction of an investment lifetime. Today, young workers may begin accumulating savings in a corporate 401(k) thrift plan or an Individual Retirement Account in their mid-twenties, and are likely to be enjoying the fruits of their savings at age 75 and beyond. Over 50 years, at, say, a more normal historical return of 10%, $10,000 grows to $1,174,000. At 8%, $10,000 grows to

$469,000. The difference: a staggering $705,000, a value added that is 70 *times* the initial stake. The magic of compounding writ large!

To be sure, the past 15 years may have been too good to be true for indexing, but even a 1% advantage, extended over the decades, would represent a priceless enhancement to performance. That said, and despite the success of indexing, it remains quite possible for a relative handful of mutual fund investors to outpace a market index fund, either by selecting a single fund that tops the index over a 50-year period, or perhaps by choosing a winning fund over one decade, then a winner over the next decade, and so on over a half century. Only time will tell.

Alas, the possibilities of success in picking these winners are not encouraging. If the odds in favor of a mutual fund with a typical cost structure significantly outpacing a market index are (as recent history suggests) about 1 in 10 over a decade, the odds of doing so in two consecutive decades are 1 in 100; in three decades, 1 in 1,000; in four decades, 1 in 10,000; and in five decades, 1 in 100,000.

Selecting the best performers from among the thousands of mutual funds out there today is a formidable task, for only a few funds—and they are incredibly difficult to identify *in advance*—will succeed in overcoming both: (1) the pull of gravity represented by the power of regression to the mean; and (2) the fiscal drag of high advisory fees and heavy transaction costs. Index fund theory and practice alike suggest that combing past performance records or analyzing present portfolio structures to select future winners is rarely worth the effort. The herculean odds in doing so confirm Alexander Pope's words:

> "Hope springs eternal in the human breast:
> Man never is, but always to be blest."

But it is not at all certain that the past record is too good to be true. Indeed, the past, never a certain prologue to an inevitably speculative future, may even prove to have *understated* the dimension of index investment success. First, as Good and Hermansen note, on an *after-tax basis* index funds have provided even better relative returns, given that their low portfolio turnover structure minimizes the current realization of taxable capital gains. Second, the index fund performance domination has come despite giving actively managed funds the benefit of a very large doubt, for the records of those funds that did not survive the full period—the poorer performers—are ignored. (The authors cite evidence that this "survivor bias" overstates mutual fund returns by nearly 1.5% per year.) Third, and perhaps most importantly, the mutual fund industry has grown from infant to colossus during the past two decades. In the years to come, it may well prove even more difficult for fund portfolio managers, now owning more than 20% of all U.S. equities, to distinguish themselves. It seems more likely that the managers of the giant funds will become mere faces in the crowd.

That said, the mounting and persuasive evidence that mutual fund *costs* should be given the same attention as *risk* and *return* (together, in my view, "the eternal triangle of investing") may well cause the industry to look to its own interests and reduce costs in the years ahead. Not even a sweeping and astonishing 33% industrywide cost reduction (taking the average annual equity fund expense ratio from 1.5% to 1.0%) would eliminate the wide advantage enjoyed by a low-cost index fund. But enlightened self-interest may well compel the major fund groups to share at least some of the awesome economies of scale in fund management with too-long-deprived fund shareholders. In this sense, one of the major roles of indexing may be to act as a catalyst for change in the mutual fund industry.

Whether that change happens or not—or whether it matters—is only a matter of speculation. What is, I think, far easier to predict is that the index wave is just beginning. A decade from now, index funds will be offered, one way or another, by all of the industry titans, though they may have been dragged, kicking and screaming, into the indexing arena. And they will have to offer, not just a single fund modeled on the Standard & Poor's 500 Index, but a whole array of funds in different segments of the stock and bond markets.

In all, Walter Good and Roy Hermansen have provided us with a remarkable compendium of indexing—theory and practice, basics and variations, and asset allocations—the first study of its kind. It is with a high level of confidence that I predict it will not be the last book on the subject, as index funds of all varieties come into their own—a new force for the individual investor. *Index Your Way to Investment Success* is a landmark book. I commend it to you.

JOHN C. BOGLE
Chairman of the Board
The Vanguard Group of Investment Companies
August 27, 1997

PREFACE

The proliferation of index mutual funds in recent years offers individual investors expanding opportunity to participate in the rewards of indexing. Over most of the past quarter century, retirement and endowment funds have led the way. Since the introduction of indexing in the 1970s, these professionally managed institutions have increased their aggregate investment in stock and bond index funds to *more than $1 trillion.* In comparison, holdings of index funds by individual investors are still very small—*but they are now growing at a much faster rate.* Assets of index mutual funds broadly available to individual investors have expanded from $4 billion as recently as 1990 to more than $58 billion by 1996.

The authors have shaped this book to meet the needs of a broad spectrum of individual investors, irrespective of portfolio size. The potential contribution of indexing to investment performance, as documented here, is almost certain to surprise most readers—those with multimillion-dollar portfolios as well as those just beginning to invest. After identifying the full extent of the benefits, we show the investor how to incorporate indexing in an individually designed investment program. As indicated below, customizing the portfolio allows for wide differences in the market value of portfolio assets:

- Although most examples refer to a $100,000 portfolio, they readily adapt to much larger or much smaller portfolios.

- We also show how to get started, even if the initial investment is as small as a few thousand dollars—or even a few hundred dollars.

- For larger portfolios, we identify adjustments to improve diversification and increase flexibility.

- For the investor delegating portfolio management to an outside advisor, the index-fund framework presented in the book offers tools urgently needed to manage the manager. They include a commonsense way of gauging portfolio risk and a simple method of evaluating portfolio performance.

Acknowledgments

The authors thank the many industry sources that have generously made available information and advice. For detailed information on the more than 7,000 individual mutual funds, we have relied on *Morningstar Principia for Mutual Funds*. In a related area, The Investment Company Institute has provided a wealth of data on investor participation in mutual funds. Michael J. Clowes, Editor of *Pensions & Investments*, has served as an indispensable source of statistics on institutional investment management. Wayne H. Wagner, President of the Plexus Group and a leading consultant to institutional investors on trading costs, has shared his special expertise in this area.

Sponsors of the leading investment indexes have provided updating of data as well as historical background. For information on domestic equity indexes, we thank Dow Jones & Company Inc., Standard & Poor's Corporation, Wilshire Associates, Inc. and Frank Russell Company. We depended on Morgan Stanley Capital International for information on a widely recognized family of foreign stock indexes. Lehman Brothers made available information on the firm's extensive family of bond indexes.

Mutual fund families that offer index funds to the individual investor provided supplementary information as well as extensive background in fund prospectuses. Of the 10 leading fund families (as determined by total assets under management), we very much appreciate help from the four that offer one or more index funds:

The Vanguard Group, Fidelity Management and Research Company, T. Rowe Price, and Merrill Lynch Asset Management. A number of other fund families also provided helpful information. They include Schwab Funds and Galaxy Funds, each of which offers four or more index mutual funds.

We express special appreciation to The Vanguard Group of Investment Companies, which pioneered index mutual funds and continues as the industry leader by a wide margin. We benefited from the help of John C. (Jack) Bogle, Chairman of the Board; George U. ("Gus") Sauter, Managing Director, Core Management Group; and Kenneth E. Volpert, Principal, Fixed Income Group. James H. Gately, Managing Director, Individual Investor Group, and John S. Woerth, Communications Manager, Corporate Communications, provided additional perspective. Jack Bogle and Gus Sauter, as readers of our draft, contributed many useful observations. We particularly thank Jack Bogle for writing the foreword to our book.

Several distinguished readers, in addition to Jack Bogle and Gus Sauter, contributed valuable insight, each approaching the subject of indexing from a different vantage point. We are very fortunate to have had the advice of Jack R. Meyer, President and Chief Executive Officer, Harvard Management Company; Burton G. Malkiel, Chemical Bank Chairman's Professor of Economics, Princeton University; and R. Charles Tschampion, CFA, Managing Director, General Motors Investment Management Corporation. We greatly appreciate their help.

Ellen Schneid Coleman, Executive Editor at Prentice Hall, early recognized the growing importance of indexing for individual investors. We very much appreciate her wise counsel as we wrote. We also thank Barry Richardson, Development Editor, for his careful reading of our draft and his many suggestions.

WALTER R. GOOD

ROY W. HERMANSEN

HOW LESS BECOMES MORE

Surging Index Funds

A growing number of investors—first, institutions and, more recently, individuals—are discovering the benefits of indexing. Index funds held by institutional investors (retirement plans and endowment funds) have grown from around $10 billion in 1980 to more than $1 trillion by the end of 1996. Although the rate of increase for institutional investors has moderated in recent years, individual investors are now beginning to move into index funds at an extremely vigorous pace. Index mutual funds broadly available to individual investors amounted to only $4 billion as recently as 1990. By year end 1996—just 6 years later—their market value had increased to more than $58 billion.

What accounts for the rapidly increasing acceptance of index funds? On first encounter, indexing may seem to offer *much less* than does traditional investing. Indexing uses *much less* financial and economic information, *much less* forecasting of market price changes and *much less* buying and selling of securities. As investors increasingly recognize the benefits of indexing, however, they begin to understand how *less can become more—even much*

1

more. The purpose of this book is to identify the benefits of indexing and to show you how these benefits can contribute to your investment success.

How Indexing Differs from Active Investing

Before we consider the benefits of indexing, let's first look at the difference between index funds and actively managed funds. Indexing and active investing differ from each other in a very fundamental way.

The goal of an index fund is to match the total return (income plus market price appreciation) of a designated index. To this end, it may replicate all of the issues represented in the index, or, alternatively, rely on a sampling technique. Careful design permits the sample to reflect key characteristics of the index with fewer issues than are included in the index itself.

The goal of active investing, in contrast, is to achieve investment returns superior to that of the index fund. Pursuit of this goal implies superior forecasting skill—sufficiently superior to overcome index fund advantages relating to costs, deferral of capital gains taxes, and risk control. Rigorous performance measurement has increasingly demonstrated how difficult it is to identify superior forecasting skill before the fact.

Forecasting, as the central element in active management, may take various forms that do not necessarily wear the label. The most clearly defined examples include specific targets for both the price and the time horizon. A forecaster, for example, may conclude that the broad stock averages will rise by about 20% over the coming year, or, alternatively, that a particular stock is likely to double, say, in two years. More commonly, a forecast refers in a less precise way to valuation or relative attraction. To conclude that stocks are overvalued implies increased likelihood of unfavorable market performance. Similarly, "attractive" stocks are generally expected to provide better outcomes than those rated "unattractive." A decision to delegate investment responsibility to an external portfolio manager also represents an exercise in forecasting. Institutional investors have traditionally focused on selecting the portfolio manager most likely to demonstrate superior skill in anticipating the financial markets. The challenge, according to this view, is to forecast the winning forecasters. The individual investor encounters the same forecasting challenge in choosing a mutual fund.

Not Just the S&P 500

Although the most widely held index mutual fund aims to match the return of the S&P 500, other index funds are rapidly gaining market share. They target major segments of the publicly traded markets for domestic stocks, foreign stocks, and domestic bonds.

To illustrate the application of indexing to various segments of the financial markets, this book relies on the Vanguard family of index funds. As the pioneer in introducing index mutual funds to the individual investor, The Vanguard Group offers by far the most extensive line at the current time. Since we do not recommend specific investments, Appendix 7-1 also lists other index mutual funds broadly available to individual investors at year end 1996. The accompanying toll-free telephone numbers enable you to secure prospectuses and other up-to-date information needed to compare alternative index mutual funds.

How Big Are the Benefits?

How big are the benefits of indexing? Although they vary with the circumstances, they often amount to considerably more than you may realize. Many investors, especially those with portfolios of moderate size, pay too little attention to four items that subtract directly from mutual fund returns, as listed in Table I-1. Chapters 3 and 4 provide details concerning how each of these items reduces the return that the investor actually realizes from investment in a mutual fund. By way of overview, we briefly comment here on the combined burden these factors place on returns. Application of the principles presented in this book will almost always reduce this burden by a significant amount. For many investors, savings can average 2% to 3% *per year*—and more.

Table I-1: Four areas of potential savings.

Opportunity for Savings	Explanation
Loads, front end or deferred	Sales charge
Expenses	Management, administration, distribution
Transaction costs	Brokerage commissions plus market impact
Personal income taxes	Both ordinary income and capital gains

These savings do not take into account additional index fund benefits in the area of risk management. Actively managed funds, striving to achieve superior performance, may also generate returns that fall far short of the corresponding index fund returns. Because an index fund stresses diversification within the market segment that it represents, it controls risk better than a less-well-diversified portfolio.

The savings made possible by indexing expand dramatically over the longer term. Savings of 2% to 3% per year may seem modest in comparison with the extraordinary stock-market gains in recent years. The S&P 500 registered a total return of almost 23% in 1996 and a compound annual rate of more than 15% for the decade ended 1996. A more realistic benchmark for gauging the future outlook, however, is the average over a much longer period. For the S&P 500, the compound annual rate of return over 1926–1996 amounted to 10.7%. If a mutual fund could achieve this return *before* deductions for expenses, transaction costs, and sales load, the net return to the shareholder *after* these deductions and allowance for personal income taxes would be much lower.

To underscore the cumulative impact of annual savings of 2% to 3% per year, Figure I-1 traces the growth of investor wealth over 20 years. Suppose that you invest $10,000 in each of three different equity mutual funds. For purposes of this example, all three funds provide exactly the same rate of return of 10% annually before deductions for expenses, transaction costs, and sales loads. The first bar on the left assumes that your investment in the index equity mutual fund returns 8% *after* personal income taxes. The return reflects very limited expenses, negligible transactions costs, and the absence of sales load. Meanwhile, your tax burden benefits from deferral of most capital gains taxes to the end of the holding period. Fund A (middle bar) and Fund B (at the right) identify the two actively managed mutual funds. Your net return after taxes from either Fund A or B is significantly lower than from the index fund. Not only are there substantially larger deductions for expenses and transaction costs, but a sales load may provide a further disadvantage. In addition, a higher tax burden results from less advantageous scheduling of realized capital gains.

Over an extended period, moderate differences in annual rate of return result in startling differences in total wealth. With an annu-

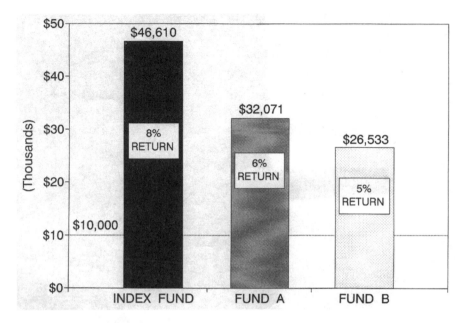

Figure I-1: BENEFITS OF INDEXING (20-YEAR AFTER-TAX COMPARISONS). Comparison of index equity mutual fund with actively managed mutual fund assumes no difference in returns before costs and taxes. It illustrates how savings in costs, together with deferral of capital gains taxes, can add to investor wealth over the longer term.

al rate of return two percentage points less than for the index fund, Fund A provides a compound annual rate of return of only 6% after taxes. For Fund B, the annual rate of return is three percentage points less than for the index fund, or 5% after taxes. These rates of return compounded over 20 years mean that the index fund would grow to $46,610 compared with $32,071 for Fund A and $26,533 for Fund B.

Identifying the Benefits

The advantages of indexing are cumulative. In any one year, no single benefit may seem very significant, but they add up to a formidable total over an extended period. We identify here benefits in three areas: cost savings, tax deferral, and risk control. Details follow in Chapters 3 and 4.

Cutting Costs

Expense savings provide the most readily identifiable cost advantage of index funds, but differences in transaction costs and sales loads may contribute even more to holding down costs. Expenses include management fees and administrative and distribution costs. Transaction costs, which accumulate as securities are bought and sold, reflect the spread between purchase and sale prices realized by the market maker, as well as commissions charged by brokers. Accordingly, transaction costs subtract from market value. A sales load—which applies to about 60% of actively managed equity mutual funds—is often too easily overlooked. Because it is usually a one-time charge, the investor is likely to omit the annualized cost from assessment of year-to-year investment returns. For equity mutual funds, the expense ratio, which is a matter of public record, likely amounts to 0.5 to 2.0 percentage points more than for the competing low-cost index fund. Transaction costs account for an additional significant difference, with estimates often ranging between 0.5 to 2.0 percentage points and, in certain circumstances, even more. The burden of the sales load on annual rate of return can cover a much wider range, depending not only on the magnitude of the load, but also the holding period over which the charges are allocated. We defer specific examples of the reduction of investment returns as a result of the sales load to Chapters 3 and 4. For a tax-deferred portfolio such as an IRA or 401(k) account, expenses, transaction costs, and the annualized charge for the sales load subtract directly from investment return.

Reducing the Tax Burden

For a taxable portfolio, the index mutual fund is likely to benefit further in comparison with the actively managed mutual fund because of sharply different policies concerning realization of capital gains. Index funds, reflecting a very low level of turnover, ordinarily generate very little capital gains taxes from year to year. To the extent the fund defers such taxes, more assets are available to earn returns. Other things equal, the compound rate of return is higher over the holding period even after allowance for payment of the taxes that eventually come due on redemption of the shares. The benefits are even greater if the capital gains taxes never come due for any one of several reasons. The investment may pass into an estate or, as a gift, to a tax-exempt recipient. Other possibilities include change in the taxable income of the shareholder or revision in the tax code.

For the more extended holding periods, the index fund advantage resulting from deferral of capital gains taxes is only partially offset by the deductibility for tax purposes of expenses, transaction costs, and sales loads. Since the higher expenses associated with active investing subtract from ordinary income, they result in a corresponding reduction in taxes on ordinary income. Similar arithmetic applies to the differential in transaction costs between index mutual funds and actively managed mutual funds. Because the much higher transaction costs ordinarily reported by actively managed funds subtract from market value, they correspondingly reduce the potential for realized capital gains and the taxes thereon.

The index fund tax advantage varies with applicable tax bracket, the holding period, and the characteristics of the actively managed fund. At one extreme, the tax advantage disappears because the investments are held in a tax-deferred account [such as a 401(k) plan or an IRA] or turnover for the actively managed fund may be extremely low. For most taxable accounts, however, the long-term tax advantage of index funds is likely to be significant. Deferral of capital gains taxes, after allowance for liability at the end of the holding period, may benefit the annual rate of return by a large fraction of 1%. Absent liability for capital gains at the end of the holding period, the index fund advantage relating to capital gains taxes may amount to significantly more. While personal income taxes reduce the index fund advantage relating to expenses, transaction costs, and sales loads, the net result of income taxes (including deferral of capital gains taxes) is likely to increase the index fund advantage as the holding period lengthens.

Indexing Limits Risk

In the absence of superior forecasting skill, index funds limit risk in two ways. One way concerns *superior diversification*. The other way derives from *tight restrictions on incremental risk taking*.

Superior Diversification.   An index fund, reflecting broad diversification, will be much less volatile than the individual stocks included in it. Many of the stocks in the index will provide higher returns while at least as many will likely lag the performance of the index. The investor, if he or she has no way of distinguishing the prospective winners and losers, wisely diversifies by purchasing the stocks representing the entire index. The same logic applies to mutual funds that are less well diversified than the index from which the manager makes selections. Other things equal, lack of diversification signals increased risk.

Tight Restrictions.   A well-managed index fund provides a high degree of protection against unanticipated risk taking because its composition is so predictable. The investor in an index fund, in attempting to understand future risks for the fund, benefits from past history of the index. Should the index fund manager stray very far from the securities that represent the relevant index, the resulting discrepancy in performance would immediately stand out.

The manager of an actively managed mutual fund, striving to achieve performance superior to the index despite higher expenses and transaction costs, does not encounter the same tight restrictions. An actively managed mutual fund may revise the risk characteristics of the fund through substantial departures from previous practice, as permitted by the broad limits of the prospectus. For example, an equity fund manager may shift from high-quality, large-capitalization (large-cap) stocks to much more volatile small-capitalization (small-cap) issues or reshape a broadly diversified portfolio to concentrate heavily on one or two favored industries. Conversely, unusual buildup of cash or bonds in an equity portfolio to protect against lower stock prices risks lost opportunity if stock prices suddenly begin a strong uptrend. Shareholders may not recognize the evolving risk until trouble develops.

A portfolio of several stocks owned directly by the individual investor, as an alternative to mutual funds, may result in even higher risk. Apart from the risks associated with limited diversification, the investor acting on judgments concerning individual issues may drift into increased risk without fully realizing the expanding downside potential.

Using Index Funds as a Tool

To recognize the advantages of index funds does not automatically provide sound investment management. Consider the range of challenging questions that every investor must still confront:

- Which index funds should you hold?
- When should you change the mix?
- To what extent should you substitute an actively managed fund for all or part of an index fund?
- How should you measure the success of active strategy?

Emphasis on *index funds* rather than *indexes* underscores an important difference. An index fund, in contrast to the index on which it is based, describes an actual investment. Consideration of the return from the index fund therefore requires allowance for expenses, transaction costs, and also possible tax consequences. Investment managers for large tax-exempt funds may ignore such differences, since, in their situation, index fund expenses and transaction costs may constitute a very small percentage of assets, and taxes are not an issue. For the individual investing in an index mutual fund, however, the burden of expenses, if not transaction costs, becomes more significant, and tax considerations are likely to be important. By incorporating an allowance for these items in our assessment of the outlook for index mutual funds, we also emphasize their significance in comparisons of index funds with alternative investments.

How Much Risk?

Development of a long-term investment plan constitutes the most important single investment decision that you are likely to make. Among individual investors, it may also be the most widely neglected part of the investment decision process. The long-term plan defines how aggressive the investor wants to be and how much risk he or she is willing to accept. For any investor—individual as well as institutional—the composition of the long-term plan constitutes a statement of investment objectives. Long-term plans differ markedly from one investor to another because their objectives differ. Investing with the wrong plan—or no plan—courts investment disaster.

Index funds provide an effective framework for identifying the target. How would you arrange your investment portfolio for the longer term if index funds were the only investment option? What allowance should you make for expenses, transaction costs, and taxes? Chapters 6 and 7 show you, in easy steps, how to develop an answer. The resulting long-term plan does not preclude other investment vehicles, but *index funds define the standard that alternative investments must exceed.*

Staying Out of Big Trouble

Risk management follows from development of your long-term plan. Reflecting your objectives, the long-term plan defines the combination of index funds that would provide a level of risk acceptable to you. To contain risk at the level incorporated in the long-term plan requires that your actual investment portfolio conform to the index funds represented in your plan. To control risk, you control departures from the plan. For example, you may identify what you consider to be a particularly attractive investment opportunity. Or you may differ with the marketplace concerning the pricing of stocks or bonds or various segments of these broad groups. The resulting departures from your long-term plan entail incremental risks as well as opportunities for incremental gain. We shall explain how to contain these special risks at acceptable levels.

Raising the Hurdle

Appreciation of the benefits of indexing does not preclude active investing, but it raises the hurdle that such investments must clear. Our approach to indexing leaves room for departures from indexing with the aim of exploiting superior forecasting skill—to the extent it can be identified. In this application, indexing serves the investor in two ways. First, it provides a more rigorous standard for selection of other investment vehicles. The key issue is whether the proposed investment offers better overall prospects than the index fund that it would replace. Second, the same index fund provides the benchmark for evaluating the returns of the active investment after the fact. Positive or negative performance depends on how well net returns, including differences in the tax burden, compare with those for the relevant index fund.

Flowering of a New Industry

Indexing differs so dramatically from traditional investing that it might be described as a new industry. It operates from very different assumptions concerning the workings of the financial markets. It permits the investor to keep most of the fees and charges that traditional investing transfers to various specialists in marketing, trading, and decision making. It stresses deferral of capital gains taxes and pays particular attention to risk control. To underscore the impact of this innovative approach on the practice of traditional investing, we look to the experience of the large financial institutions that have led the way in the use of index funds.

When Indexing Had No Friends (Almost)

When first offered to institutional investors more than 25 years ago, indexing encountered heated resistance. Wells Fargo Bank pioneered index funds, offering its first product in 1971. (Barclays Global Investors, having acquired the index fund operations initially established by Wells Fargo Bank, continues to serve the institutional market as the leading manager of index funds.) The early years generated much more negative reaction than marketing success. Acceptance of indexing in the second half of the 1970s by a few large pension funds, including AT&T, changed the prevailing mood only marginally. Even though additional indexers gradually entered the business, by 1980 total holdings of index funds amounted to less than 1% of the market value of publicly traded domestic stocks. Most institutional investors would have nothing to do with index funds, and, seeing indexing as a challenge to common sense, they often presented their conclusions in less than diplomatic language. By way of example, consider the following *Fortune* magazine report of a meeting in early 1976, when indexing was just beginning to find a role in a few large pension funds:

> ...Richard Posner [then professor at the University of Chicago Law School] gave a talk at a conference on pension fund investing at New York's Plaza Hotel. Posner was by far the least popular speaker at the conference. As the drift of his message began to get across to the audience, an angry buzz filled the Terrace Room; before he had finished speaking, many in the audience were no longer listening, but denouncing him to others at their tables. Subsequent speakers warmed themselves to the group by starting off with slighting references to Posner's remarks.

The reason for this ill will was all too clear. The audience consisted mainly of professional money managers, most of whom pride themselves on their ability to offer superior investment performance. Posner's message was that they are wasting their time. It is impossible to beat the market averages, he insisted, and efforts to do so are expensive and self-defeating. The managers would do better, Posner argued, by investing their customers' assets in "index funds"—portfolios that duplicate broad stock market averages like the Standard and Poor's 500.[1]

Although many encounters such as the Plaza Hotel meeting were repeated in the 1970s, the academic studies cited by the proponents of indexing resulted in very few early conversions. Many institutional investors simply paid little attention, dismissing as gobbledygook the theoretical arguments quoted from academic journals. Some, comparing indexing to the many investment fads that come and go, quickly dismissed it as just plain silly, if not outrageous. Others, building on hasty but erroneous impressions, contrived straw men that could easily be demolished. Triumphantly, they would ask: "*If everyone indexed*, how could indexing work?" or, alternatively, "*If stocks are always worth the market price*, please explain the severe losses that would have been incurred by an index fund bought at the market peak in 1929."

While some institutional investors saw merit in the sobering message directed to traditional investment managers, they also recognized practical constraints. Application of indexing to day-to-day investment management requires judgments hardly ever addressed by theoreticians. Since, in practice, index funds fall short in varying degrees from the theoretical model, decision makers have to determine which indexes best serve the client's purpose. Several early efforts ran into trouble because they attempted to match a poorly chosen index. Other major challenges include allocation of assets among the various index funds, timing of the initial commitments, and rebalancing as market prices change. An ongoing practical issue, moreover, concerns the coordination of indexing with other forms of investment management. The evidence in favor of indexing, although it does not preclude opportunity to gain advantage through superior forecasting, makes clear that such gains are much more difficult to achieve than most institutional investors have wanted to believe. Index fund theory, nevertheless, leaves the door open for truly superior forecasting—if it can be

---

[1]A. F. Ehrbar, "Index Funds—An Idea Whose Time Is Coming," *Fortune,* June 1976, p. 145. Copyright © 1976 Time Inc. All rights reserved.

identified—and for investment decision makers who are able to find ways to make it pay.

From the vantage point of the early 1970s, an observer might well have asked if indexing would ever be taken seriously. More than a few institutional investors initially regarded index funds as a "nutty" idea. Pioneer indexers, on occasion, made mistakes in the choice of the index, which not only embarrassed them but also served to underscore their folly in the eyes of their critics. Established trust law, which required trustees to act prudently in putting funds at risk, added to the misgivings. Is it prudent to buy any issue included in an index without careful consideration of the outlook for its market price? The lonely few who accepted the broad outlines of the argument in favor of indexing faced another obstacle. They recognized the enormous practical differences between index fund theory and day-to-day investment management. For many clients, meanwhile, owning an index fund was like flying in an airliner without a pilot. Who would be in charge when trouble developed?

Burgeoning Growth

Despite the less than warm welcome initially accorded index funds, conditions were in place by the 1970s to open the door to burgeoning growth. In the long history of investing, there were no index funds prior to the 1970s. Advancing computer technology, while reshaping many aspects of active investing, also played a decisive role in making a place for index funds.

- Computer processing of market price data served academic researchers in developing and testing the theories that underlie indexing. By the end of the 1960s, these studies began to receive attention, not only in academic journals, but also in the financial press. Increasingly, MBA candidates in the leading business schools became familiar with the evolving evidence. As they gradually took over responsibility for investment management, they brought with them increasing recognition of the merits of indexing.

- Computer capability facilitated translation of index fund theory into the practical creation and maintenance of index funds. During the early 1970s, the standard index fund matched the S&P 500, but soon the choice broadened considerably. Table I-2 provides a partial listing of indexes now represented in institutional funds. Custom indexes may be designed to reflect an area of the investment spectrum otherwise not adequately tracked by a standard index.

- Huge savings in transaction costs permitted by introduction of negotiated commissions in the early 1970s reflected in part efficiencies made possible by advancing computer technology. While institutional investors took advantage of the bargaining power associated with large volume, indexers successfully argued for even better terms. Instead of buying or selling one stock at a time based on perceived market opportunity, they could package hundreds of individual issues in a single large transaction. Even more important, they secured concessions because such trades are "informationless." The broker—when bidding for index fund business—does not have to allow for the risk that the buyer or seller taking the other side of the trade benefits from an information advantage.

- The computer has contributed in a major way to advances in performance measurement. As evolving performance measurement highlighted shortfalls in the returns of active management, pressure mounted to try indexing. For institutional decision makers, practical results count far more than theory. Few were willing to argue the subtleties of index fund theory, but all are accountable for results. For these institutional investors, accountability means that they back away from what, in practice, does not work and try something new if it demonstrates promise.

Table I-2: Broadening application of index funds.

Index	Description
Wilshire 5000	Total domestic stock market
S&P 500	Large-cap stocks
Wilshire 4500	Medium-to-small-cap stocks
Russell 2000	Small-cap stocks
MSCI EAFE	Major foreign stocks
MSCI Europe	Major European stocks
MSCI Pacific	Major Australian, Asian, and Far Eastern stocks
MSCI Emerging Markets	Foreign stocks other than major markets
Lehman Bros. Aggregate Bond	Total domestic taxable fixed income issues
Lehman Bros. Treasury Bond	Total U.S. Treasury issues
Custom indexes	As required

Individual Indexing

Individual investment in index funds, despite the early institutional lead, is now growing at a much more rapid rate. Initially, index funds were marketed exclusively to large institutional investors. Even after introduction of the first index mutual fund in 1976, offerings available to the individual investor were very limited for many years. A very important development in the 1990s has been the widening access to index mutual funds.

Figure I-2 traces the explosive growth of index mutual funds in recent years. As shown in Panel A, the number of index funds broadly available to the individual investor, still only 3 as recently as 1986, increased to 71 by year end 1996. Assets in these funds, as plotted in Panel B, have risen even more dramatically. They amounted to $58.5 billion in 1996, an increase of more than one hundredfold since 1986.

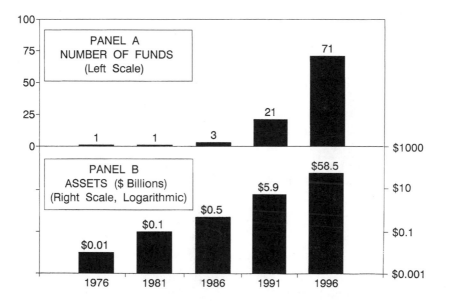

Figure I-2: **INDEX MUTUAL FUNDS**. The number of index mutual funds serving the individual investor and assets in these funds have grown explosively over the last 20 years. (*Sources: Morningstar Principia for Mutual Funds, January 1997*, Morningstar, Inc., Chicago, IL, © 1997; The Vanguard Group of Investment Companies, Valley Forge, PA.)

Potentially Greater Benefits

Will individual investors, with the proliferation of index mutual funds, follow the institutional pattern in their use of indexing? The reasons cited below point to a broadly affirmative answer. They explain how indexing provides potentially greater benefits to individuals than to institutions in three areas:

- One area concerns the *access to information* required to gain advantage through superior forecasting. In general, individual investors, even if they read the *Wall Street Journal* faithfully and subscribe to various newsletters and other services, cannot duplicate the information resources available to the institutional investor. The latter benefits from continuing help from an array of outside portfolio managers and advisors, and, sometimes, from an in-house staff of full-time investment specialists.

- A second area concerns *expenses,* as reflected in the mutual fund expense ratio, and *transaction costs,* which subtract directly from market values. Even if individual investors arrived at exactly the same decisions at exactly the same time as the institutional decision maker, they would ordinarily incur significantly higher transaction costs. Most individual investors managing their own investments do not generate the trading volume necessary to secure cost savings to match those secured on most institutional trades. If the individual investor turns to mutual funds to secure professional management, the issue shifts from transaction costs to the expense ratio. For the same type of portfolio, the individual buyer of a mutual fund will almost always incur a heavier burden of management fees and other expenses than will a large institution operating in the same area. (We defer consideration of sales loads and redemption fees, which may further burden the performance of the individual investor, to Chapters 3 and 4.) The disadvantage to the individual investor, however, can be greatly narrowed when the mutual fund provides indexing.

- The third area involves *personal income taxes,* which individuals pay and tax-exempt institutions do not. Index funds, because they make no attempt to switch holdings in anticipation of changes in the investment outlook, defer realization of capital gains and the accompanying tax liability to a much greater extent than do most actively managed funds. It is easy to overlook this significant tax advantage of index funds, since published comparisons of returns do not take it into account.

Increasing Need for Effective Management

While individuals are likely to benefit even more than institutional investors from indexing, the need for more effective management of their investments is also increasing:

- A major shift is underway from retirement plans managed by the employer (defined benefit plans) to those managed by the individual, such as 401(k) plans and IRAs. In the mid 1980s, individually managed plans accounted for 30% of retirement assets. Now the percentage is about 50%—and rising.

- Recent low unemployment rates have done little to reduce concerns about retirement security resulting from corporate downsizing. No longer are corporate employees so sure that the company-defined benefit plan will provide income for their retirement.

- Prospective revisions in Social Security income payments and the cost of Medicare further underscore the need for sound financial planning for retirement. Almost all observers agree that future legislation will in some way curtail benefits under these programs.

How This Book Is Organized

In examining the contribution of indexing to investment success, we differentiate between the key issues that ultimately determine the broad pattern of successful investing and the many refinements that may (or may not) enhance investment return. We stress the limited number of key issues that matter most for all investors. Ultimately, investment success for individual investors, as well as for large financial institutions, depends on how well these key issues are understood and addressed.

Part 1. Understanding Index Funds

The initial two chapters place index funds in the broad perspective of traditional investment management. Chapter 1 examines index design. Serving as an example, the S&P 500 illustrates how key characteristics facilitate use of this index in an index fund. A final section turns to indexes representing other areas of the financial markets. Chapter 2 shows how index funds are established and maintained. It identifies mutual fund groups that provide the individual investor with families of four or more index funds.

Part 2. Assessing the Benefits

The examination of mutual funds in Chapter 3 (stocks) and Chapter 4 (bonds) explains how indexing achieves savings in expenses, transaction costs, and sales loads, along with reduction in the burden of personal income taxes. A series of examples reflect various alternatives. Chapter 5 explores the efforts of actively managed funds to achieve advantage through superior forecasting skill. It does not rule out opportunities to gain advantage through the exercise of such skill but shows why the odds are less favorable than so many investors imagine.

Part 3: Investing in an Uncertain World

The three chapters in Part 3 describe, in easily understood steps, how to use index funds in portfolio management. Chapter 6 addresses the hard investment decision that looks so easy, that is, the establishment of objectives. It includes a commonsense method of adjusting risk to support the investor's purposes. Chapter 7 shows how to implement the plan determined in the previous chapter. Our approach equips the individual investor, making use of an array of index funds, to aim for above-average investment success. Chapter 8 opens the door to superior forecasting skill. Our approach is designed to exploit the benefits of superior forecasting—to the extent the investor is able to identify it—but also provides for containing the damage if, this time, forecasting fails.

Part 4: Responding to Change

Part 4 recognizes individual investing as a continuing management responsibility. Appreciation of the merits of indexing does not eliminate the need for investment decision making. Even if much of this responsibility is delegated, the investor cannot completely avoid oversight. Chapter 9 focuses on the monitoring of performance. Every investor needs to check progress at designated intervals. Since self-deception ranks among the most expensive of luxuries, the method of keeping track of investment results is critical. Chapter 10 presents an agenda to serve as a checklist of *what* to do and *when* to do it. The purpose is to provide a discipline to assure timely implemenation. The last two items on the agenda address obstacles that, sooner or later, are likely to get in the way—and how to deal with them. Chapter 11, by way of review, summarizes the reasons for placing your investment program in an index fund framework.

Framework for Investment Success

In summary, this book aims to show you how to use indexing as the framework for a successful investment program. Index funds provide very-low-cost participation in the returns of the publicly traded financial markets. They also serve as building blocks in investment planning and as the standard for measuring the success of active investing. This book helps you identify which index funds best serve your purposes, when to buy them, and, where appropriate, how to coordinate indexing with active investing.

PART 1

UNDERSTANDING INDEX FUNDS

chapter one

INDEX DESIGN

Which Index?

The usefulness of an index fund depends on the design of the underlying index as well as on day-to-day fund management. This chapter begins with examination of three index characteristics that bear in an important way on operation of the index fund. By way of illustrating the significance of these characteristics, we compare the S&P 500, a broadly based common stock index, with two competing measures of stock prices. Finally, we consider other major indexes suitable for use in index funds, including those that represent areas of the financial markets other than domestic stocks.

Differing Index Characteristics

For the purpose of an index fund, three characteristics of the index are particularly significant: (1) the issues included in the index, (2) the weighting of the issues, and (3) the liquidity of their trading markets.

Consistency with Fund Objective

The starting point, too often overlooked by investors, is the consistency of the issues covered by the index with the index fund objective. Your objective in committing assets to an index fund may be to match the combined returns of domestic common stocks. Alternatively, for reasons of either portfolio diversification or strategy, as discussed in Chapters 7 and 8, you may look for a more specialized index fund. The fund may aim to match an index representing a particular area of the domestic stock market, or various segments of either the foreign stock markets or the domestic bond markets.

By way of example, suppose the purpose of the index is to track the domestic stock market. One possibility would be to index the 100 domestic stocks with the largest market capitalizations (price per share multiplied by the number of shares outstanding). These large-cap stocks—the 100 largest—together account for close to half the market value of all publicly traded domestic stocks. No matter how the stocks are weighted, however, returns for the 100 largest will at times diverge substantially from the combined returns of the thousands of other publicly traded domestic stocks. During a particular year, the 100 largest might register a decline in market value of, say, 5%, while the combined market value of the remaining stocks rises by 10%. Under such circumstances, an index fund based on an index of the 100 largest stocks fails dramatically to serve as a broad measure of the stock market.

Lack of suitability of an index for one purpose does not necessarily disqualify it for other purposes. Clearly, there are better indexes than the 100 largest for representing all publicly traded stocks. For another purpose, however, the index may appropriately track the 100 largest or other limited segments of the stock market. Examples include very-small-cap stocks or stocks in an industry classification such as electric utilities or banking. Similar conclusions apply to foreign equities or the fixed income markets, where, again, the first criterion is the consistency of the index with the fund purpose. A stock index relating to a specific foreign country or geographic region, while useful for implementing a particular strategy, does not adequately represent the international equity market. In much the same way, an index of short Treasury notes or long corporate bonds will likely prove to be a misleading measure of the fixed income market.

Weighting of Index Components

The method of weighting the issues in an index determines how the changing market price of each issue will influence the overall index. Comparison of equal weighting with market-value weighting provides a good example.

If index issues are equally weighted, the market price change for a very-small-cap stock will affect the index just as much as the same percentage price change for General Electric or other large-cap stock. Over designated intervals, such as a day, week, or month, the change for the index reflects the average of the percentage changes for the component issues. For the stocks in the index, differing rates of price change over the measurement interval result in corresponding changes in respective weights. To restore equal weighting, rebalancing begins each new measurement cycle.

Market-value weighting provides a sharp contrast to equal weighting. The influence of each issue in the index depends on its total market value (price per share multiplied by the number of shares outstanding). Because changes in market value produce proportional changes in the index, a price change for the small-cap stock will affect the index much less than the same price change for General Electric.

For application to index funds, market-value weighting offers two important advantages. First, it supports the overall objective of indexing. The index fund aims to track the combined return of all outstanding shares of the securities in a designated market or market segment. Market-value weighting—assuming the issues in the index adequately represent the market segment—is consistent with this objective. Second, market-value weighting simplifies day-to-day management of the index fund. As market prices rise or fall, changes in the market value of the index fund parallel changes in the index. Since market price changes do not automatically require rebalancing, there are corresponding savings in the number of transactions and resulting transaction costs.

Market Liquidity

Although transaction costs have no bearing on the calculation of the index itself, they burden the index fund that aims to match the index. The cost per transaction, to be examined more closely in Chapters 3 and 4, depends in large part on market liquidity. The cost tends to be low for large-cap stocks trading in highly liquid markets, but it rises substantially for issues traded in less liquid markets.

S&P 500 in Perspective

The S&P 500 index fund serves to demonstrate the importance of the index characteristics outlined in the foregoing. Despite the more rapidly growing investment in other index funds in recent years, the S&P 500 version continues as the most widely held of all index funds. Widespread acceptance of the S&P 500 index fund reflects in large part the characteristics of the underlying index. The S&P 500 is market-value weighted, as are almost all indexes targeted by index funds. At the same time, it represents a convenient tradeoff between market coverage and market liquidity. Two comparisons that follow show how the characteristics of the S&P 500 facilitate its application to index funds. (Appendix 1-1 provides additional background.)

- Comparison of the S&P 500 with the Dow Jones Industrial Average (DJIA) highlights major differences in both the issues representing domestic stocks and the way these issues are weighted.

- We then compare the S&P 500 with the Wilshire 5000. The latter provides much broader coverage of domestic stocks, but, as a result, also opens the way to higher transaction costs.

While many investors look to each of these indexes to gauge broad changes in domestic stock prices, the S&P 500 occupies a special place in the development of index funds. For the general public, the DJIA is much better known and more widely followed. The Wilshire 5000 is just as familiar as the S&P 500 to institutional investors. Table 1-1 compares these domestic stock market indexes in terms of the proportion of total market value of publicly traded common stocks that each represents. The Wilshire 5000, widely accepted as an approximate measure of the entire domestic stock market, serves as the benchmark against which the market coverage of other indexes is compared. (Although the name remains unchanged, the total number of issues included in the index has increased over the years to about 7400.)

Comparing the S&P 500 with the DJIA

To explain the leading role of the S&P 500 in the implementation of index funds, we first focus on comparison with the DJIA. The 500 stocks in the S&P 500 provide much broader representation of the

Table 1-1: Stock market indexes as percentage of total market value of publicly traded domestic stocks (1996).

Index	Number of Issues	% Market Value
Wilshire 5000	7368	100%
S&P 500	500	70
DJIA	30	16

domestic stock market than do the 30 stocks in the DJIA. The S&P 500, moreover, is market-value weighted while the DJIA is not.

Table 1-2 lists the 30 stocks that made up the DJIA at the beginning of 1997, all of which are also included in the S&P 500. For each issue, the first two columns show the then-current market price and the number of shares then outstanding. The third column indicates the total market value for each issue, calculated by multiplying market price (column 1) times the number of shares outstanding (column 2). Columns 4 and 5 compare the weights accorded each issue in the two competing indexes. The S&P 500 weighting of 0.0% for Bethlehem Steel reflects rounding to one decimal point of 0.02%. The order of the listings reflects the differences in weightings for the two indexes, as shown in the far-right column.

Broader Representation of the Stock Market. As a gauge of stock prices, the S&P 500 provides broader representation of the stock market than does the DJIA. The S&P 500 demonstrates a substantial advantage in each of three areas:

- Table 1-2 underscores the *greater breadth* of the S&P 500 in terms of both number of issues and market value. It shows that the DJIA, with 30 issues, accounts for about 24% of the market value of the S&P 500. The market value at the beginning of 1997 for the 500 issues in the S&P 500 amounted to $5.6 trillion compared with $1.3 trillion for the DJIA.

- The S&P 500 also covers a *greater range of market capitalization*. The market value at the beginning of 1997 for the 30 issues included in both the S&P 500 and DJIA ranged from $163 billion to $1 billion, with an average of $44 billion. For the remaining 470 issues in the S&P 500, the range of market capitalization extended from $108 billion to $23 million, with an average of $9 billion.

Table 1-2: Comparison of S&P 500 with DJIA at the beginning of 1997.

DJIA Stocks	Share Price	Shares (millions)	Value (billions)	Weighting DJIA	S&P500	Difference
International Business Machines Corp.	152	518	$ 78	7.2%	1.4%	5.8%
The Boeing Co.	107	358	38	5.1	0.7	4.4
J.P. Morgan & Co., Inc.	98	185	18	4.7	0.3	4.3
Texaco Inc.	98	264	26	4.7	0.5	4.2
Procter & Gamble Co.	108	682	73	5.1	1.3	3.8
Philip Morris Cos., Inc.	113	814	92	5.4	1.6	3.8
E.I. du Pont de Nemours & Co.	94	563	53	4.5	0.9	3.5
Eastman Kodak Co.	80	333	27	3.8	0.5	3.4
Minnesota Mining & Manufacturing Co.	83	418	35	4.0	0.6	3.3
Caterpillar, Inc.	75	191	14	3.6	0.3	3.3
United Technologies Corp.	66	240	16	3.2	0.3	2.9
Allied Signal Inc.	67	283	19	3.2	0.3	2.9
Aluminum Co. of America	64	173	11	3.0	0.2	2.8
Exxon Corp.	98	1242	122	4.7	2.2	2.5
The Walt Disney Co.	70	675	47	3.3	0.8	2.5
Chevron Corp.	65	652	42	3.1	0.8	2.3
The Goodyear Tire & Rubber Co.	51	155	8	2.5	0.1	2.3
American Express Co.	57	474	27	2.7	0.5	2.2
Merck & Co., Inc.	80	1205	96	3.8	1.7	2.1
General Motors Corp.	56	756	42	2.7	0.7	1.9
Sears, Roebuck & Co.	46	392	18	2.2	0.3	1.9
Union Carbide Corp.	41	127	5	1.9	0.1	1.9
General Electric Co.	99	1646	163	4.7	2.9	1.8
International Paper Co.	41	300	12	1.9	0.2	1.7
McDonald's Corp.	45	698	32	2.2	0.6	1.6
Woolworth Corp.	22	134	3	1.0	0.1	1.0
AT&T Corp.	42	1620	68	2.0	1.2	0.8
Westinghouse Electric Corp.	20	604	12	0.9	0.2	0.7
Bethlehem Steel Corp.	9	112	1	0.4	0.0	0.4
The Coca-Cola Co.	53	2488	131	2.5	2.3	0.2
Total	2097		$1329	100.0%	23.6%	76.4%

Source: Computed using data from Dow Jones & Company, Inc., New York, NY and Standard & Poor's Corporation, New York, NY.

- As a matter of policy, the S&P 500 provides *wider industry diversification*. The DJIA, reflecting the definition of the index as a measure of industrial stocks, limits representation of stocks in the transportation, utility, and financial sectors. The S&P 500, without such limits on industry diversification, routinely includes issues in all major industry classifications.

Advantage of Market-Value Weighting. For application to index funds, a major advantage of the S&P 500 is the method of weighting the component issues. The weighting in the S&P 500 corresponds to the market value of each issue. Since the beginning-1997 market value of the outstanding common shares of General Electric was $163 billion, the S&P 500 accorded General Electric a weight of $163 billion divided by the aggregate market value of $5.6 trillion. The result, as shown in column 5 of Table 1-2, is 2.9%. For the DJIA, the weighting reflects the price per share of each issue, also shown in Table 1-2. The sum of the share prices for the 30 DJIA stocks at the beginning of 1997 was 2097. The weight of General Electric stock was therefore the price per share—then 99—divided by 2097, equal to 4.7%.

The S&P 500 provides an example of how market-value weighting accomplishes the purposes of an index fund better than other weighting methods. To avoid the risk of below-average performance, indexing aims to secure the average return of all investors in the market segment represented by the index. At the beginning of 1997, the $5.6-trillion market value of stocks in the S&P 500 corresponded with an index level of 741. If the combined market value of these stocks were to rise 10%, the S&P 500 would also increase by 10%, no matter which stocks registered an increase or decrease in market value. Holders of an S&P 500 index fund would participate proportionally in the combined market appreciation of all stocks in the index. In a similar way, they would also share proportionally in all dividend payments to shareholders.

The weightings for the individual issues in the DJIA present a sharp contrast to the weightings for those in the S&P 500. At the beginning of 1997, the DJIA, then at 6448, represented stocks with a combined market value of $1.3 trillion. If the market value of these 30 DJIA stocks were to rise by 10%, the DJIA could rise either more or less, depending on which stocks accounted for the increase in market value. General Electric, at one extreme, accounted for more

Table 1-3: How the DJIA masks differences in market-value weightings (December 31, 1996).

	Share Price	Value (billions)		Share Price	Value (billions)
General Electric	99	$163	Boeing	107	$ 38
			Texaco	98	26
			Eastman Kodak	80	27
			Caterpillar	75	14
			Allied Signal	67	19
			Alcoa	64	11
			Goodyear	51	8
			International Paper	41	12
			Union Carbide	41	5
			Woolworth	22	3
Total	99	$163		646	$163

than 12% of the total market value of the stocks in the DJIA but less than 5% of the weight in the index itself. At the other extreme, as shown in Table 1-3, a group of 10 stocks together accounted for approximately the same market value as General Electric but provided 31% of the weight in the index. From the levels at the beginning of 1997, a 10% rise in the market price of General Electric would have accounted for a 30-point increase in the DJIA. In contrast, a 10% increase for the 10 stocks *with about the same aggregate market value* would have increased the DJIA by 199 points—or by six times as much as for General Electric. The widely different responses by the DJIA would have masked very similar increases in the aggregate market value of the DJIA stocks.

Market-value weighting not only conforms to the purpose of indexing but also facilitates tracking. For an S&P 500 index fund with total assets of $100 million at the beginning of 1997, holdings of General Electric stock, reflecting its weight in the index of 2.9%, would amount to $2.9 million. Similarly, the holdings of Union Carbide, with an index weight of 0.1%, would amount to $0.1 million. Barring significant sale of newly issued shares or buyback of outstanding shares, the market value of each holding automatically adjusts as market prices change. In the absence of cash flow in and out of the fund or changes in the stocks in the index, reinvestment of dividends would provide the main reason for incurring transaction costs. Since dividends for the S&P 500 now amount to less than 2% annually, they generate only a very small amount of transaction costs over the course of a year.

A DJIA index fund, in contrast, would require more turnover in order to track the index. The market value of a DJIA index fund and the DJIA would move together as prices of the individual issues changed from day to day until either the composition of the index changed or a stock split took place. Substitution of one stock for another in the DJIA, as in the S&P 500, makes necessary a rebalancing of the component issues. The replacement of any one stock in the index is likely to exert a greater impact on the DJIA, with only 30 issues, than on the S&P 500, which holds so many more issues. A much more important difference between the DJIA and the S&P 500 relates to stock splits. While stock splits require no action on the part of an S&P 500 index fund, they make necessary the immediate reduction of the weighting accorded the stock in a DJIA index fund. As the split in the price of one DJIA stock reduces its index weight by as much as 50% or more, the other stocks in the index become candidates for offsetting adjustments.

By way of example, the stock of IBM split 2 for 1 in May 1997. Overnight, the weight of IBM in the DJIA dropped from 8% to 4.2%. An index fund tracking the DJIA would have had to reduce the holding of IBM shares accordingly. To compensate, the fund would have also increased holdings of the remaining 29 DJIA stocks.

Comparison with the Wilshire 5000

Comparison of the S&P 500 with the Wilshire 5000 directs attention to the influence of market liquidity on transaction costs. (Comments concerning the Wilshire 5000 throughout this book refer to the version of this index that, like the S&P 500, is market-value-weighted. Although Wilshire also offers an equally weighted version, index funds focus on the market-value-weighted index.) Representing many more issues than the S&P 500, the Wilshire 5000 also accounts for a larger proportion of the market value of domestic stocks outstanding. An index fund based on the Wilshire 5000, as the most comprehensive domestic equity index, provides the investor with almost complete coverage of publicly traded domestic stocks.

While the main advantage of the Wilshire 5000 is the comprehensive coverage of the equity market, its main disadvantage is the much less liquid markets in which many of the smaller-cap stocks trade. As a result, the transaction costs incurred in moving in or out of stocks included in the Wilshire 5000 is greater in proportion to market value than for those in the S&P 500. The S&P 500, although accounting for about 70% of the total market value of the Wilshire 5000, includes 500 stocks. For the most part, these stocks are large-capitalization issues that trade in highly liquid markets. The Wilshire 5000, in contrast, numbers 7400 issues, most of them trading in much less liquid markets. (Appendix 1-2 provides additional details concerning the Wilshire 5000.)

Either the Wilshire 5000 or the S&P 500, as discussed in Chapter 7, may contribute in various ways to the index fund portfolio plan. To broaden market coverage, the portfolio may hold the S&P 500 index fund in combination with other stock index funds representing smaller-cap stocks. A Wilshire 5000 index fund, meanwhile, will almost always attempt to limit the burden of transaction costs through the application of sampling techniques. Rather than hold all 7400 stocks, the fund may carefully select a fraction, such as 20%, to represent the total population of stocks.

Other Market-Value Weighted Indexes

Index funds increasingly make use of indexes other than the S&P 500. The index fund that aims to match the Wilshire 5000, as described in the foregoing, permits the investor in one fund to participate in the broad range of issues that constitute the domestic stock market. Other index funds target medium- or small-cap domestic stocks, foreign stocks, and also domestic bonds. By way of example, we look to leading indexes in each of these categories.

Medium- and Small-Cap Indexes

Two indexes occupy a particularly prominent position in the indexing of medium- and small-cap domestic stocks. Index mutual funds using either the Wilshire 4500 or the Russell 2000 account for about 90% of the assets held in such funds as of the beginning of

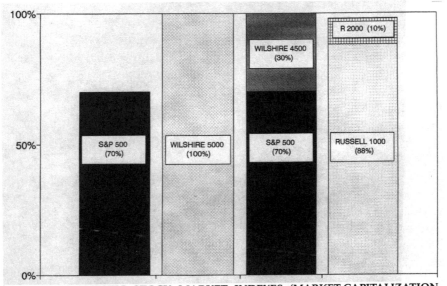

Figure 1-1: DOMESTIC STOCK MARKET INDEXES (MARKET-CAPITALIZATION WEIGHTED). How the S&P 500 index compares with the Wilshire and Russell indexes. (*Sources:* Standard & Poor's, New York, NY, a Division of The McGraw-Hill Companies; Wilshire Associates, Inc., Santa Monica, CA; Frank Russell Company, Tacoma, WA.)

1997. In addition to these two indexes, we comment on more recent introductions in this area by Standard & Poor's Corporation. In view of the leading role of the S&P 500 index funds, the S&P Mid-Cap 400 and the S&P SmallCap 600 seem likely to receive rapidly increasing acceptance in the years ahead.

To place the Wilshire 4500 and the Russell 2000 in the perspective of broader stock market indexes, we turn to Figure 1-1. The first bar on the left depicts the market value for the S&P 500, accounting for close to 70% of the total for publicly traded domestic stocks. The second bar represents the Wilshire 5000. The approximately 7400 issues with aggregate market value of $8 trillion provide a widely accepted proxy for 100% of the publicly traded domestic stock market. The third and fourth bars identify the market value of each of the two smaller-cap indexes within the context of a larger index family.

The Wilshire 4500, the upper component of the third bar, comprises the issues in the Wilshire 5000 other than those representing the S&P 500. The lower (and larger) segment approximates the S&P 500, since it includes all the stocks in the S&P 500 with company headquarters in the United States. At the beginning of 1997, there were 490 such companies. The Wilshire 4500 consists of the remaining 6900 stocks, mainly medium- and small-capitalization stocks. As indicated graphically, the Wilshire 4500, combined with the S&P 500 in appropriate proportions (about 70/30), approximates the Wilshire 5000. (Comments concerning the Wilshire 5000 in Appendix 1-2 also address the Wilshire 4500.)

The Russell 2000 represents the 2000 issues with the smallest market capitalizations in the Russell 3000. The bar at the far right represents the Russell 3000—made up of the 3000 largest issues as determined by market capitalization—and two subindexes. The Russell 1000 consists of the 1000 largest-capitalization issues in the Russell 3000. It includes most of the stocks in the S&P 500, and the remaining 500 issues represent, for the most part, much smaller market capitalizations. As a result, the combined market value of all stocks included in the Russell 2000 amounts to only 10% of that for all publicly traded stocks. An index fund based on the Russell 2000 represents smaller-capitalization stocks, on average, than does the Wilshire 4500. (Appendix 1-3 presents supplementary information on the Russell 2000.)

Standard & Poor's has introduced in recent years two indexes to supplement the S&P 500 in representing the domestic stock market. The S&P MidCap 400 covers middle-capitalization stocks, while the S&P SmallCap 600 tracks small-cap issues. (S&P uses the term *middle-cap* to identify much the same population of stocks as described in this book as *medium-cap*.) The design of these indexes aims to facilitate their use in the management of index funds as well as in the performance measurement of specialized portfolios. Exclusion of highly illiquid issues or issues priced at less than $1 per share helps to control costs per transaction. Because market capitalization is not the sole criterion for inclusion in the index, fluctuations in market prices do not mechanically determine that one issue must substitute for another. For the index fund tracking the index, the resulting reduction in turnover further contributes to limiting transaction costs. (Appendix 1-4 provides further perspective concerning the MidCap 400, while Appendix 1-5 addresses the specific features of the SmallCap 600.)

Up-to-date information on stock market indexes other than the DJIA are becoming increasingly accessible in the business sections of daily newspapers as well as in the financial press. While individual investors have long regarded the DJIA as the primary measure

STOCK MARKET DATA BANK   12/31/96

MAJOR INDEXES

†12-MO HIGH	†12-MO LOW	DAILY HIGH	DAILY LOW	CLOSE	NET CHG	% CHG	†12-MO CHG	% CHG	FROM 12/31	% CHG
DOW JONES AVERAGES										
6560.91	5032.94	30 Industrials 6553.60	6448.27	x6448.27	−101.10	−1.54	+1270.82	+24.55	+1331.15	+26.01
2315.47	1882.71	20 Transportation 2282.80	2254.75	2255.67	−24.97	−1.09	+255.30	+12.76	+274.67	+13.87
238.12	204.86	15 Utilities 235.05	232.46	x232.53	−2.59	−1.10	+5.10	+2.24	+7.13	+3.16
2059.18	1655.55	65 Composite 2054.57	2025.61	x2025.83	−28.15	−1.37	+314.35	+18.37	+332.62	+19.64
714.26	564.39	DJ Global-US 711.90	700.54	700.56	−11.19	−1.57	+119.76	+19.59	+119.13	+20.49
NEW YORK STOCK EXCHANGE										
398.86	321.41	Composite 397.42	392.29	392.30	−5.12	−1.29	+60.59	+18.27	+62.79	+19.06
503.23	403.39	Industrials 500.34	494.38	494.38	−5.96	−1.19	+78.04	+18.74	+81.09	+19.62
266.69	236.63	Utilities 262.73	259.50	259.91	−2.82	−1.07	+5.43	+2.13	+7.01	+2.77
358.60	294.40	Transportation 356.01	351.13	352.30	−3.25	−0.91	+47.87	+15.72	+50.34	+16.67
358.18	263.70	Finance 357.65	351.04	351.17	−6.48	−1.81	+75.87	+27.56	+76.92	+28.05
STANDARD & POOR'S INDEXES										
757.03	598.48	500 Index 753.95	740.74	740.74	−13.11	−1.74	+120.01	+19.33	+124.81	+20.26
887.95	702.07	Industrials 883.96	869.97	869.97	−13.86	−1.57	+142.32	+19.56	+148.78	+20.63
213.83	184.66	Utilities 200.81	198.81	198.81	−2.00	−1.00	−4.54	−2.23	−3.77	−1.86
257.41	207.94	400 MidCap 255.58	254.35	255.58	+0.22	+0.09	+36.90	+16.87	+37.74	+17.32
145.65	115.48	600 SmallCap 145.49	144.29	145.48	+0.84	+0.58	+23.58	+19.34	+24.38	+20.13
162.77	129.15	1500 Index 162.20	159.81	159.81	−2.36	−1.46	+25.60	+19.07	+26.57	+19.94
NASDAQ										
1316.27	988.57	Composite 1291.88	1285.45	1291.03	+3.28	+0.25	+232.38	+21.95	+238.90	+22.71
1193.13	908.41	Industrials 1109.99	1098.37	1109.63	+7.99	+0.73	+141.08	+14.57	+144.95	+15.03
1465.43	1196.03	Insurance 1471.08	1461.70	1465.43	+1.55	+0.11	+179.74	+13.98	+172.79	+13.37
1273.46	990.65	Banks 1274.12	1266.52	1273.46	+2.49	+0.20	+265.98	+26.40	+264.05	+26.16
591.59	441.77	Nat. Mkt. Comp. 580.78	577.98	580.39	+1.35	+0.23	+106.31	+22.42	+109.22	+23.18
486.92	368.88	Nat. Mkt. Indus. 452.63	447.93	452.48	+3.19	+0.71	+57.71	+14.62	+59.18	+15.05
OTHERS										
614.99	526.60	Amex 583.48	581.24	583.28	−0.18	−0.03	+32.31	+5.86	+35.05	+6.39
401.21	318.24	Russell 1000 399.47	393.75	393.75	−5.67	−1.42	+62.67	+18.93	+64.86	+19.72
364.61	301.75	Russell 2000 362.61	359.23	362.61	+2.62	+0.73	+45.72	+14.43	+46.64	+14.76
425.72	340.20	Russell 3000 424.61	419.44	419.44	−5.12	−1.21	+65.33	+18.45	+67.53	+19.19
377.41	321.64	Value-Line(geom.) 375.95	374.78	375.32	−0.61	−0.16	+42.06	+12.62	+44.28	+13.38
7295.57	5850.20	Wilshire 5000 ...	...	7198.29	−75.91	−1.04	+1102.19	+18.08	+1141.09	+18.84

† Based on comparable trading day in preceding year.

Figure 1-2: The financial press routinely reports widely followed stock indexes, as illustrated by this example (*Source: The Wall Street Journal,* January 2, 1997, page C-2. Reprinted by permission of *The Wall Street Journal,* © 1997 Dow Jones & Company, Inc. All Rights Reserved Worldwide.)

of stock prices, institutional investors are much more likely to rely on the S&P 500 for this purpose. At the same time, institutional investors increasingly look to additional indexes to define specific segments of the stock market. As a result, the financial press routinely list a broad range of indexes. Figure 1-2 provides an example.

Beyond Domestic Equities

In addition to domestic equities, index mutual funds also address international financial markets and domestic bonds. A leading family of indexes serves as an example in each market.

Morgan Stanley Capital International (MSCI) maintains a family of indexes representing various segments of foreign stock markets. Index funds that invest abroad are likely to focus particularly on the MSCI Europe, Australasia, and Far East Index (EAFE). It consists of the MSCI Europe Index and the MSCI Pacific Free Index, either of which may serve independently as the basis for an index fund. (Indexes designated as *free* exclude issues unavailable for purchase by foreigners.) The MSCI Emerging Markets Free Index (EMF) includes stocks of companies domiciled in less developed economies throughout the world. (While the names of these indexes suggest the geographical areas that they represent, Appendix 1-6 provides additional details concerning the specific countries and the method of stock selection.)

Lehman Brothers (LB) compiles bond indexes that serve as the basis for many institutional bond index funds and also for several bond index mutual funds. The LB Aggregate Bond Index represents the broad public market for taxable notes and bonds (in contrast to tax-exempt issues, such as those issued by states and municipalities) and mortgage and other asset-backed securities. (Appendix 1-7 explains more fully the composition of the LB Aggregate Bond Index.)

Appendix 1-1: S&P 500 Index

Although the S&P 500 includes 500 issues, the 100 with the largest market values account for more than 60% of the weight in the index. Table 1-4 compares the weightings of the issues by quintiles, reflecting market values as of December 31, 1996. Immediately following, Table 1-5 identifies the 25 stocks in the index with the largest market values on the same date.

Standard & Poor's brochure, *The S&P 500 Index*, provides additional background information (updated through 1996 by Standard & Poor's Corporation):

- The primary objective of the Standard & Poor's 500 Composite Stock Price Index, known as the S&P 500, is to be the performance benchmark for the U.S. stock market performance.

- The Index is a market-value-weighted index (shares outstanding times stock price) in which each company's influence on Index performance is directly proportional to its market value.

- The S&P 500 does not contain the 500 largest stocks. Although many of the stocks in the Index are among the largest, there are also some relatively small companies in the Index. Those companies, however, are generally leaders within their industry group.

- S&P identifies important industry groups within the U.S. economy and then allocates a representative sample of stocks within each group to the S&P 500. There are four major industry sectors within the Index: Industrials, Utilities, Financial, and Transportation.

- The origins of the S&P 500 Index go back to 1923 when Standard & Poor's introduced a series of indices which included 233 companies and covered 26 industries. The index as it is now known was introduced in 1957. Today, the S&P 500 encompasses 500 companies representing 105 specific industry groups.

Table 1-4: Weighting of stocks in S&P 500, December 31, 1996.

Market Value	Weight
First 100	64%
Second 100	17
Third 100	10
Fourth 100	6
Fifth 100	3
Total	100%

Source: Standard & Poor's, New York, NY, a Division of the McGraw-Hill Companies.

Table 1-5: S&P 500 largest 25 holdings ranked by market value, December 31, 1996.

Rank	Stock	Weight
1	General Electric Co.	2.9%
2	The Coca-Cola Co.	2.3
3	Exxon Corp.	2.1
4	Intel Corp.	1.9
5	Microsoft Corp.	1.7
6	Merck & Co., Inc.	1.7
7	Philip Morris Cos., Inc.	1.6
8	Royal Dutch Petroleum Co., ADR	1.6
9	International Business Machines Corp.	1.4
10	Procter & Gamble Co.	1.3
11	AT&T Corp.	1.2
12	Johnson & Johnson	1.2
13	Bristol-Myers Squibb Co.	1.0
14	Pfizer, Inc.	0.9
15	E.I. du Pont de Nemours & Co.	0.9
16	Wal-Mart Stores, Inc.	0.9
17	Hewlett-Packard Co.	0.9
18	American International Group, Inc.	0.9
19	Citicorp	0.9
20	Mobil Corp.	0.9
21	The Walt Disney Co.	0.8
22	PepsiCo Inc.	0.8
23	GTE Corp.	0.8
24	Chevron Corp.	0.7
25	General Motors Corp.	0.7
	Total	32.2%

Source: Standard & Poor's, New York, NY, a Division of the McGraw-Hill Companies.

Appendix 1-2: Wilshire 5000

*Excerpt from Wilshire 5000 Notes:**

> The Wilshire 5000 Equity Index measures the performance of all U.S. headquartered equity securities with readily available price data.... The Wilshire 5000 base is its December 31, 1980 capitalization of $1,404.596 billion. Therefore, the index is an excellent approximator of dollar changes in the U.S. equity market.... Wilshire Associates created the Wilshire 5000 in 1974 to aid in performance measurement. Month end history was created back to December 1970. Beginning December 1979, the index was calculated daily.

Additional information from company spokesperson:

> The Wilshire 4500 consists of the stocks in the Wilshire 5000 less the 490 issues that are also included in the S&P 500. The Wilshire 5000 excludes 10 stocks included in the S&P 500 because they are not headquartered in the United States. As shown in Table 1-6, the Wilshire 4500 accounts for 93% of the issues but only 30% of the market value of the Wilshire 5000.

Table 1-6: Comparison of Wilshire 5000 and Wilshire 4500, December 31, 1996.

Wilshire Index	5000	4500	4500/5000
Market Value (billions)	$7888	$2399	30%
Number of Stocks	7368	6878	93%

Source: Wilshire 5000® Notes, Wilshire Associates Incorporated, Santa Monica, CA. Wilshire 5000® is a registered service mark of Wilshire Associates Incorporated.

Appendix 1-3: Russell 2000

Excerpt from Russell US Equity Indexes, *Frank Russell Company, Tacoma, WA, June 30, 1996.*

Russell 3000® Index measures the performance of the 3,000 largest US companies based on total market capitalization, which represents approximately 98% of the investable US equity market. As of the latest reconstitution, the average market capitalization was approximately $2.3 billion. The index had a total market capitalization range of approximately $138 billion to $162 million....

Russell 2000® Index measures the performance of the 2,000 smallest companies in the Russell 3000 index, which represents approximately 10% of the total market capitalization of the Russell 3000 index. As of the latest reconstitution, the average market capitalization was approximately $421 million. The largest company in the index had an approximate market capitalization of $1.0 billion.

Appendix 1-4: S&P MidCap 400 Index

Excerpts from Standard & Poor's brochure:

- The Standard & Poor's MidCap 400 Index measures the performance of the mid-size segment of the U.S. stock market. The Index is based on 400 stocks chosen on the basis of market capitalization, liquidity and industry group representation.

- The Index is market-value-weighted (shares outstanding times stock price), so that each company's influence on Index performance is directly proportional to its market value.

- S&P identifies important industry groups within the U.S. economy and then allocates a representative sample of stocks within each group to the S&P MidCap 400. There are four major industry sectors within the Index: Industrials, Utilities, Financials, and Transportation.

- Standard & Poor's employs selection criteria to ensure continued recognition by investors as a representative and investable benchmark.

- At no time will stocks in the S&P MidCap 400 also be included in the S&P 500.

Appendix 1-5: S&P SmallCap 600 Index

Excerpts from Standard & Poor's brochure (updated January 9, 1997 by Standard & Poor's Corporation):

The S&P SmallCap 600 Index has been designed to be both a benchmark of small capitalization stock performance and an investable portfolio of small cap stocks for passive replication purposes. The Index complements the S&P 500 Composite, a broad index covering leading publicly traded companies in leading industries in the U.S. economy, and the MidCap 400 Index, a benchmark of leading publicly traded companies in secondary industries in the U.S. economy.

Essentially, the S&P 500 represents the large capitalization segment of the market, the MidCap 400 covers the middle capitalization segment and the SmallCap 600 completes coverage of the U.S. equities market by capturing the economic and industry characteristics of small stock performance. Together, the 1,500 stocks that comprise the three S&P Indexes have a combined market value that is about $6.6 trillion. This accounts for roughly 81% of the total market value of the approximately 7,500 stocks that make up the domestic equities market. Thus, around 6,000 issues account for the remaining 19% of the market and many of these stocks are highly illiquid....

Development of the Index (S&P SmallCap 600) began ... shortly after S&P introduced the S&P MidCap 400 Index in June 1991. S&P extensively surveyed active and passive small cap managers, quantitative research analysts, academics and traders about their definitions of small cap companies in terms of market value size. The results revealed a consensus average market value range of $80 million to $600 million at market levels at year-end 1993. (It should be noted that there are almost as many definitions of small cap stocks as there are small cap managers.)

S&P converted the range into percentiles of the entire domestic market in order to account for fluctuations in performance over time. The $600 million upper bound converted into the 50th percentile, while the $80 million lower bound became the 83rd percentile. This percentile range was used to calculate the Index back history and is being used to select future Index constituents. For example, ten years ago, the 50th and 83rd percentiles would have yielded a market value range of $250 million for the largest companies and $35 million for the smallest companies in the small cap segment of the domestic stock population.

With these overall guidelines, S&P developed screening criteria to select stocks from its Index Selection Database. ... To select the 600 companies for the new small cap index, S&P applied the target percentile range to the ... stock Index Selection Base. By doing this, S&P created its own version of the small cap population, a universe of about 1,850 issues. The small cap population is broken down further into 11 economic sectors including: Basic Materials, Energy, Capital

Goods, Consumer Cyclicals, Consumer Staples, Technology, Transportation, Utilities and Financials. New sectors as of July 1, 1996 are Communications Services and Health Care. The following screens are then used to select the 600 companies for the Index:

1. Candidates must trade on either the New York, American or NASDAQ stock exchanges.

2. Companies must have a trading history of at least six months in order to be considered.

3. Stocks that do not trade on any three days during a 12 month period are removed. The same screen—three days without trades—applies to companies that qualify but have a trading history less than twelve months but more than six months.

4. Companies with stock prices below $1.00 are removed from consideration.

5. Share turnover has to exceed 20% on an annualized basis for a company to be included. Share turnover is calculated as the annual trading volume as a percent of the total common shares outstanding.

6. Companies with high ownership concentrations are reviewed. Companies that have 50% or more of their total common shares outstanding owned by another corporation or one individual are not considered. Companies that have 60% or more of their shares owned by insiders, or in combination with other corporations' holdings, are also not included.

7. Companies in bankruptcy or in severe financial distress, such that their continuance as a going concern is highly doubtful, are eliminated from consideration.

8. Bid/Ask spreads as a percentage of the last sale are calculated for 30 days for survivors of the above screens and only those companies with spreads that are 5% or less are considered. The ratio is calculated as an average of 30 days trading activity.

Candidates that pass these screens are selected based on the need to balance the economic sector weightings relative to the weightings of the small cap population. Only those companies that have the tightest bid-ask spread ratios within an underweighted sector are selected. Thus, economic sector exposure is a key index maintenance criteria.

Appendix 1-6: Morgan Stanley Capital International (MSCI) Indexes*

Excerpts from MSCI brochure (updated February 25, 1997 by Morgan Stanley spokesperson):

MSCI Europe, Australasia and Far East (EAFE) Index

The Morgan Stanley Capital International EAFE Index is a market capitalization weighted equity index composed of a sample of companies representative of the market structure of the following twenty countries: Australia, Austria, Belgium, Denmark, Finland, France, Germany, Hong Kong, Ireland, Italy, Japan, Malaysia, Netherlands, New Zealand, Norway, Singapore, Spain, Sweden, Switzerland and the United Kingdom. Constituent stocks are selected on the basis of industry representation, liquidity and sufficient float. As of December 31, 1996, the EAFE Index was composed of 1098 companies.

MSCI Europe Index

The Morgan Stanley Capital International Europe Index is a market capitalization weighted equity index composed of a sample of companies representative of the market structure of the following fourteen countries: Austria, Belgium, Denmark, Finland, France, Germany, Ireland, Italy, Netherlands, Norway, Spain, Sweden, Switzerland, and the United Kingdom. Constituent stocks are selected on the basis of industry representation, liquidity and sufficient float. As of December 31, 1996, the Europe Index was composed of 573 companies.

MSCI Pacific Free Index

The Morgan Stanley Capital International Pacific Free Index is a market capitalization weighted equity index composed of a sample of companies representative of the market structure of the following six countries: Australia, Hong Kong, Japan, Malaysia, New Zealand and Singapore. Constituent stocks are selected on the basis of industry representation, liquidity and sufficient float. The "Free" version of this index excludes those shares in otherwise free markets which are not purchasable by foreign investors. As of December 31, 1996, the Pacific Free Index was composed of 525 companies.

---

*Used with permission of Morgan Stanley Capital International (MSCI), Morgan Stanley & Company, Inc., New York, NY. MSCI data is the exclusive property of Morgan Stanley & Company, Inc. and may not be reproduced or redisseminated without the prior written permission of Morgan Stanley.

MSCI Emerging Markets Free (EMF) Index

The Morgan Stanley Capital International Emerging Markets Free (EMF) Index is a market capitalization weighted equity index composed of a sample of companies representative of the market structure of the following 26 countries: Argentina, Brazil, Chile, China (Free), Columbia, Czech Republic, Greece, Hungary, India, Indonesia, Israel, Jordan, Korea (Free), Malaysia, Mexico (Free), Pakistan, Peru, Philippines (Free), Poland, Portugal, South Africa, Sri Lanka, Taiwan, Thailand, Turkey, and Venezuela (Free). The base date for this index is December 31, 1987. Constituent stocks are selected on the basis of industry representation, liquidity, sufficient float, and avoidance of cross-ownership. In addition, the "Free" version of this index excludes those shares in otherwise free markets which are not purchasable by foreign investors. As of December 31, 1996, the EMF Index was composed of approximately 1016 securities.[1]

---

[1]For the Vanguard Emerging Markets Portfolio, the fund prospectus (revised May 19, 1997) provides the following description: The Portfolio "seeks investment results that parallel those of the Morgan Stanley Capital International (MSCI)—Select Emerging Markets (Free) Index, an index of companies located in 14 Asian, Latin American, African, and European countries. These Portfolios use statistical procedures to invest primarily in common stocks found in their indexes."

Appendix 1-7: Lehman Brothers (LB) Aggregate Bond Index

Source: Lehman Brothers, Lehman Family of Indices, Index Definitions, *June 1995, page 1:*

The Lehman Brothers Aggregate Index includes fixed rate debt issues rated investment grade or higher by Moody's Investors Service, Standard & Poor's Corporation or Fitch Investors Service, in that order. All issues have at least one year to maturity and an outstanding par value of at least $100 million. Intermediate indices include bonds with maturities up to 10 years, and long-term indices include those with maturities of 10 years or longer. Price, coupon, paydown, and total return are reported for all sectors on a month-end to month-end basis. All returns are market value-weighted inclusive of accrued interest.

The Aggregate Bond Index is made up of the Government/Corporate Index, the Mortgage-Backed Securities Index, and the Asset-Backed Securities Index. ... The Government/Corporate Bond Index includes the Government and Corporate Bond Indices.

The Government Bond Index is made up of the Treasury Bond Index (all public obligations of the U.S. Treasury, excluding flower bonds and foreign targeted issues) and the Agency Bond Index (all publicly issued debt of U.S. Government agencies and quasi-federal corporations, and corporate debt guaranteed by the U.S. Government). ... The Corporate Bond Index includes all publicly issued, fixed rate, nonconvertible investment grade, dollar-denominated SEC-registered corporate debt. ... The Mortgage-Backed Securities Index includes 15- and 30-year fixed rate securities backed by mortgage pools of the Government National Mortgage Association (GNMA), Federal Home Loan Mortgage Corporation (FHLMC) and the Federal National Mortgage Association (FNMA). ... The Asset-Backed Securities Index is composed of credit card, auto, and home equity loans.

chapter two

TURNING AN INDEX INTO AN INDEX FUND

Overview of Index Fund Operations

Chapter 2 provides an overview of index fund operations. To demonstrate the principles involved, let's first look at how an institutional investor would manage a single large index fund. Then let's turn to the additional requirements of managing an index mutual fund. For the latter, a particular challenge is the day-to-day management of uneven cash flows in and out of the fund. A final section reviews the growing list of fund families that make available the building blocks for an index fund portfolio. The list highlights fund families that offer four or more index funds, each representing differing segments of the financial markets.

Indexing for a Large Financial Institution

A single S&P 500 index fund, internally managed by a large institutional investor, illustrates how an index fund operates. Let's assume initial investment of $200 million to allow for efficiencies of scale in trading and fund management. In the interest of simplicity, the example excludes subsequent additions or withdrawals and also coordination of transactions with other index funds. Under these circumstances, the manager of the institutional index fund focuses on the three principal challenges: (1) making the initial investment, (2) timely reinvestment of dividend income, and (3) adjustment for substitutions in the index or other factors that affect the weightings of the individual securities that make up the index.

Making the Initial Investment

With an initial investment of $200 million, the fund is large enough to include all the issues in the S&P 500. In attempting to replicate the index, the fund manager balances two competing goals. One goal is to match the weightings in the index as closely as possible. To the extent that the matching is less than perfect, the fund return risks lagging that of the index by something more than transaction costs. The other goal is to limit transaction costs, since they directly subtract from total return. If the only concern were matching the index—without regard for transaction costs—the manager would aim to duplicate the precise weighting of each issue in the index, completing all transactions at the closing market prices as soon as cash becomes available for investment. To hold down transaction costs, however, orders are likely to be rounded to 100-share lots (or even 1000 shares). Suppose, for example, the precise weighting of a stock priced at 36 amounts to $513,036, calling for 14,251 shares. Rounding to 14,300 shares would result in overweighting of about 3/10 of 1%. Since shares of almost all stocks in the fund would be overweighted or underweighted by very small percentages, the individual tracking errors in one direction are likely to offset in large part those in the other direction. Although a small net tracking error is likely in any single year, the annual tracking errors partially offset each other over longer periods.

Brokers handling trades for index funds are ordinarily willing to negotiate much more favorable terms than for other investors. The index fund manager, communicating by computer, submits to the broker a list of the issues to be purchased. The broker, in competition with other brokers, provides a bid to complete all transactions at a designated price, such as the closing market price. The commission may amount to as little as 2 or 3 cents per share—or even less—depending on such factors as the size of the order and the anticipated difficulty of completing individual transactions.

The broker is able to guarantee transaction prices at very low commission rates for several reasons. First, the trades involved in the order are *informationless*. The broker does not have to worry that the client, in presenting a buy order, has information that will push up the price before completion of the order. Second, *spreading the order over a large number of issues* reduces the risk to the broker. If the broker unexpectedly has to pay up for one stock, very likely another stock becomes available at a lower-than-expected price. Third, *hedges in the futures market* can at least partially protect the broker against changes in the general level of stock prices before transactions are completed. S&P 500 futures, reflecting the high degree of liquidity in trading markets, usually serve this purpose.

Sampling to Save Transaction Costs

Carefully controlled sampling enhances savings in transaction costs but not without risk of net increase in tracking error. Up to now, we have assumed that the separately managed fund replicates the stocks in the S&P 500 Index. Sampling, which relies on a selected group of the issues to represent the entire index, provides another possible choice. Reduction in the number of transactions through sampling is likely to provide more-than-corresponding savings in transaction costs as the fund manager, in choosing between alternative transactions, takes into account differences in prospective transaction costs. To cushion the impact of sampling on tracking error, the method of sample selection is critical.

The early days of indexing provide a simple illustration of how a poorly selected sample may result in unexpected difficulties. One of several index fund managers that entered the market in the 1970s aimed to meet the goals of an S&P 500 index fund by holding only the 250 stocks with the largest market capitalizations. Although these large-capitalization issues accounted at that time for about 90% of the total market value of the stocks in the index, they sometimes performed very differently from the small-capitalization issues that were omitted from the index fund. The method was abandoned soon after a period when the fund return badly lagged that of the S&P 500, reflecting a period of higher average returns for small-capitalization issues than for those with larger capitalizations.

To sample successfully requires a reliable method of matching sample characteristics with index characteristics. Index funds that track indexes with many more issues than the S&P 500 are virtually certain to rely on sampling techniques. A policy of holding all of the stocks in the Wilshire 5000 or the Russell 2000 would raise transaction costs to unacceptable levels. Although sampling methods vary considerably, they are likely to incorporate such measures as industry classification, market capitalization, or financial benchmarks.

For an S&P 500 index fund, the choice between holding all the stocks in the index or a carefully selected sample depends on the circumstances. Very large index funds are likely to hold all the stocks in the index, while smaller funds, especially where the cash inflows and outflows are relatively unpredictable, may determine that sampling is the better alternative. An S&P 500 index fund, for example, may hold all of the 250 stocks in the index with the largest market capitalizations, but sample the remaining 250. The largest 250 trade in highly liquid markets and currently represent 87% of the total market value of the index stocks. The remaining 250 stocks, incurring higher transaction costs in less liquid markets, account for about 13% of the market value represented by the index. This approach limits sampling errors to a small part of the fund (13% of the market value). At the same time, it more than proportionally reduces transaction costs, since it samples the 250 stocks that represent the higher average trading costs.

Reinvesting Dividends

Cash dividends, unless passed along directly to the client, require prompt reinvestment. The example presented here, as explained earlier, assumes a single institutional index fund, managed independently of other funds and experiencing neither cash additions nor withdrawals. Accordingly, there is no opportunity to combine dividend reinvestment with other cash flows. Under such circumstances, transaction costs would become unacceptable if the fund reinvested the cash dividends as received each day in each of the 500 issues according to their respective weights. A simple alternative is to accumulate cash dividends in a short-term investment fund (STIF)—much like the money market funds familiar to individual investors—for specified periods, such as a month. Purchase of S&P 500 futures contracts to represent the cash in the STIF account may be used to provide a temporary hedge against a rise in stock prices. At the end of the month (or other designated period), the fund manager moves the accumulated cash into the stock market. In the absence of special factors affecting the weightings in the index, rounding rules determine the stocks to be purchased. (As discussed in the earlier section on weightings, rounding rules save transaction costs by rounding the order for each issue up or down to the nearest 100 or 1000 shares.) For example, one stock that has been slightly underweighted because of the last application of the rounding rule may now serve as a candidate for purchase. Another stock, slightly overweighted until now, will be passed over until a subsequent round of cash reinvestment.

Adjusting for Index Revisions

Revisions in index weightings periodically provide further reason for adjustment in fund weightings. The most widely publicized adjustment results from substitution of one stock for another in the index. Sponsors of the index may do so for any one of several reasons:

- A stock may no longer trade because of merger or takeover.
- The underlying company may deteriorate to the point that the market value of its stock no longer represents a significant market segment.
- Newer stocks in rapidly growing industries warrant weight in the index, displacing established issues that have become less representative of the current market.

Whatever the reason for the change, the burden of transaction costs resulting from such revisions in the index is small. Substitutions in the S&P 500 are infrequent, and, when they occur, they affect only a small portion of the market value of an index fund with 500 issues. Over the past 5 years, for example, substitutions in the S&P 500 have averaged 19 per year—only about 4% of the 500 issues included in the index. The weight of these issues in the index, reflecting a tendency toward below-average market capitalizations, ordinarily amounts to considerably less than suggested by the number of issues.

Other revisions in the index do not necessarily require immediate adjustment in the index fund. Consider, for example, an increase in the market value of a stock from $5 billion to $5.2 billion as a result of the public sale of $200 million of newly issued shares. The resulting 4% increase in market value means that the stock's weighting in the S&P 500 will increase in proportion. Alternatively, suppose a $200 million buyback of shares reduces the market value for another stock from $5 billion to $4.8 billion. As a result, the 4% decline in the S&P 500 weighting means a proportional reduction in the weighting in the index fund. In either example, the change in market capitalization is much smaller than if the index had eliminated the stock itself. For the example of our $200 million separately managed index fund, transactions could be deferred until the next opportunity to reinvest dividends. Where newly issued shares have increased total market value of outstanding shares, a disproportionate part of the dividend reinvestment can be concentrated in these shares. Where the buyback of shares has reduced total market value, the inflow of funds avoids adding to the holding until balance has been restored.

Mutual Funds: Indexing for Individual Investors

Although index mutual funds build on investment-industry experience with institutional index funds, the two products differ in several respects:

- Administrative expenses for the index mutual fund are necessarily much greater than for the separately managed institutional index fund.

- Management of cash flows, depending on the individual decisions of many different shareholders and prospective shareholders, is more complex.

- In marketing the index mutual fund, shareholder service and convenience rank high in importance, sometimes overshadowing significant differences in the expenses that burden returns.

- The index mutual fund combines the investment technology involved in the management of the institutional index fund with other considerations that apply to the operation of mutual funds in general.

Higher Administrative Expenses

Administrative expenses for the index mutual fund, as for other mutual funds, reflect the broad client base. Where the institutional index fund in our previous example serves only one large client, the index mutual fund aims to serve many thousands of shareholders. As new shareholders buy into the fund, at least a few existing shareholders withdraw for one reason or another. Each shareholder transaction, whether initially to establish an account or subsequently to add or to withdraw funds, requires record keeping and communications, including costs of toll-free telephone lines and mailings. In addition, index mutual funds incur administrative expenses in several areas that do not apply to management of the institutional index fund. They include fixed costs relating to preparation of fund prospectuses, mandatory dissemination of periodic reports, and legally required meetings of directors and shareholders.

Managing Cash Flows

To minimize the burden of transaction costs, the index mutual fund may impose various limitations on cash flows. Both index mutual funds and separately managed institutional index funds offset cash flows into and out of the fund to the extent possible in order to control transaction costs. For the index mutual fund, the challenge is greater because of the diversity of the client base and the continuing opportunity for new clients to invest in the fund and established shareholders to withdraw. If, on a certain day, the cash inflow, including cash dividends, amounts to $1.5 million, but withdrawals total $1 million, only the net addition to the fund of $0.5 million generates transaction costs.

To avoid undue disruptions from market timers, withdrawals may be limited during a specified time period or, through imposition of penalties, discouraged. For example, the Dreyfus S&P 500 Index Fund imposes a 1% fee on redemptions within six months after opening an account. In other cases, an allowance for transaction costs may be charged to the client as new funds are added. In such event, the client that generates the transactions pays the costs rather than the investors already established in the fund. A transaction fee—payable to the portfolio and not to the management company—ordinarily applies to index funds involved in markets where transaction costs are high. For example, Vanguard imposes a transaction fee for purchases of shares of 0.5% for the Extended Market Portfolio (index fund representing medium- and small-cap domestic stocks) and 0.75% for the Total International Portfolio (combination of foreign-stock index funds).

Note that a fee for transaction costs differs fundamentally from a sales load, either front end or deferred. When an investor acquires shares of the fund, the transaction fee, added directly to fund assets for the benefit of existing shareholders, offsets the transaction costs specifically related to the newly acquired shares. In contrast, the sales load, with no proceeds to shareholders, supports the fund's marketing program. It compensates the fund management company and/or the broker, the financial planner, or other sales agent for the selling effort.

Marketing Index Mutual Funds

For the index mutual fund, marketing depends on shareholder service and convenience as well as performance relative to the designated index. Whether delivered by a mutual fund to the individual investor or as a separately managed fund to a large financial institution, indexing must achieve an acceptable level of tracking (that is, an acceptably close match between the returns of the index fund and the returns of the target index). The standards for the shareholders in the index mutual fund, however, are likely to be more flexible than for the client of a separately managed institutional index fund. A simple example suggests the reason. If an incremental tracking error lowers investment return of a $100-million institutional index fund by only 1/10 of 1%, the net reduction amounts to $100,000. The comparable reduction for a shareholder with $10,000 invested in an index mutual fund is $10. The institutional investor cannot easily tolerate an avoidable loss of investment return amounting to $100,000. The shareholder in the index mutual fund, in contrast, may accept the $10 reduction in return in exchange for the convenience of dealing with the family of funds that holds his or her other investments.

Portfolio Building Blocks

While the examples thus far have featured the S&P 500, index mutual funds based on many other indexes have become available in recent years. At year end 1996, Morningstar—a leading mutual fund reference service—listed 71 index mutual funds with initial purchase requirements of no more than $5000. Together, they provide the individual investor with a range of portfolio building blocks. Let's look at five fund families that offer index mutual funds—three included among the ten leading mutual fund companies and two others, each independently offering four different index funds. These five fund families account for 26 of the 71 index mutual funds broadly available for purchase by the individual investor at year end 1996. Combined assets for the 26 funds amounted to $53.1 billion, more than 90% of the $58.5-billion total for index mutual funds broadly available to individual investors.

Among the leading fund families, two initiated major new index fund programs during 1997. Fidelity, which has sponsored an S&P 500 index fund since 1990, has announced plans to introduce three additional index funds to serve individual investors. Merrill Lynch, not previously represented in index funds, introduced a total of four index funds in early 1997. Because of the very important role of each of these firms in serving the individual investor, we include a comment on each in our survey of fund organizations that offer a family of four or more index funds.

The Vanguard Group

Although an increasing number of fund families have introduced index mutual funds in recent years, The Vanguard Group, as the pioneer in bringing indexing to the individual investor, remains the leader by a wide margin. Now the second largest mutual fund family, Vanguard accounts for 9% of the total assets of equity and bond mutual funds (excluding money market funds), but 81% of index mutual fund assets. Morningstar lists 15 index mutual funds that Vanguard offers to individual investors. To bring the Vanguard total of funds to 16, as shown in Table 2-1, we have added to the Morningstar list the Vanguard Total International Equity Index Portfolio. Introduced during the first half of 1996, the Total International Portfolio holds shares in the European, Pacific (Free), and Select Emerging Markets (Free) portfolios, with weightings pro-

Table 2-1: Index mutual funds offered by The Vanguard Group in 1996.

Fund Name	Matching Index
Large-Cap Domestic Stocks	
Vanguard Index 500	S&P 500
Vanguard Index Growth	S&P 500/BARRA Growth
Vanguard Index Value	S&P 500/BARRA Value
Small-Cap Domestic Stocks	
Vanguard Index Extended Market	Wilshire 4500
Vanguard SmallCap Stock	Russell 2000
Vanguard REIT Index	Morgan Stanley REIT
Total Domestic Stock Market	
Vanguard Index Total Stock Market	Wilshire 5000
International Stocks	
Vanguard Total International	MSCI Europe, Pacific (Free) & Select Emerging Markets (Free)
Vanguard Intl. Equity European	MSCI Europe
Vanguard Intl. Equity Pacific	MSCI Pacific (Free)
Vanguard Intl. Equity Emerg. Mkt.	MSCI Select Emerging Markets (Free)*
Domestic Bonds	
Vanguard Total Bond Market	Lehman Bros. Aggregate Bond Index
Vanguard Long-Term Bond	Lehman Bros. Mut.Fd. Long Gov./ Corp. Index
Vanguard Intermediate-Term Bond	Lehman Bros. Mut. Fd. Interm. Gov./ Corp. Index
Vanguard Short-Term Bond	Lehman Bros. Mut. Fd. Short Gov./ Corp. Index
Domestic Stocks and Bonds	
Vanguard Balanced Index	Wilshire 5000 (60%) plus Lehman Brothers Aggregate Bond (40%)

Source: Fund prospectuses (all funds other than REITS, May 19, 1997; REIT Index Fund, May 30, 1997), The Vanguard Group of Investment Companies, Valley Forge, PA.

*Footnote to Appendix 2-4 defines the Vanguard "Select" version of the MSCI Emerging Markets (Free) Index.

portional to the market values represented by each index. Table 2-1 does not include two institutional index funds, each with a minimum initial purchase requirement of $10 million.

As you can see by the range of offerings in Table 2-1, Vanguard provides the investor with considerable flexibility in indexing the various segments of the financial markets. The Vanguard Balanced Index provides broadly diversified representation of both the domestic stock and bond markets. Alternatively, investors may hold various combinations of domestic stock and bond funds to adjust allocation of assets to their particular objectives. They may also supplement these holdings with index funds representing foreign stock markets.

Schwab Funds

With the addition of an S&P 500 index fund during 1996, Schwab offers four index mutual funds. Together, they provide representation in domestic stocks (ranging from large- to small-cap) and in foreign stocks. Table 2-2 identifies each of these funds along with the matching index.

Table 2-2: Index mutual funds offered by Schwab Funds in 1996.

Fund Name	*Matching Index*
Large-Cap Domestic Stocks	
Schwab 1000	Schwab 1000
Schwab 500	S&P 500
Small-Cap Domestic Stocks	
Schwab Small-Cap Index	Schwab Small-Cap
International Stocks	
Schwab International Index	Schwab International

Source: Fund prospectuses, February 28, 1997, Schwab Funds, Charles Schwab & Co., Inc., San Francisco, CA.

Galaxy Funds

Galaxy Funds sponsors four index mutual funds, representing both the domestic stock and bond markets. As listed in Table 2-3, these funds offer participation in the market for U.S. Treasury bonds as well as both large- and small-capitalization stocks in the domestic market. Galaxy also manages an industry index fund specializing in electric utility stocks.

Table 2-3: Index mutual funds offered by Galaxy Funds at December 31, 1996.

Fund Name	Matching Index
Large-Cap Domestic Stocks	
Galaxy II Large Company Index	S&P 500
Small-Cap Domestic Stocks	
Galaxy II Small Company Index	Russell Special Small Company
Industry Stock Funds	
Galaxy II Utility Index	Russell 1000 Utility
Domestic Bonds	
Galaxy II U.S. Treas. Index	Salomon Bros. Bond Index—U.S. Treasuries

Source: Fund prospectuses, August 1, 1996, The Galaxy Funds, Fleet Financial Group, Inc., Rochester, NY.

Fidelity

Fidelity, as the largest fund family in terms of assets under management, is in a strong position to offer a highly competitive group of index funds. Table 2-4 lists the Spartan Market Index fund, previously available as the Fidelity Market Index Fund, along with the three new additions to become available under the *Spartan* name. The new Spartan funds will maintain low expense ratios but are expected to require a minimum initial purchase of $25,000.

Table 2-4: Fidelity plans the introduction of three additional index funds.

Fund Name	Matching Index
Large-Cap Domestic Stocks	
Spartan Market Index*	S&P 500
M/S-Cap Domestic Stocks	
Spartan Extended Market Index**	Wilshire 4500
Total Domestic Stock Market	
Spartan Total Market Index**	Wilshire 5000
International Stocks	
Spartan International Index**	MSCI EAFE

*Previously Fidelity Market Index, fund prospectus, June 20, 1997, Fidelity Investments, Boston, MA.
**To be introduced.

Table 2-5: Index mutual funds offered by Merrill Lynch during 1997.

Fund Name	Matching Index
Large-Cap Domestic Stocks	
Merrill Lynch Large-Cap Index Series	S&P 500
Small-Cap Domestic Stocks	
Merrill Lynch Small-Cap Index Series	Russell 2000
International Stocks	
Merrill Lynch International Equity Index Series	MSCI EAFE (GDP weighted)
Domestic Bonds	
Merrill Lynch Aggregate Bond Index Series	Lehman Bros. Aggregate Bond

Source: Fund prospectuses, Merrill Lynch Asset Management, New York, NY, January 31, 1997.

Merrill Lynch

Table 2-5 lists the four index mutual funds that Merrill Lynch introduced during 1997. The entry of Merrill Lynch into this market seems particularly significant in view of the firm's leading position in financial services. Merrill Lynch not only ranks as the largest brokerage firm, but also qualifies as the sixth leading mutual fund family. Merrill Lynch offers the new index funds to 401(k) plans, but also makes them available to individual investors.

Fund Families

Table 2-6, listing the ten leading fund families at year end 1996, identifies those that offer index mutual funds to individual investors. The rankings reflect assets under management other than money market funds. The list excludes those funds limited to institutional use or requiring a minimum initial purchase of more than $5000. By way of perspective, we also list separate data for Schwab and Galaxy as well as aggregate data for the remainder of the mutual fund industry.

Broadening Choices

The choice of index mutual funds available to individual investors seems certain to broaden further in the years ahead. The number of

Table 2-6: Index mutual funds offered by fund families in 1996.

Fund Family	All Stock & Bond Funds		Index Funds	
	# Funds	Assets (billions)	# Funds	Assets (billions)
Most Assets				
Fidelity	193	$ 317	1*	$ 1.6
Vanguard	68	188	16	47.4
American Funds Group	25	171	0	0.0
Franklin/Templeton	155	124	0	0.0
Putnam	144	107	0	0.0
Merrill Lynch	262	69	0*	0.0
T. Rowe Price	55	58	1	0.8
IDS Mutual Funds	52	49	0	0.0
Dean Witter	53	45	0	0.0
AIM Family of Funds	36	44	0	0.0
By Way of Comparison				
Schwab	16	3	4	2.5
Galaxy	20	2	4	0.8
All Others	5176	879	45	5.4
Total	6255	$2056	71	$58.5

Source: *Morningstar Principia for Mutual Funds, January 1997,* Morningstar, Inc., Chicago, IL © 1997.

*New index funds introduced or planned for introduction during 1997.

such funds keeps increasing as total assets have grown at a dramatic rate. As individual investors increasingly recognize the advantages of indexing, they will stimulate continuing response on the part of the mutual fund industry. Understandably, most fund families, preferring to market products that permit higher management fees and other revenues, are unlikely to promote index funds in a substantial way anytime soon. An increasing number of fund families, nevertheless, are likely to offer a line of index mutual funds as a necessary means to keep shareholder investments in house, particularly in competition for 401(k) assets. Individual investors who seek to acquire shares in one or more index mutual funds will likely hold other mutual funds. And many of these investors prefer the convenience of maintaining their mutual fund investments with one fund group.

PART 2

ASSESSING THE BENEFITS

chapter three

MEASURING THE COSTS

First of Two Key Issues

Why would anyone want to invest in an index fund? Clearly, it would be better to own the winners in the index—and to avoid the losers. That's the aim of *active management*. As the traditional approach to investing, active management expects to reap the rewards of superior forecasting skill. Why, then, should the investor settle for indiscriminate buying of every issue that happens to be in the index?

Addressing the first of two key issues that bear on the role of indexing in investment management, Chapter 3 examines the cost savings achieved by stock index funds in relation to active management. Chapter 4, which immediately follows, considers bond index funds with the same end in view. Chapters 3 and 4 in combination provide the background for the review in Chapter 5 of the second key issue: the goal of active management, which is to benefit from superior forecasting skill. Together, these chapters direct attention to a central question that everyone with assets to invest in the financial markets should be asking: *What is the likelihood that the special forecasting skill at your command will overcome the cost advantages of indexing?* Part 2 establishes indexing as the framework for the management of financial assets, but also identifies circumstances that call for departure from the index fund framework.

Focusing on Mutual Funds

Since individual investors increasingly make use of mutual funds to meet their investment goals, let's focus primarily on how index mutual funds compare with actively managed mutual funds. For most individual investors, mutual funds provide the most effective way of developing an appropriately diversified investment portfolio. As estimated by the Investment Company Institute, 37% of all households owned one or more mutual funds by April 1996.[1] Even for very wealthy individuals, mutual funds now account for a rapidly growing proportion of their total investments, as reported recently by *The New York Times:*

> Not so long ago, the wealthy hired someone to manage their money. Along with a certain snob appeal, they could count on portfolios created just for them and on ready access to a cadre of elite managers. Mutual funds were the investments of commoners.
>
> No more. The wealthy are moving into mutual funds—as are heavily larded institutions.
>
> Among the converts (to mutual funds) is an 83-year-old New York business man who has moved part of his $150 million portfolio into mutual funds since opening an account in 1987 with Ron Baron, president of Baron Capital, Inc., a New York money manager who started two mutual funds. "I bet 10 years ago he wouldn't have invested in funds," Mr. Baron said.
>
> Consultants say the trend is pronounced. "There's been a sea change over the last five years," said Michael Stolper, whose San Diego firm tracks investment managers and publishes a mutual fund newsletter. Private money management always was a vanity business," Mr. Stolper explained. "It really had a lot to do with being able to hold up your head at cocktail parties," he said. But now, "mutual funds have been legitimized as investments for the wealthy."
>
> The Institute for Private Investors, based in Summit, N.J., held a symposium in June about private accounts and mutual funds for its members, 60 percent of whom oversee portfolios of $50 million or more. "I was startled by the interest and enthusiasm shown by our very wealthiest clients," said Charlotte B. Beyer, the group's founder. "When I started in the business, mutual funds were considered crass."
>
> Graystone partners of Chicago, which tracks money managers and advises America's wealthiest families, conducted a survey at the end of last year that showed its target clients, who have $100 million in assets, are looking to put a bigger share of their assets in mutual funds within five years. "The average wealthy family that we work with has over 200 accounts," David B. Horn, the managing director of Graystone, said. "You have to look for efficient ways to invest these accounts." Mutual funds can be an efficient way. ..."[2]

---

[1]"Fundamentals, December 1966," *Investment Company Institute,* Washington, DC, p. 1.

[2]Carole Gould, "Private Money Managers or Mutual Funds? The Gap Narrows," *The New York Times,* September 17, 1995, p. F-7. Copyright © 1995 by The New York Times Co. Reprinted by permission.

Cost Advantage of Indexing

To demonstrate the cost advantage of index mutual funds, let's examine in this chapter domestic equity funds in considerable detail. While this analysis does not specifically address the index fund cost advantage for foreign stock portfolios, the same principles apply—only more so. For the mutual fund shareholder, both the charges included in the expense ratios and the transaction costs tend to increase the overall cost differentials between index funds and actively managed funds. Sales loads, moreover, burden returns for about 60% of actively managed equity funds.

Indexing Domestic Equities

Let's examine separately two segments of the domestic equity market based on market capitalization. Among index funds, those that match the S&P 500 represent large capitalization (large-cap) stocks. Therefore, S&P 500 index funds should be compared with actively managed funds holding issues with similarly large market capitalization.

The index that represents virtually all the publicly traded equity market apart from the S&P 500 is the Wilshire 4500. It consists of two-thirds medium-capitalization (medium-cap) and one-third small-capitalization (small-cap) stocks. To reflect its composition, the corresponding market segment is identified with medium/small-cap (m/s-cap) stocks.

For both index and actively managed mutual funds, the designation as *large-cap* or *m/s-cap* depends on the median market capitalization as defined by Morningstar, a leading source of mutual fund statistics. For each individual stock, the market capitalization reflects market price per share multiplied by the number of shares outstanding. To identify the median market capitalization for each fund, Morningstar weights each issue by market value. Based on this definition, *"Half of the fund's money* [our italics] is invested in the companies larger than our median market capitalization calculation, and half is invested in smaller issues."[3] Following the definition provided by Morningstar, Table 3-1 classifies equity mutual funds with a median holding in excess of $5 billion as large-cap.

---

[3]*Morningstar Principia for Mutual Funds, January 1997,* Morningstar, Inc., Chicago, IL, © 1997.

Table 3-1: Domestic equity mutual funds, 1996.

	Actively Managed Funds	*Index Fund Benchmark*
Large-Cap >$5 Billion		
Number of Funds	359	1
Aggregate Market Value	$703.0 billion	$30.3 billion
Average Median Cap	$13.4 billion	$24.6 billion
M/S-Cap <$5 Billion		
Number of Funds	321	1
Aggregate Market Value	$249.6 billion	$2.1 billion
Average Median Cap	$1.9 billion	$1.3 billion

Source: *Morningstar Principia for Mutual Funds, January 1997,* Morningstar, Inc., Chicago, IL, © 1997.

The remainder of the funds—both medium-cap and small-cap—are grouped together under the heading m/s-cap funds. Together, the two categories include 680 domestic equity funds. We have limited the sample to funds with assets in excess of $100 million and minimum initial purchase of no more than $5000. The data exclude funds restricted to institutional use, enhanced index funds, which combine active management with indexing; and conventional index funds. The average median capitalization reflects equal weighting for the funds in each category irrespective of net assets.

For each of the actively managed categories, the table displays an *index fund benchmark.* Because the purpose of the benchmark is to focus on indexing generally available to individual investors, those index funds requiring high-minimum investment or marketed primarily to financial institutions have been excluded. For the large-cap category, the Vanguard Index Trust 500 Portfolio, an index fund that replicates the S&P 500, serves as the benchmark. While a number of competing funds have become available during the past few years, the Vanguard 500, introduced in 1976, still accounts for about 75% of the market value of funds that serve our objective. For similar reasons, the Vanguard Index Trust Extended Market Portfolio represents the m/s-cap category of index funds included in Table 3-1. It is the only index mutual fund of significant size that focuses on the broad range of the domestic stock market not included in the S&P 500. These two Vanguard funds in combination (70% S&P 500 and 30% Extended Market) approximately match the market performance of the entire domestic stock market. (Chapter 7 provides details concerning additional index fund benchmarks.)

Confronting Sticker Shock

In addressing the costs of investing, let's draw on an analogy from the automobile showroom. The prospective automobile buyer, when considering a new model, routinely examines the window sticker to determine the total cost. For investors, there is no comparable sticker. Yet every approach to investing entails costs—some hidden, others overlooked, and still others recognized but too easily ignored.

Investors may search the mutual fund prospectus for expense ratios and sales loads, or they may look to the broker's confirmation statement to identify commissions. But these documents, even when scrutinized by the conscientious investor, do not come close to telling the whole story. To provide perspective on the cost savings offered by indexing, the last section of this chapter presents a series of mutual fund "window stickers." Investors who have never itemized index fund cost savings are likely to be surprised. They may even experience what observers of the automobile industry describe as "sticker shock." Our window sticker will compare costs in four categories:

- **Reported Expenses.** Mutual funds report in the prospectus the expenses that management charges against ordinary income. Parts of these expenses pay for the investment research, decision making, and portfolio implementation that determine the fund's investment performance. Administrative expenses cover such mundane activities as record keeping and mailings to shareholders. Other expenses include payments for services of directors, auditors, lawyers, and custodians of securities—as well as for state and local taxes. For about half of the equity mutual funds, the expense ratio also includes 12b-1 expenses (advertising and marketing costs authorized by the Securities and Exchange Commission under the Investment Company Act of 1940).

- **Transaction Costs.** The mutual fund prospectus, although it does not identify transaction costs, provides sufficient information to permit useful estimates. Publicly disclosed data on turnover records the total number of annual purchases or sales (whichever is smaller) in relation to total holdings. Turnover data, together with an estimate of the cost per transaction, serve to estimate transaction costs. Since transaction costs subtract directly from shareholder asset value, they correspondingly reduce shareholder returns.

- **Sales Load.** About 60% of actively managed equity mutual funds require a one-time payment either to purchase the fund or to redeem it. Because the front-end load or the deferred load burdens the investment only at the beginning or end of fund ownership, investors may overlook the resulting reduction in the annual rate of return over the life of the holding.

- **Capital Gains Taxes.** A shareholder of a mutual fund becomes liable for taxes on capital gains realized and distributed by the fund. The fund passes net realized capital gains along to shareholders each year in order to maintain its exemption from taxes on capital gains. To the extent shareholders are able to defer payment of capital gains taxes, they benefit. Tax deferral means more money to invest until the taxes are actually paid.

Narrowing the Expense Ratio

Indexing avoids most of the expenses incurred by actively managed funds. For indexing, there is no need for high-priced portfolio managers; the analytical work of security analysts; the travel budgets required to interview company managements; or payment for the advice of strategists, economists, or other consultants. Portfolio management of index funds is much less labor intensive than that of actively managed funds.

The goal of the index fund manager—to duplicate the returns of the index—provides further incentive for frugality in fund management. Suppose, for example, the annual performance of the index fund manager were to fall 0.3% (3/10 of 1%) short of that for the index. If the index fund, through intense cost control, could reduce management expenses by 0.1 percentage point, the improvement in the performance match becomes a visible competitive advantage.

In contrast, the actively managed fund, as it aims to concentrate on the winners and to avoid the losers, expects to perform differently from the index that serves as its performance benchmark. If it succeeds, returns may exceed those of the benchmark index by several percentage points. Alternatively, fund performance, when reflecting a lack of forecasting success, may lag the benchmark index by several percentage points. In this framework, who would notice if the management expenses of perhaps 1.0 to 1.5 percentage points were to decline—or rise—by 0.1 percentage point?

Shareholders seem to have paid little attention to the rise in the overall expense ratio over the last several years despite the huge increase in mutual fund assets. In response to this development, a *Wall Street Journal* columnist observed:

> This is a disgrace, especially in an industry that has enjoyed spectacular growth and booming profits. ...
>
> Over the past 10 years (ended 1995), annual expenses at diversified U.S. stock funds have risen to 1.41% from 1.21%, ... Arguably, these numbers don't tell the whole story. Average expenses have been driven up by the introduction of many newer, smaller funds, though the numbers have also been held down by the proliferation of funds for institutional investors, which typically have low expenses. ...
>
> If you exclude funds introduced in the past 10 years and those that are open only to institutional investors, what do you find? At stock funds, expenses over the past decade have dipped slightly to 1.19% from 1.21%, despite an almost five-fold increase in average fund assets. Economies of scale? The benefits clearly aren't trickling down to stock-fund holders.[4]

How Much Savings?

Table 3-2 underscores the contrast between expense ratios for actively managed mutual funds and index mutual funds holding stocks with similar market capitalization. Comparisons of actively managed funds with index fund benchmarks—even allowing for considerable variation from fund to fund—present an unambiguous conclusion: *Management expenses for actively managed funds are almost always much higher than for the benchmark index fund.*

Table 3-2: Expense ratios (expenses as percentage of assets) for equity mutual funds, 1996.

	Actively Managed Funds	*Index Fund Benchmark*	*Difference*
Large-Cap	1.16%	0.20%	0.96%
M/S-Cap	1.43	0.25	1.18

Source: Morningstar Principia for Mutual Funds, January 1997, Morningstar, Inc., Chicago, IL, © 1997.

[4]Jonathan Clements, "Keeping an Eye on Mutual Fund Costs Can Pay Large Dividends for Investors," *The Wall Street Journal*, August 27, 1996, p. C-1. Reprinted by permission of *The Wall Street Journal*, © 1996 Dow Jones & Company, Inc. All Rights Reserved Worldwide.

Based on the averages for each category of actively managed funds, the annual savings for the corresponding index fund benchmarks cluster around 1 percentage point. (Expense ratios for the benchmark index funds assume total holdings of Vanguard funds of at least $10,000. Until holdings reach this level, Vanguard imposes a supplementary fee on each account of $10 per year.) Since the average expense ratios do not reflect the wide range of variation among actively managed funds, we urge the investor to consult the fund prospectus to identify the details of the expense ratio for the specific fund. Figure 3-1, displaying graphically the distribution of expense ratios for the two categories of actively managed equity mutual funds, highlights the range of variation.

Assessing Transaction Costs

Most investors routinely underestimate transaction costs. They are generally aware of the commission charged by brokers, since, where applicable, brokerage statements issued to confirm trades explicitly identify commission charges. (We ignore provision for taxes, delivery fees, or other miscellaneous charges since they tend to be relatively small.) Yet total transaction costs almost always exceed commission charges by a considerable margin. A survey of a number of studies of transaction costs reached the following conclusion:

> Think of transaction costs as an iceberg, with the commission being the tip above the surface. *The major parts of transaction costs are unobservable.* They do not appear in accounting statements, and they appear only indirectly in manager evaluations. Even formal studies cannot clearly gauge the size and relative importance of transaction cost components.[5]

Identifying Hidden Costs

The bid-and-ask spread provides a simple example of how hidden costs add to total transaction costs. Suppose a buyer and a seller, working through their individual brokers, simultaneously com-

---

[5]Jack L. Treynor and Wayne H. Wagner, "Implementation of Portfolio Building: Execution," included in John L. Maginn and Donald L. Tuttle, *Managing Investment Portfolios*, The Association for Investment Management and Research, Charlottesville, VA, © 1990, Chap. 12, p. 35.

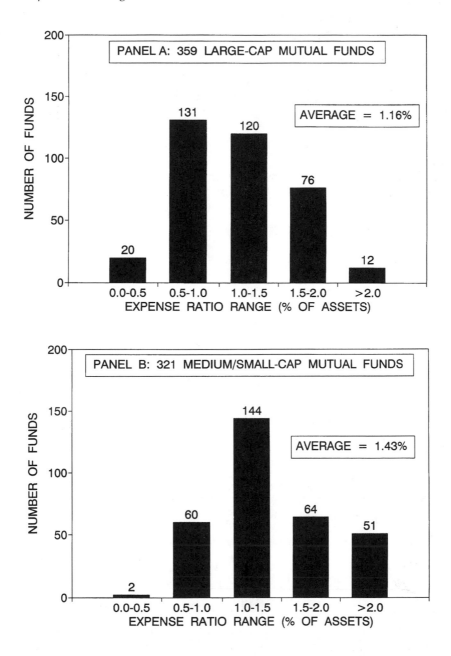

Figure 3-1: EXPENSE RATIO. For most actively managed equity funds, expense ratios range between 0.5% and 2.0% (1996 data). (*Source: Morningstar Principia for Mutual Funds, January 1997*, Morningstar, Inc., Chicago, IL © 1997)

plete transactions in a stock that last traded at 20. The seller receives the bid price of 19 7/8 before deduction of commissions, while the buyer pays the offering price of 20 1/8 before addition of commissions. In this simple example, the seller and buyer together pay 1/4 of a point ($0.25) in addition to their respective commission charges. If we divide the $0.25 equally between buyer and seller, the transaction costs for each amount to commission charges *plus* $0.125.

As a practical matter, useful estimates of hidden costs of trading entail analysis of a large number of transactions. For a single transaction, identification of the hidden charges as market prices change presents a daunting challenge. Purchase of a stock at 20 1/8 that last traded at 20 does not in itself provide an answer. Suppose, since the last trade at a price of 20, market demand for the stock has risen—or fallen. Even if we knew, as suggested in our simple example, prices for a simultaneous purchase and sale, how should the cost be allocated between buyer and seller? Perhaps the buyer in this one instance paid too much or a too eager seller accepted too little. These questions become more manageable, however, through the application of statistical techniques to a large number of transactions.

For any investment portfolio, the burden of transaction costs depends on two key factors. One of these factors is the *average cost per transaction,* reflecting both the broker's commissions and the hidden costs. The other factor is *turnover,* the ratio of purchases or sales (whichever is smaller) to average monthly assets over the year. Multiplication of the cost per transaction times *twice* the turnover estimates *total transaction costs.* Allowing for major differences in market capitalization, Table 3-3 compares estimated transaction costs for equity index funds with those for actively managed equity funds.

Cost per Transaction. As market capitalization declines, cost per transaction tends to rise. One reason is the relationship between market capitalization and market liquidity, reflecting the tendency for trading volume to rise with market capitalization. As shown in Table 3-1, the average median capitalization of holdings for large-cap actively managed funds is *7 times* the comparable figure for m/s-cap funds. It follows—other things equal—that brokers more easily fill purchase and sale orders for large-cap stocks than for m/s-cap stocks.

Table 3-3: Total transaction costs as percentage of net assets (cost/transaction × turnover × 2) for domestic equity mutual funds, 1996.

	Actively Managed Funds	*Index Fund Benchmark*	*Difference*
Large-Cap			
Cost/Transaction	0.40%	0.25%	0.15%
Annual Turnover	71	4	67
Total Trans. Costs	0.57	0.02	0.55
M/S-Cap			
Cost/Transaction	0.80%	0.50%	0.30%
Annual Turnover	92	15	77
Total Trans. Costs	1.47	0.15	1.32

Source (for turnover data): *Morningstar Principia for Mutual Funds, January 1997,* Morningstar, Inc., Chicago, IL, © 1997.

A second reason is the risk to the market maker, who temporarily may hold purchases from the seller until an offsetting sale to a buyer is completed. A similar risk develops if the market maker, to fill a purchase order, temporarily takes a short position. On average, long or short positions in m/s-cap stocks not only may have to be held longer because of the thin markets, but they often are exposed to greater volatility. Accordingly, the hidden component of transaction costs reflects adjustment of the market maker's margin to compensate for the higher level of risk.

Index funds achieve much lower average cost per transaction than do actively managed funds. There are two key reasons:

- Index fund orders are "informationless," since the index fund manager makes no effort to act on information not yet incorporated in market prices. Brokers, relieved of the risk of a client information advantage, compete to handle index fund transactions on terms very favorable to the client.

- Index mutual funds avoid costs for research and certain other services that brokers frequently provide institutional clients. The absence of these charges permits further savings on broker commissions.

Reflecting the combination of these factors, savings for index funds in costs per transaction, as estimated in Table 3-3, are likely

Table 3-4: Comparison of Table 3-3 estimates of cost per transaction with recent (1996) Plexus Group estimates.

Market Cap	Table 3-3 Estimates	Plexus Group Estimates		
		NYSE	*NASDAQ*	*AMEX*
Large	0.40%	0.40%	0.47%	0.19%
M/S	0.80			
Medium		0.60	0.90	0.63
Small		1.02	1.47	1.09

to average about 0.15 percentage point (for large-cap stocks) to around 0.30 percentage point (for m/s-cap stocks).

Estimates of the costs per transaction reflect our survey of research in this area. A report by the Plexus Group, a highly respected consultant to institutional investors, provides a recent (August 1996) example. Table 3-4 compares our estimates in Table 3-3 with the more detailed data provided by the Plexus Group.[6] While the market-capitalization categories in the two series are not precisely the same, they are close enough to highlight areas of broad agreement. For the large-cap stocks, our estimate for cost per transaction of 0.40% closely matches the Plexus figures for large-cap stocks listed both on the New York Stock Exchange (0.40%) and NASDAQ (0.47%). Our m/s-cap stocks include many of the same issues as the combined Plexus categories for medium-cap and small-cap stocks. The m/s-cap estimate for cost per transaction of 0.80% is intermediate between the NYSE and the AMEX figures for medium- and small-cap stocks as listed by Plexus. Since each of the estimates represents an average, the cost of a particular transaction or set of transactions may differ substantially. Variations depend not only on the characteristics of the particular stock, but also on such factors as market conditions, the skill of the trader, and time constraints relating to the trade.

Turnover. Most of the differences in total transaction costs shown in Table 3-3 reflect sharply different levels of turnover. For an actively managed mutual fund, the primary reason for purchase or sale of securities is the changing attractiveness of the issues in the

---

[6]"Quality of Trade Execution in Comparative Perspective: AMEX vs. NASDAQ vs. NYSE," Plexus Group, Los Angeles, CA, August 1996.

fund. The active manager may adjust holdings because of change in market price, change in prospects for the company underlying the stock, or change in anticipated market conditions. Annual turnover for these reasons often accounts for 25% to 100%—or even more—of the shares in the fund. As indicated by Figure 3-2, turnover in 1996 exceeded 100% for 24% of the large-cap funds and 34% of the m/s-cap funds.

The index mutual fund, in contrast, ordinarily reports a much lower level of annual turnover despite three kinds of transactions routinely required by the index fund format.

- As money flows in and out of the fund, the index fund manager must maintain a very-close-to-fully-invested position at all times. Money will flow into the fund as stocks included in the fund pay cash dividends or the public buys additional shares. Money will flow out of the fund as shareholders collect cash dividends (rather than automatically reinvest them), shareholders redeem shares, or management withdraws funds for normal expenses. Only the net purchases (purchases less sales) or net sales (sales less purchases) on a given day need affect transaction costs, since offsetting orders will cancel out.

- Index fund management, particularly for large-cap funds that hold all or most of the issues in the designated index, will adjust the holdings in the fund to correspond to changes in the index. For example, an S&P 500 index fund will sell the stock eliminated from the S&P 500 and buy the issue to be added. Since such changes occur only a few times each year, the impact on transaction costs remains extremely small. From time to time, much smaller adjustments may reflect company buybacks of outstanding shares or the issuance of new shares (as a result of public financing or acquisition through exchange of shares).

- Market price changes will require periodic rebalancing where a limited number of issues represent an index with many more issues. M/s-cap index funds (as well as many large-cap index funds) rely on a sample that includes only a portion of the many issues that make up the index. As time passes and prices change relative to each other, the sample requires revision to maintain diversification that closely matches that of the issues in the index.

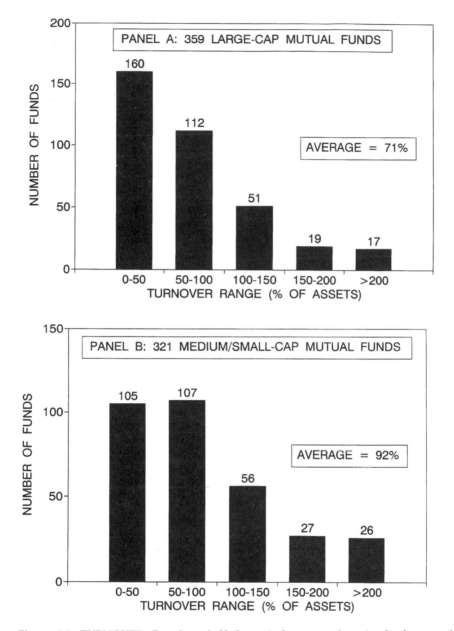

Figure 3-2: TURNOVER. For about half the actively managed equity funds, annual turnover ranges between 50% and 150% (1996 data). (*Source: Morningstar Principia for Mutual Funds, January 1997*, Morningstar, Inc., Chicago, IL, © 1997.)

Transaction-Cost Advantage

Index funds, benefiting from extremely tight control of both cost per transaction and turnover, are able to achieve very large savings in total transaction costs. Since our data identify a single figure for each of the four fund categories, savings will differ in degree depending on the particular circumstances. For comparison of a benchmark index fund with a particular actively managed alternative, the reader may develop his or her own estimate by multiplying 2 times the turnover reported in the fund prospectus times the cost per transaction as estimated in Table 3-3. In the absence of such calculation, however, Table 3-3 suggests a broad rule of thumb. For large-cap stocks, the actively managed mutual fund may incur total transaction costs that average about 0.5 percentage point higher than for the index mutual fund. A comparable rule of thumb for m/s-cap stocks makes use of a round-figure estimate of 1 percentage point. For either category, the investor using the rule of thumb should keep in mind that it represents a single point within a considerable range. As turnover rises and median market capitalization diminishes, the number could be much higher. Conversely, lower turnover and larger median capitalization would tend to lower the differential in transaction costs.

Pay Now or Pay Later

Front-end and deferred loads represent one-time expenses paid by investors in about 60% of the actively managed equity mutual funds. In either case, the proceeds support the fund's marketing effort. A further advantage of index mutual funds is their widespread availability absent such charges:

- For the front-end load, the shareholder pays at the time the investment is made. Consider, for example, an investment of $10,000 in a fund with a load of 5%. After deduction of $500 to provide for the load, the money actually invested in the fund amounts to $9500.

- Alternatively, the deferred load takes the form of a fee to be paid later on redemption of the fund's shares. The redemption schedule may permit decreases in the percentage deduction as the time horizon increases. If the deferred load amounts to 5% during the first year, it may drop by 1 percentage point in each successive year until it entirely disappears.

Sales loads differ fundamentally from transaction fees. The purpose of the sales load is to pay for marketing expenses, including the sales commission. No part of the load is returned to fund shareholders. In contrast, the transaction fee, since it aims to offset the transaction costs incurred on behalf of the new investor in the fund, is paid directly to the fund. It therefore adds to net asset value as an offset to the cost of acquiring shares for the new entrant to the fund. While sales loads average around 5%, transaction fees are usually 1% or less. The Vanguard Extended Market Fund, which serves as the benchmark index fund for m/s-cap stocks, charges a transaction fee amounting to 0.5%. For the Vanguard Total International Portfolio, also a benchmark fund, the transaction fee is 0.75%. In our comparisons of actively managed funds with benchmark index funds, we spread the cost of both the load and the transaction fee over the holding period.

Table 3-5 summarizes data concerning loads for the 680 actively managed domestic equity mutual funds with net assets in excess of $100 million. The expense ratio *includes* 12b-1 expenses, also shown as a percentage of assets. The Securities and Exchange Commission au-

Table 3-5: Sales loads and 12b-1 expenses for actively managed, domestic equity mutual funds, 1996.

	No. Funds	Total Assets (billions)	12b-1 Expenses (%)	Expense Ratio* (%)	Average Load (%)
Large-Cap					
Front-End Load	172	$367	0.22%	1.10%	5.09%
Deferred Load	68	71	0.95	1.76	4.51
No Load	119	265	0.08	0.91	0.00
Total	359	$703	0.31%	1.16%	3.29%
M/S-Cap					
Front-End Load	115	$ 95	0.25%	1.31%	4.90%
Deferred Load	63	39	0.97	2.12	4.00
No Load	143	116	0.08	1.23	0.00
Total	321	$250	0.32%	1.43%	2.54%

Source: Morningstar Principia for Mutual Funds, January 1997, Morningstar, Inc., Chicago, IL, © 1997.

*Includes 12b-1 expenses.

thorizes 12b-1 expenses to support marketing efforts. For the averages of the two broad fund categories, as shown in the table, variations in 12b-1 expenses account for most of the variations in expense ratios.

Front-End Loads: Translating a One-Time Expense into an Annual Rate

How much does a front-end load burden the annual rate of return? The answer depends on the length of the holding period as well as the size of the load. Table 3-6 provides examples based on three common levels of load. Since the annual cost of the load spread over short holding periods, such as one or two years, appears prohibitively large, buyers of load funds are likely to look to much longer time horizons. Note, however, that many "long-term investors" liquidate all or part of their holdings much sooner than initially anticipated. Reasons may include a change in personal financial circumstances, a revision in the shareholder's view of the attractiveness of the fund, or even a recommendation from an advisor who is compensated for switching the client from one load fund to another. A long holding period, moreover, narrows the *annual* cost but, because it is spread over more years, increases the *total* cost as the investment appreciates in value. If the load amounts to 5% of the initial investment, it will still reduce the value of the fund at the time of liquidation by 5% of what it otherwise would be. Suppose a $10,000 investment, in the absence of a load, would grow fivefold to $50,000 over 20 years. With a 5% load, the net asset value of the investment immediately declines to $9500 at the time of purchase. After 20 years, the fivefold increase in the net asset value brings the total to $47,500, indicating that the cost of the load has increased to $2500.

Table 3-6: Annual cost of front-end load assuming 10% compound annual rate of return for the fund.

Load	Holding Period (Years)				
	1	2	5	10	20
4%	4.40%	2.22%	0.89%	0.45%	0.22%
5	5.50	2.79	1.12	0.56	0.28
6	6.60	3.35	1.35	0.68	0.34

Assessing the Annual Cost of Deferred Loads

Data on front-end loads also provide a broad indication of the special costs associated with deferred loads. Although each 1 percentage point paid as a deferred load burdens the shareholder in exactly the same way as an equal percentage paid as front-end load, the deferred load may seem less burdensome than a front-end load for two reasons:

- The initial rate for the deferred load, as a percentage of the value of the fund shares, may be lower than the rate for the front-end load.

- More important, the deferred load may phase out over several years. If so, the buyer of fund shares usually expects to avoid the deferred load by sufficiently extending the holding period.

Even if the shareholder discovers reasons for selling the shares much sooner than initially intended, the deferred load itself will likely amount to less than an alternative front-end load. *After allowance for differences in expense ratios, however, the true cost of the deferred-load alternative may exceed that for the fund with the front-end load.* Where a fund offers its shares subject either to a front-end load or to a schedule of declining redemption fees, it may adjust the expense ratio to compensate for differences in the anticipated proceeds. As indicated in Table 3-5, expense ratios for funds with deferred loads average about 0.75 percentage point higher than expense ratios for funds with front-end loads. This difference primarily reflects larger allowances for 12b-1 marketing expenses. Depending on the specific numbers—the amount of the front-end load, the schedule of deferred loads, the holding period, and the expense ratios—the shares with the front-end load may prove less costly than the deferred-load alternative.

Tax Savings

To this point, we have examined cost comparisons between actively managed funds and index funds without allowance for personal income taxes. For a tax-deferred account, such as an IRA or 401(k) plan, income taxes are clearly not an issue. In contrast, investors that own mutual funds in a taxable personal account become liable for income taxes on dividend distributions, both ordinary income and capital gains, as well as capital gains taxes on redemption of the shares. Since comparisons of mutual funds usually ignore income taxes, investors too often do not take taxes into account in choosing between competing equity mutual funds.

Allowance for personal income taxes requires restatement of the index fund advantage. Ordinary income taxes partially offset expenses (included in the expense ratio) since expenses subtract directly from distributions of income dividends (taxable at the ordinary rate). Similarly, allowance for capital gains taxes partially offsets the burden of transaction costs and sales loads. Since these charges reduce net asset value, they also reduce the potential for realization of capital gains and accompanying capital gains taxes. The index fund cost advantage after allowance for personal income taxes, nevertheless, may exceed the cost advantage before taxes. We direct attention to differences in turnover between index funds and most actively managed funds by way of explaining the implications for capital gains taxes.

Deferral of Capital Gains Taxes

For equity mutual funds in a taxable account, deferral of capital gains taxes ordinarily contributes in a significant way to the index fund cost advantage. A capital gain is realized on sale of a security that has increased in price since purchase. The index fund, reflecting very low turnover, realizes a correspondingly low level of capital gains. Other things equal, the shareholder benefits, since tax regulations defer liability for capital gains taxes until the year in which sale of the appreciated security takes place. Actively managed funds ordinarily generate much higher turnover than index funds, as they continually seek to switch issues perceived as less attractive to those that seem to offer better prospects. Although gains and losses will partially offset each other, the net balance will likely result in a much higher level of realized capital gains—and shareholder capital gains taxes.

To estimate future differentials in realized capital gains, we focus on turnover and market price appreciation. While several other factors may heavily influence realized capital gains in any specific year, these two factors dominate the longer-term average. The history of the past two decades provides an example. Over the 20 years ended 1996, turnover for domestic equity funds averaged 59.5% per year. The compound annual rate of market price appreciation for the S&P 500 over the same interval amounted to 10.1%. Multiplying average turnover (59.5%) times average market price appreciation (10.1%) suggests that realized capital gains averaged about 6.0% annually. This estimate approximates the realized capital gains of 6.3% annually that these funds reported for this period.[7]

Estimating Future Tax Deferrals

Despite the wide range of variables bearing on liabilities for capital gains taxes from year to year, the index fund advantage becomes clear when viewed in long-term perspective. To illustrate, we compare actively managed funds with index fund benchmarks over a series of holding periods. The underlying assumptions take into account both current circumstances and historical experience:

- **Total Returns for Domestic Stocks.** Our assumptions provide a 10% rate of return for both large-cap and m/s-cap stocks. This return is broadly consistent with the record of the S&P 500 over its history since 1926. Since ordinary-income dividends in recent years have accounted for a much smaller proportion of total return than in earlier periods, we assume that they will average only 3 percentage points of the total return for large-cap stocks and 1.5 percentage points for m/s-cap stocks. Accordingly, the long-term assumptions for market price appreciation—at 7.0% and 8.5% for large-cap stocks and m/s-cap stocks, respectively— moderately exceed the historical averages.

- **Personal Income Taxes.** Guided by tax rates as revised by the Taxpayer Relief Act of 1997, we assume an intermediate rate of 31% on ordinary income and the 20% rate on capital gains.

- **Fund Operations.** Table 3-7 brings together fund operating data previously displayed in Tables 3-2 and 3-3. Except for the sales load, each statistic represents the average for the stock category

---

[7]Calculated from *1997 Mutual Fund Fact Book, 37th Edition,* Investment Company Institute, © 1997, pp. 60, 75 and 79.

Table 3-7: Comparisons of fund operating data, 1996.

	Large-Cap Stocks		M/S-Cap Stocks	
	Act. Mgd.	*Index Fd.*	*Act. Mgd.*	*Index Fd.*
Expense Ratio	1.16%	0.20%	1.43%	0.25%
Total Transaction Costs	0.57	0.02	1.47	0.15
Turnover	71	4	92	15
Front-end load	5	No load	5	No load

identified by the heading. We include a sales load in this illustration since about 60% of actively managed equity funds impose such charges on new purchases. As indicated in Table 3-5, the front-end load is by far the most common version, and the rates for front-end loads, both large-cap and m/s-cap funds, average very close to the 5% assumption shown in the table.

Increasing Advantage as Holding Period Lengthens

Deferral of capital gains taxes provides increasing advantage as the holding period extends into the future. To illustrate, we project fund returns to reflect the assumptions listed in Table 3-7. Comparing actively managed no-load funds with their corresponding index fund benchmarks, Table 3-8 indicates the variations in the tax burden due to differing rates of capital gains distributions.

Other things equal, tax payments that reflect annual capital gains distributions are more burdensome than those deferred until re-

Table 3-8: Annualized cost of personal taxes on capital gains distributions increases with holding period.

Holding Period (Years)	*5*	*10*	*20*	*30*
Large-Cap Stocks				
Actively Managed Fund	0.10%	0.22%	0.39%	0.50%
Benchmark Index Fund	0.01	0.01	0.03	0.04
Index Fund Advantage	0.09%	0.21%	0.36%	0.46%
M/S-Cap Stocks				
Actively Managed Fund	0.14%	0.28%	0.51%	0.67%
Benchmark Index Fund	0.03	0.06	0.12	0.16
Index Fund Advantage	0.11%	0.22%	0.39%	0.51%

demption of the shares at the end of the holding period. For each designated fund, Table 3-8 identifies how much this tax burden reduces the annual rate of return. For both the representative large-cap and the m/s-cap funds included in our example, the index fund advantage relating to the deferral of capital gains taxes approximates 0.4 percentage point over a 20-year holding period. It amounts to a greater percentage for longer holding periods and a lesser percentage for shorter holding periods. Appendix 3-1 provides further details.

Adding Up the Costs

In addressing mutual fund shares, this chapter focuses on the *cost* of active management without attempting to assess its *worth*. For the purposes of comparing costs, we assume that both the actively managed fund and the benchmark index fund hold securities that, overall, achieve exactly the same return (income and market price appreciation). In this chapter, we add up the costs incurred, directly or indirectly, by shareholders of the actively managed fund and the corresponding benchmark index fund. The difference represents the index fund cost advantage. It does not in itself, however, prove that the index fund is a better investment. Suppose the actively managed fund skillfully selects investments with total returns more than sufficient to offset the index fund cost advantage. The actively managed fund, since it would achieve the greater net return to the shareholder, would then hold the advantage in terms of *worth*.

The fundamental question confronting the prospective buyer of an actively managed mutual fund concerns the relationship between the incremental costs of active management and the likelihood that the active fund management will more than offset these incremental costs. In order to assess the overall worth of the actively managed mutual fund for your own purposes, you logically start with the costs in relation to the index fund benchmark. This final section of Chapter 3, borrowing language from the auto industry, presents a series of "window stickers" that discloses the estimated incremental costs paid by fund shareholders to gain the benefits of active management. The purpose of the window sticker is to show the reader how these incremental costs add up. (Chapter 4 addresses the same issue for bond mutual funds.) We leave to Chapter 5 our response to the other key question: How likely is active management to add sufficient value to exceed the incremental costs generated by actively managed funds?

Reading the Window Sticker

The window stickers presented here in Figures 3-3 through 3-10, addressing eight representative actively managed funds, incorporate assumptions that we have reviewed in earlier sections of this chapter. By way of summary, Table 3-9 lists the funds, comparing variations in the index fund cost advantage over a specific holding period of 20 years. The individual window stickers that follow, each presented in graphic form, provide greater detail. They identify the components of the overall cost advantage—expenses, transaction costs, sales loads, and deferral of capital gains taxes. In addition, they trace the changes in these components together with the overall cost advantage as the holding period varies from 5 to 30 years.

For any particular actively managed fund held by any specific shareholder, the index fund cost advantage may be either higher or lower than indicated by the window sticker selected as the closest match. At best, investment returns for either large-cap or m/s-cap

Table 3-9: Index fund cost advantage based on projected total investment return at an annual rate of 10% over 20-year holding period (equal rates before expenses, other costs, and personal income taxes).

Actively Managed Fund (Window Sticker #)	Projected Return		Index Fund Advantage
	Actively Managed	Index Bench.	
Large-Cap			
5% Front Load, Taxable (1)	6.3%	8.1%	1.8%
No Load, Taxable (2)	6.5	8.1	1.6
5% Front Load, Tax Deferred (3)	8.0	9.8	1.8
No Load, Tax Deferred (4)	8.3	9.8	1.5
M/S-Cap			
5% Front Load, Taxable (5)	5.5%	8.2%	2.7%
No Load, Taxable (6)	5.7	8.2	2.5
5% Front Load, Tax Deferred (7)	6.8	9.6	2.8
No Load, Tax Deferred (8)	7.1	9.6	2.5

stocks will not conform exactly to the assumptions included in the table, even over an extended time horizon. Personal income tax rates are likely to change again, as they have several times in recent years. Even if current tax brackets persist, many mutual fund shareholders will pay taxes at higher or lower marginal rates than indicated by our assumptions.

Despite such limitations, the window stickers provide broad perspective concerning the index fund cost advantage over a range of differing circumstances. They follow in the same order as listed in Table 3-9. Each window sticker consists of two panels. Panel A traces the index fund cost advantage (percent annual rate) in relation to the designated actively managed fund over periods ranging from 5 to 30 years. Panel B illustrates the implications for shareholder wealth of the indicated cost advantage over three differing time horizons. Together, the two panels underscore important differences in the costs that deduct from mutual fund returns, depending on the fund characteristics, the tax status of the shareholder, and the holding period. At the same time, they alert the investor to the substantial handicap that almost all actively managed funds must overcome to achieve performance equal to—or better than—the corresponding index fund benchmark.

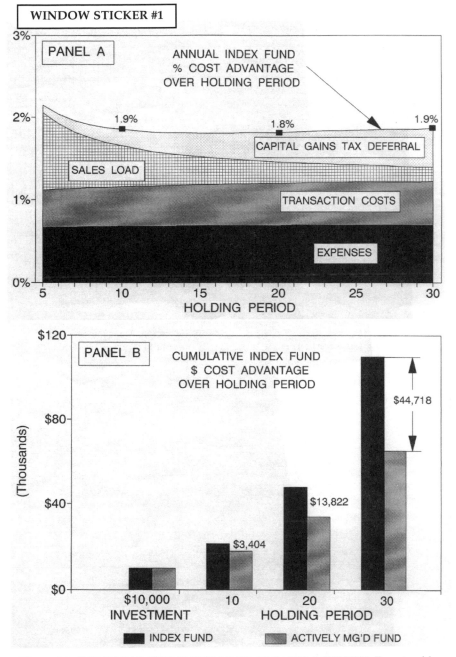

Figure 3-3: LARGE-CAP, FRONT-END LOAD, TAXABLE ACCOUNT. For a taxable account, cost advantage of benchmark index mutual fund compared with composite of actively managed, large-cap mutual funds, assuming a front-end sales load.

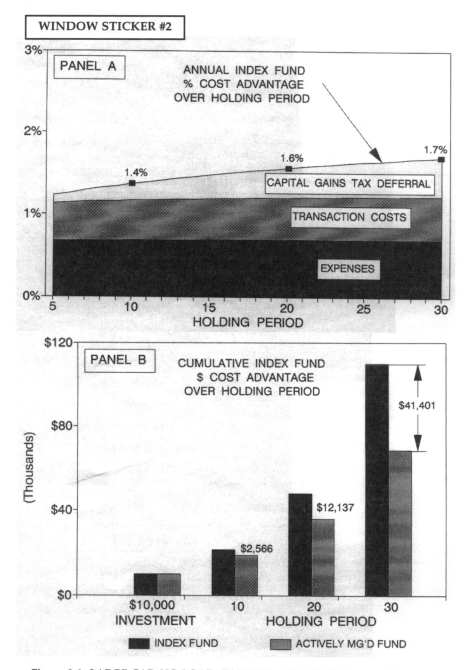

Figure 3-4: LARGE-CAP, NO-LOAD, TAXABLE ACCOUNT. For a taxable account, cost advantage of benchmark index mutual fund compared with composite of actively managed, large-cap mutual funds, assuming no sales load.

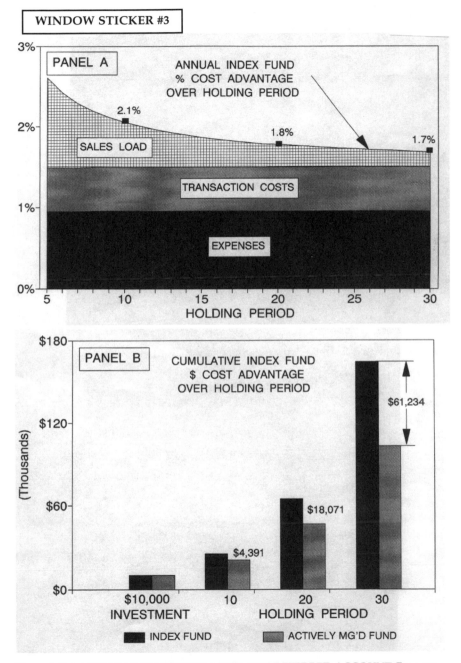

Figure 3-5: LARGE-CAP, FRONT-END LOAD, TAX-DEFERRED ACCOUNT. For a tax-deferred account, cost advantage of benchmark index mutual fund compared with composite of actively managed, large-cap mutual funds, assuming a front-end sales load.

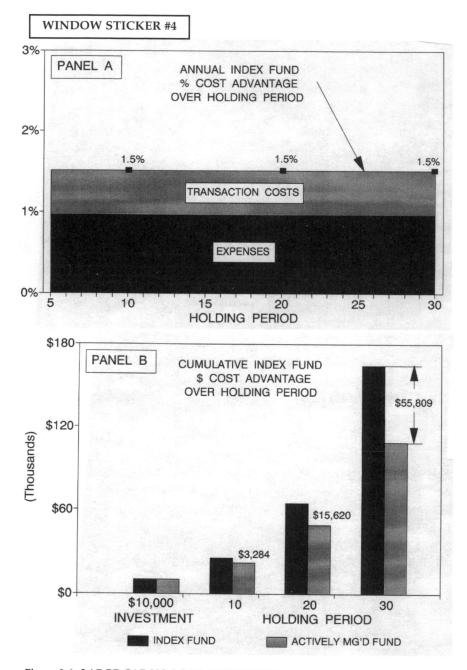

Figure 3-6: LARGE-CAP, NO-LOAD, TAX-DEFERRED ACCOUNT. For a tax-deferred account, cost advantage of benchmark index mutual fund compared with composite of actively managed, large-cap mutual funds, assuming no sales load.

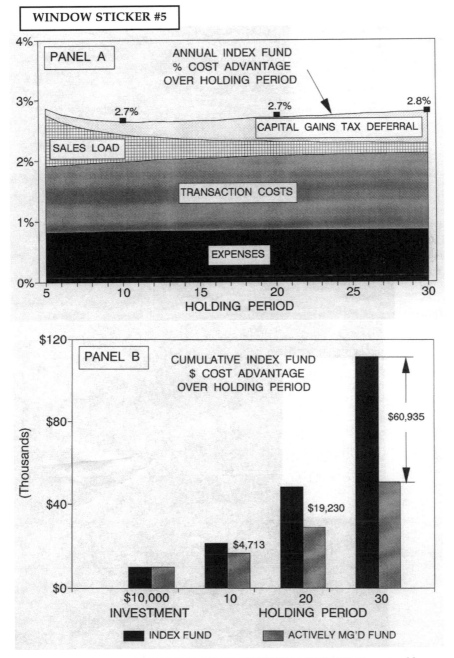

Figure 3-7: M/S-CAP, FRONT-END LOAD, TAXABLE ACCOUNT. For a taxable account, cost advantage of benchmark index mutual fund compared with composite of actively managed, m/s-cap mutual funds, assuming a front-end sales load.

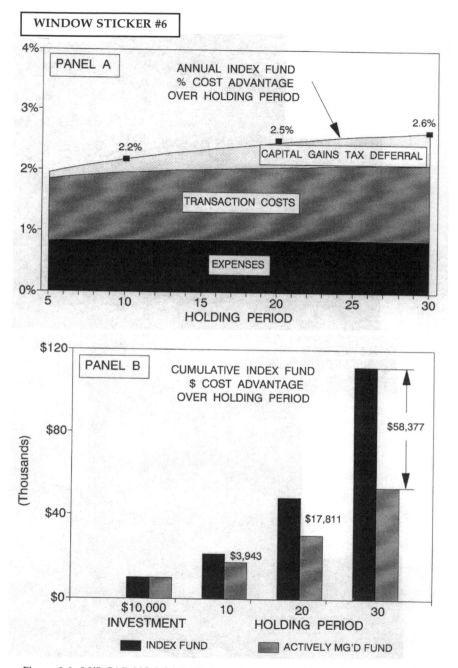

Figure 3-8: M/S-CAP, NO-LOAD, TAXABLE ACCOUNT. For a taxable account, cost advantage of benchmark index mutual fund compared with composite of actively managed, m/s-cap mutual funds, assuming no sales load.

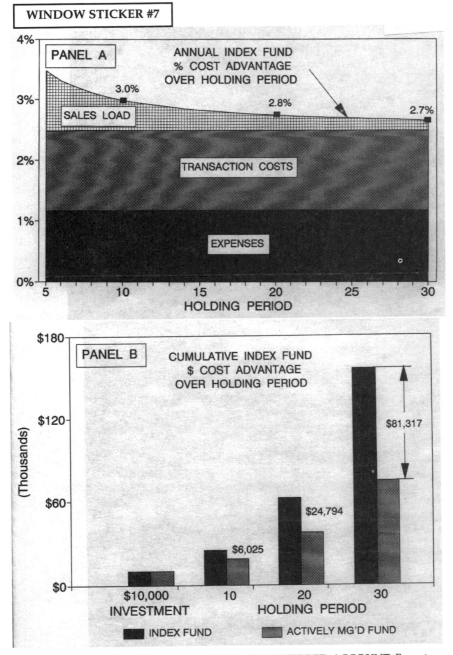

Figure 3-9: M/S-CAP, FRONT-END LOAD, TAX-DEFERRED ACCOUNT. For a tax-deferred account, cost advantage of benchmark index mutual fund compared with composite of actively managed, m/s-cap mutual funds, assuming a front-end sales load.

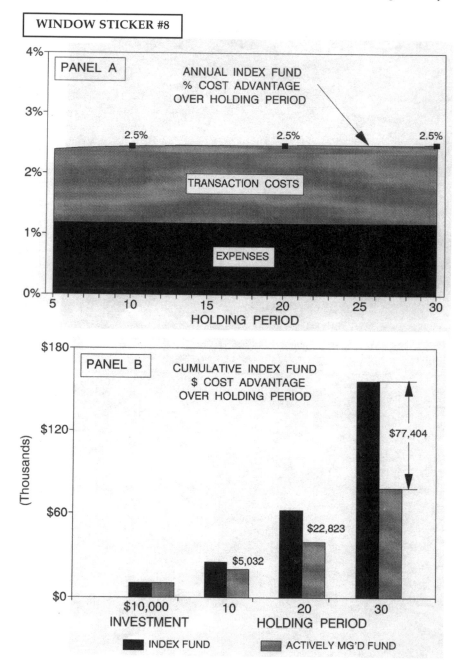

Figure 3-10: M/S-CAP, NO-LOAD, TAX-DEFERRED ACCOUNT. For a tax-deferred account, cost advantage of benchmark index mutual fund compared with composite of actively managed, m/s-cap mutual funds, assuming no sales load.

Appendix 3-1: Deferral of Capital Gains Taxes

To illustrate the index fund advantage relating to capital gains taxes, we first examine a no-load, actively managed, large-cap mutual fund. The underlying assumptions are identified in Table 3-7 and the three paragraphs that precede it. Section (I) of Table 3-10 addresses the compound rate of return for this fund over four designated holding periods. **Line (1)** imposes, for purposes of comparison, a hypothetical condition: deferral of taxes on capital gains distributions to shareholders until redemption of the shares at the end of the holding period. **Line (2)**, removing this condition, provides for subtraction of capital gains taxes from capital gains distributions before reinvestment. As highlighted on **line (3)**, the returns shown on line (2) are lower than those shown on line (1).

Table 3-10: How deferral of taxes on capital gains distributions contributes to the index fund advantage.

Holding Period (Years)	5	10	20	30
(I) Actively Managed Large-Cap Fund				
(1) Capital Gains Taxes Deferred	6.56%	6.72%	6.96%	7.12%
(2) Capital Gains Taxes Paid as Required	6.46	6.50	6.57	6.62
(3) Tax Burden on Capital Gains Distributions	0.10%	0.22%	0.39%	0.50%
(II) Index Large-Cap Fund				
(4) Capital Gains Taxes Deferred	7.70%	7.89%	8.17%	8.35%
(5) Capital Gains Taxes Paid as Required	7.69	7.88	8.14	8.31
(6) Tax Burden on Capital Gains Distributions	0.01%	0.01%	0.03%	0.04%
(III) Actively Managed M/S-Cap Fund				
(7) Capital Gains Taxes Deferred	5.82%	5.97%	6.22%	6.40
(8) Capital Gains Taxes Paid as Required	5.68	5.69	5.71	5.73
(9) Tax Burden on Capital Gains Distributions	0.14%	0.28%	0.51%	0.67%
(IV) Index M/S-Cap Fund				
(10) Capital Gains Taxes Deferred	7.67%	7.94%	8.30%	8.53%
(11) Capital Gains Taxes Paid as Required	7.64	7.88	8.18	8.37
(12) Tax Burden on Capital Gains Distributions	0.03%	0.06%	0.12%	0.16%
(V) Index Fund Advantage				
(13) Large-Cap	0.09%	0.21%	0.36%	0.46%
(14) M/S-Cap	0.11%	0.22%	0.39%	0.51%

The next section of Table 3-10 addresses the Vanguard S&P 500 Index Fund that serves as a benchmark for the actively managed large-cap fund. As for the actively managed fund, we apply the assumptions displayed in Table 3-7 and the three preceding paragraphs. **Line (4),** subject to the same hypothetical condition imposed on the data on line (1), reflects deferral of taxes on capital gains dividends until the end of the holding period. **Line (5),** like line (2), allows for subtraction of taxes on capital gains distribution prior to dividend reinvestment. **Line (6)** identifies the differences between lines (4) and (5). Because the index fund ordinarily realizes very little capital gains each year, line (6) shows only negligible differences over the entire range of holding periods.

Sections (III) and (IV) of Table 3-10 examine m/s-cap funds, repeating the analysis applied to large-cap funds in the previous sections. For both the actively managed and the index m/s-cap funds, turnover higher than for comparable large-cap funds implies a correspondingly higher annual rate of realized capital gains.

Section (V) of Table 3-10 identifies the index fund advantage associated with deferral of capital gains taxes. **Line (13),** addressing the large-cap segment of the stock market, reflects subtraction of **line (6)** from **line (3). Line (14),** the result of subtracting **line (12)** from **line (9),** provides the comparable figure for the m/s-cap funds. For both the large-cap and m/s-cap funds that we have selected as examples, the annual index fund advantage ranges from about 0.1 percentage point for 5 years to about 0.5 point for 30 years.

chapter four

INDEXING THE BOND MARKET

Growing Segment of the Fixed Income Market

While indexing applies primarily to equity portfolios, it also accounts for a small but growing segment of the fixed income market. Our comments focus specifically on bond index mutual funds that target the individual investor (with minimum initial purchase requirements of $5000 or less). At year end 1996, there were seven such bond funds. In total, they reported net assets of $4 billion, or 7% of the net assets for comparable equity index mutual funds.

Making Allowance for Income Taxes

The use of bond index mutual funds depends in part on the tax status of the portfolio. Bond index funds hold taxable fixed income securities such as those issued by corporations, the U.S. Treasury, and agencies of the federal government. In comparison with tax-exempt securities issued by state and local governments, taxable issues provide a yield advantage and generally trade in much more liquid markets.

Institutional investors, reflecting exemption from income taxes, have rapidly increased commitment to taxable bond index funds over the past decade. In the early years after introduction of indexing in 1970, they concentrated on stock index funds. By 1986, bond index funds still accounted for only $10 billion, or about 7% of total institutional index funds. Despite the late start, such funds now substantially exceed $200 billion, amounting to more 20% of all institutional index funds.

Where tax considerations permit, individual investors are beginning to follow the lead of the institutional investors. They are benefiting from bond index funds in tax-deferred accounts such as 401(k)s and IRAs. They may also hold bond index funds in personal accounts where the ordinary income tax rate is sufficiently low (examples in Chapter 7). Where personal taxes would heavily reduce the income from bond index funds, individual investors have reason to consider two alternatives: the near-index bond mutual fund or direct investment in a ladder of high-quality issues.

Near-Index Funds

Near-index bond mutual funds provide an alternative to indexing the bond market, particularly in taxable accounts. While near-index funds do not completely conform to the index fund model, they share key characteristics: very high degree of diversification (in the specified market segment), very low expense ratio, very low transaction costs, and absence of sales load. Chapter 7, which deals with the allocation of portfolio assets to index mutual funds, also addresses the use of near-index bond mutual funds.

By way of illustration, let's consider two examples of near-index funds. For a taxable account—especially where the marginal tax rate reaches the upper end of the range—the actively managed tax-exempt bond fund that meets the foregoing criteria will likely provide a better alternative than the taxable index fund. As used here, the term *tax-exempt* refers to federal income taxes. Attractiveness of the fund for a particular portfolio may depend on applicable state and local taxes.

The diversified Treasury bond fund serves as another version of the near-index fund. Because Treasury securities enjoy the full backing of the U.S. government, they receive the top credit rating. At the same time, fund expenses benefit because fund management does not have to support the cost of credit analysis. Very low costs per transaction, meanwhile, reflect the large supply of Treasury issues trading in highly liquid public markets. Income from Treasury issues, although subject to personal income taxes levied by the federal government, enjoys exemption from state and municipal taxes.

Direct Purchase of Individual Issues

Since this book focuses primarily on mutual funds, we omit consideration of direct purchase of individual notes and bonds. For the investor with the time and resources to do so, we note in passing that a well-planned program may permit further savings in costs and taxes. One approach is to buy high-quality municipal bonds with a ladder of maturities that extends 10 or 20 years into the future. When the bond with the shortest maturity is redeemed, the investor replaces it with a bond of the longest maturity planned for the ladder. In this way, the pattern of maturities remains much the same as time passes. Alternatively, the investor may buy one or more Treasury notes or bonds. For Treasury securities, the absence of potential credit problems lessens the need for diversification. Many investors, however, prefer the convenience of bond mutual funds, especially if portfolio assets are limited and little time is available for investment management.

Index Fund Advantage

To measure actively managed bond mutual funds against an index fund benchmark, we again turn to The Vanguard Group. Table 4-1, drawing on information provided by Morningstar, compares aggregate data for actively managed funds with the benchmark index

Table 4-1: Actively managed bond mutual funds compared with index fund benchmark, 1996.

	Actively Mgd. Funds	*Index Fund Benchmark*
Number	315	1
Market Value (billions)		
Total (billions)	$180	$3.0
Average (billions)	$ 0.6	$3.0
Average Maturity (years)	7.0	6.8

Source: Morningstar Principia for Mutual Funds, January 1997, Morningstar, Inc., Chicago, IL, © 1997.

fund at year end 1996. The composite of actively managed funds excludes those with assets less than $100 million, tax-exempt funds (such as those holding state and municipal bonds), and high-yield funds (with quality ratings of less than investment grade). All funds in the composite are available to the individual investor with a minimum initial purchase price of no more than $5000. The Vanguard Total Bond Market Portfolio, which aims to match the performance of the Lehman Brothers Aggregate Bond Index, serves as the broad industry benchmark. With assets of $3.0 billion, it is the largest of the bond index mutual funds, and, together with three smaller Vanguard funds, accounts for 95% of the total assets for the seven bond index mutual funds available to individuals. Consistent with the composite for the 315 actively managed bond funds, the Vanguard Total Bond Market Portfolio excludes tax-exempt issues and issues rated below investment grade. Average maturity of holdings falls in the intermediate range for both the actively managed funds (7.0 years) and the benchmark index fund (6.8 years).

Identifying Cost Savings

In addressing the expense ratio and transaction costs, Table 4-2 highlights two areas of cost advantage for the benchmark index fund. The expense ratio, as reported in the prospectus, averages about 0.7 percentage point higher for the actively managed bond funds than for the benchmark index fund. We estimate the average difference in transaction costs at 0.2 percentage points.

Our estimate of transaction costs takes into account turnover, also reported in the fund prospectus, and an estimate of average cost per transaction. Turnover for the actively managed funds averages 151%, or more than 4 times the 36% reported for the bench-

Table 4-2: Cost advantage for bond index fund benchmark reflects differences in both expense ratios and transaction costs (1996 data).

	Actively Mgd. Funds	Index Fund Benchmark	Cost Advantage
Expense Ratio	0.93%	0.20%	0.73%
Total Transaction Costs	0.30	0.10	0.20
Turnover	151	36	—

Source (for expense ratio and turnover data): *Morningstar Principia for Mutual Funds, January 1997,* Morningstar, Inc., Chicago, IL, © 1997.

mark index fund. Average costs per transaction depend in large part on the issues that are traded. Treasury securities, which account for close to half the outstanding bonds, trade in highly liquid markets at extremely low cost. Transaction costs for corporate securities average much higher, with wide variations depending on such factors as the size of the issue trading in the public market, the credit standing of the issuer, and the skill of the trader. The implication of turnover for transaction costs also depends on whether a bond, once purchased, is held to redemption at maturity or sold earlier. As shown in Table 4-2, our estimate of the transaction costs for the benchmark index fund, based on analysis of the securities held in the portfolio and the method of operation, is 0.10%. The comparable estimate for actively managed funds reflects both the much higher turnover and the likelihood that the higher turnover concentrates on issues with low costs per transaction. Accordingly, we estimate transaction costs for the actively managed bond composite at 0.30%, indicating an average index fund cost advantage of 0.20% percentage point.

Sales loads constitute a significant cost burden for shareholders in about half the actively managed bond index funds. As shown in Table 4-3, funds with a sales load (69% front end) represent half the number of funds and more than half in terms of total assets. The sales load, while ranging as high as 6.75%, averages about 4% for funds with either front-end or deferred loads. As for equity funds (see Table 3-5), the burden of the load on annual rate of return depends in large part on the holding period.

Deferral of capital gains taxes, although contributing in an important way to the index fund advantage where equities are held in taxable accounts, does not provide a comparable advantage for bond funds. Stock prices, as measured by the S&P 500, have trended upward over time—at an average annual rate of 5.9% from

Table 4-3: Comparison of load and no-load bond funds, 1996.

	Number of Funds	Net Assets (billions)	Average Load
Sales Load	158	$99	4%
No Load	157	81	—

Source: Morningstar Principia for Mutual Funds, January 1997, Morningstar, Inc., Chicago, IL, © 1997.

1926–96. As long as the resulting capital gains are not realized, investors who hold shares of an equity mutual fund defer payment of capital gains taxes. Bond prices, in contrast, have not trended upward over the long sweep of history. With stable interest rates, bond prices would remain stable, and, no matter the trend in interest rates, capital gains are no longer an issue when bonds purchased at approximately the redemption price are held to maturity. While bond mutual funds may realize significant capital gains under special circumstances, we do not include deferral of capital gains taxes in projecting the cost advantage of the bond index fund.

Adding Up the Savings

Comparison of expenses, transaction costs, and, where applicable, sales loads identify the cost advantage for bond index funds. For the purposes of projecting returns, let's assume that the actively managed fund and the benchmark index fund each hold bonds that, overall, yield the same 7% annual rate of return. This yield assumption is broadly consistent with the market rates for a diversified portfolio of fixed income securities over the past several years. The estimates make no allowance for market price appreciation, since bonds, in contrast to stocks, do not demonstrate a long-term upward trend in price.

Table 4-4 presents two examples of the bond index fund advantage over a 20-year time horizon. Both examples refer to tax-deferred accounts, since tax-exempt bond funds provide an alternative for taxable accounts. Where the personal income tax rate is sufficiently high, the tax-exempt bond will likely provide the better alternative. Tables 4-2 and 4-3 summarize the assumptions relating to expenses, transaction costs, and sales loads. For each, the assumption represents the 1996 average for the indicated sample of

Table 4-4: Bond index fund cost advantage based on projected annual return of 7% over 20-year holding period.

Actively Managed Fund (Window Sticker #)	Projected Return		Index Fund Advantage
	Actively Managed	Index Bench.	
4% Front Load, Tax Deferred (9)	5.5%	6.7%	1.2%
No Load, Tax Deferred (10)	5.8	6.7	0.9

an actively managed bond fund and the corresponding benchmark bond fund. For the actively managed load funds, the index fund advantage amounts to 1.2 percentage points per year. The comparable figure for the no-load fund is 0.9 percentage point.

Following the pattern for stock funds in the previous chapter, Figures 4-1 and 4-2 display window stickers representing bond funds. Each window sticker consists of two panels. Panel A traces the index fund cost advantage (percent annual rate) in relation to the designated actively managed fund over periods ranging from 5 to 30 years. Panel B illustrates the implications for shareholder wealth of the indicated cost advantage over three differing time horizons. Since window stickers referring to stock mutual funds display numbers 1 through 8, the two comparisons of bond mutual funds carry designations 9 and 10.

Just to Break Even!

The window stickers, despite evident limitations, provide a useful framework for comparing actively managed bond funds with the corresponding index fund benchmark. The index fund advantage for any particular fund is likely to turn out either larger or smaller than indicated by the window sticker. Averages of expenses, transaction costs, and sales loads not only vary to a degree from year to year, but individual funds may deviate significantly from the averages. Yet the window stickers for the bond funds, as for the stock funds, serve an important function. They provide a sobering glimpse of the challenge encountered by the active fund manager. They suggest how much additional return active management may have to add—on average over an extended period—just to break even!

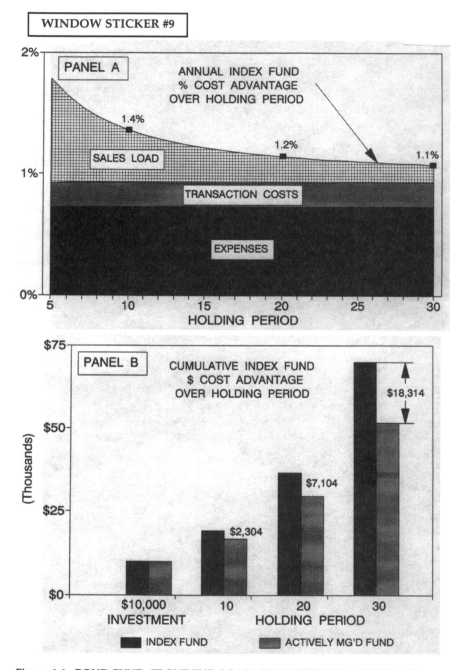

Figure 4-1: BOND FUND, FRONT-END LOAD, TAX-DEFERRED ACCOUNT. For a tax-deferred account, cost advantage of benchmark index mutual fund compared with composite of actively managed bond mutual funds, assuming a front-end sales load.

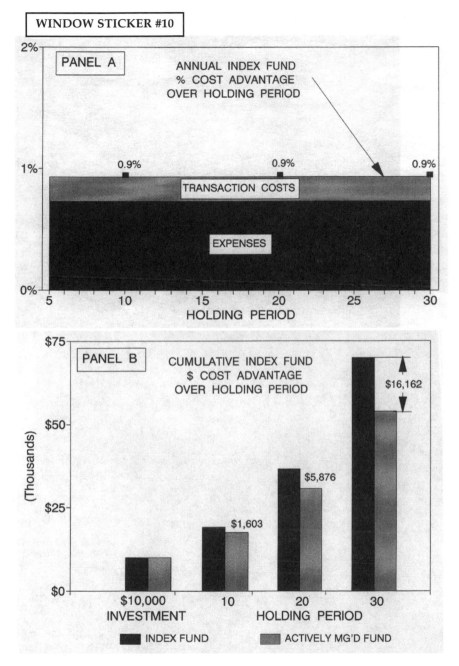

WINDOW STICKER #10

PANEL A

ANNUAL INDEX FUND
% COST ADVANTAGE
OVER HOLDING PERIOD

TRANSACTION COSTS

EXPENSES

HOLDING PERIOD

PANEL B

CUMULATIVE INDEX FUND
$ COST ADVANTAGE
OVER HOLDING PERIOD

$16,162

$5,876

$1,603

(Thousands)

$10,000
INVESTMENT

HOLDING PERIOD

■ INDEX FUND   ■ ACTIVELY MG'D FUND

Figure 4-2: BOND FUND, NO-LOAD, TAX-DEFERRED ACCOUNT. For a tax-deferred account, cost advantage of benchmark index mutual fund compared with composite of actively managed bond mutual funds, assuming no sales load.

chapter five

HOW "DUMB" MISTAKES MAKE "SMART" MARKETS

Assessing the Opportunity

On August 25, 1987, the S&P 500 reached a new high of 336. By the close on October 19, it had dropped precipitously to a 1987 low of 224. How could the S&P 500 represent proper valuation *both* at the August market peak *and* after the unprecedented one-day market plunge less than two months later? The one-day decline on October 19 exceeded 20%, bringing the total reduction in market value in just 39 trading days to more than 33%.

Viewed in the light of the subsequent course of stock prices, investors made two spectacular mistakes. First, those bullish at the top demonstrated far too much optimism and then those so bearish that they sold at the bottom were far too pessimistic. While no equally dramatic stock market event has surfaced since 1987, there has been no shortage of further investor mistakes. Day after day, many investors buy or sell stocks for the wrong reason. The buyer of one stock may expect earnings to rise, but instead they decline. The seller of another stock worries that the market price is already too high, but after the sale the price rises much higher. And on and on.

Looking for Mistakes

In this chapter, we divide investor mistakes into two groups. One group consists of *unavoidable* mistakes. These are so designated because they result from new information not foreseeable at the time the decision was made. For a very simple example, consider the influence of unusual weather on the price of an insurance company's stock. How could an investor buying the stock in July foresee that a September hurricane would decimate loss reserves? Many other examples—involving favorable as well as unfavorable surprises—affect market prices in ways that no investor could anticipate. The outcome depends on factors beyond investor control. The second group is made up of *dumb* mistakes. Our use of this label does not mean that these mistakes are necessarily made by dumb investors (since sometimes very smart people make dumb mistakes). Rather, our purpose is to contrast mistakes that could have been avoided with those that are unavoidable. A dumb mistake reflects an investor blunder rather than just plain bad luck. Suppose, for example, the investor does not do the necessary homework or lacks the background to interpret the information that is available. As a result, the investor misses, say, a critical footnote in the prospectus—or, having taken notice of it, lacks the background to recognize its full significance.

How to invest in the financial markets depends critically on the opportunities presented by dumb mistakes of other market participants. (While in Chapter 5 we focus primarily on the stock market, our comments also apply broadly to the publicly traded fixed income markets.) By definition, no investor can expect an advantage over other investors based on avoiding the unavoidable. If the only mistakes that investors made were unavoidable—purely the result of unpredictable future events—all investors, no matter the level of skill, would be completely at the mercy of chance. Active investing could claim no advantage over index funds. Dumb mistakes, in contrast, serve as the basic argument for active management. Investors bring differing levels of information, diligence, and skill to bear on investment decisions. Those who bring the most resources to the decision process expect to take advantage of dumb mistakes made by others.

But how easy is it for the well-qualified investor to take advantage of such dumb mistakes? Traditionally, investors who actively manage their assets have prided themselves on their skill in anticipating future stock prices. To do so is to imply a forecasting advantage. Index funds, in contrast, claim a different advantage. In comparison with actively managed funds, they provide savings in costs as well as significant opportunity to benefit from deferral of capital gains taxes. The challenge to the buyer of mutual funds is to weigh the opportunities for superior performance offered by actively managed funds against the cost savings provided by index funds. Our purpose in Chapter 5 is to examine the likelihood that active management will achieve incremental returns sufficient to warrant the incremental costs.

Challenging the Traditional View

Traditionally, active managers have stressed the irrationality of the financial markets, implying great opportunity for enterprising active investors. Looking back at history, they point to episodes of extreme overpricing or underpricing as evidence of investor folly. The 1929–32 stock market crash—when the S&P 500 plummeted by more than 85%—serves as the classic example. According to this traditional view, foolish optimism shared by so many investors in the late 1920s drove stock prices to unsustainable highs. Stampeding toward the opposite kind of dumb mistake, investors subsequently accounted for the extreme market low in 1932. In a similar way, traditional active management stresses the role of dumb mistakes in distorting prices of individual stocks and groups of stocks. As a widely read investment advisor observed in the 1960s:

> There are fads and styles in the stock market just as there are in women's clothes. These can, for as much as several years at a time, produce distortions in the relationship of existing prices to real values almost as great as those faced by the merchant who can hardly give away a rack full of the highest quality knee-length dresses in a year when fashion decrees that they be worn to the ankle.[1]

In recent decades, an accumulating body of investment research has challenged this traditional point of view. Much of the early research in the 1960s and 1970s focused on the performance of equity mutual funds. By way of example, Figure 5-1, updating returns of equity mutual funds through 1996, presents performance for 25

---

[1]Philip A. Fisher, *Common Stocks and Uncommon Profits,* Harper & Brothers, Publishers, New York, © 1960, p. 140. Reprinted by permission of John Wiley & Sons, Inc.

years measured against two broad stock indexes. The data includes all general equity mutual funds in existence each year. The figure at the top of each bar indicates the percentage of funds reporting returns that exceeded those of the designated index. For Panel A, the benchmark index against which the funds are measured is the S&P 500. It represents mainly large-cap stocks that account for about 70% of the market value of the domestic stock market. As indicated by the light gray bars, more than 50% of the funds performed better than the S&P 500 in only 9 of the 25 years. For Panel B, the benchmark index is the Wilshire 5000. Since it aims to represent the entire publicly traded stock market, it includes many more medium- and small-capitalization stocks than does the S&P 500. The results shown in Panel B, nevertheless, are much the same as those in Panel A. More than 50% of the funds achieved higher returns than the Wilshire 5000 in only 8 of the 25 years.

Since the wide range of participants in the financial markets commit plenty of dumb mistakes, why haven't highly qualified investment professionals, such as those that manage mutual funds, demonstrated a clear advantage over the broad market indexes? The response to this question focuses on both the highly competitive nature of our publicly traded financial markets and the tendency for dumb mistakes to offset each other. Investors too often underestimate the first factor and may totally overlook the second.

Highly Competitive Public Markets

To appreciate the intensity of the competitive challenge confronting active management, let's review how large tax-exempt institutional investors, such as retirement and endowment funds, strive to gain advantage. These specialized institutions use their large financial resources to gain access to a wide range of expert help in the following ways:

- As a starting point, they may employ in-house full-time professional investors to oversee their investments.
- Even where a large staff operates internally, they almost always delegate management of specific portfolios to outside investment firms that bring special skills in active management.

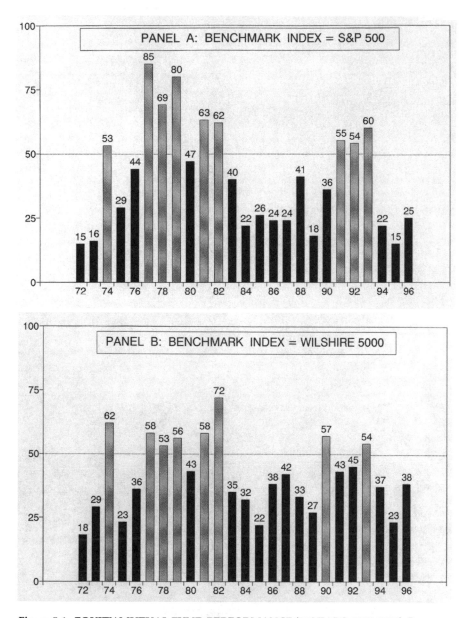

Figure 5-1: EQUITY MUTUAL FUND PERFORMANCE (25 YEARS, 1972-1996). Bars represent the percentage of funds that outperformed the specified index. The majority of funds outperformed (gray bars) the indexes in only about 1 out of 3 years over the last 25 years. (*Sources:* Lipper Analytical Services, Inc., Standard & Poor's, New York, NY, a Division of The McGraw-Hill Companies, Inc., Wilshire Associates, Inc., Santa Monica, CA.)

- The outside investment managers, in turn, supplement the work of their own experts—portfolio managers, security analysts, and market strategists—with advice from the many specialists provided by the institutional brokers as well as various independent consultants.

A brief example illustrates one of the many ways that the large financial institutions strive to keep pace with the rapidly changing events that bear on stock prices. The following *Wall Street Journal* account demonstrates how the expanding role of conference calls contributes to rapid dissemination of inputs to the decision process:

> When software giant Computer Associates International, Inc. announced a surprise $1.74 billion acquisition of Legent Corp. on May 25, Wall Street's initial reaction was negative. Soon after the stock market opened at 9:30 a.m., Computer Associates stock had fallen more than two points.
>
> But all that turned around at 10:15 a.m., when Computer Associates' President Sanjay Kumar began a conference call to 300 institutional investors and analysts extolling the transaction's benefits. The call's impact was significant. By the time it ended at 11:30 a.m., the stock was up five points.
>
> As it happened, Mr. Kumar accomplished his high tech tour de force while speaking at a pay phone at a gas station near the Long Island Expressway, where he was stuck in traffic on his way to his office. But his call was just another example of how conference calls have transformed the folkways of everyday life on Wall Street.
>
> During the past few years, conference calls have become a standard way for companies to talk over their quarterly earnings, their latest acquisition or some unfolding crisis with analysts and big investors.[2]

As illustrated by this example, intense competition rapidly exploits opportunities as they become available. Because information is so critical to investment decisions, the investment community has become particularly skilled in tracking it. Specialists serving the large institutions and other large investors not only benefit from access to company managements, but they also aggressively monitor a continuing torrent of facts, figures, and ideas. Overall, the highly qualified investment decision maker with superior information routinely competes with other highly qualified decision

---

[2]Randall Smith, "Conference Calls to Big Investors Often Leave Little Guys Hung Up," *The Wall Street Journal*, June 21, 1995, p. C-1. Reprinted by permission of *The Wall Street Journal*, © 1995 Dow Jones & Company, Inc. All Rights Reserved Worldwide.

makers with access to much the same information. This time, one highly qualified market participant may gain advantage, but next time it is likely to be someone else's turn. Even so, why shouldn't astute investors benefit significantly from a share of the opportunities created by the many dumb mistakes in the securities markets? The answer has to take into account a frequently overlooked characteristic of dumb mistakes.

How Dumb Mistakes Offset Each Other

Opportunities available to active management are further restricted by the tendency for dumb mistakes to offset each other. By way of example, suppose dumb mistakes result in both the purchase and sale of the same number of shares of the same stock. Let's say that one investor buys the stock at the market price in response to an excessively optimistic impression of the appeal of a new product. At the same time, suppose another investor sells the stock at the market price based on a very misleading fragment of evidence that sales of the company's established product lines have plummeted. Both the buyer and the seller, based on their respective views of the outlook for stock prices, are pleased to complete the transaction at prices provided by the market. This pair of dumb mistakes, because one offsets the other, does not create opportunities for other investors to benefit. The purchase does nothing to drive up the market price, neither does the sale push the market price lower. The same generalization that applies to individual stocks also applies to timing the broad market. Purchases based on misplaced optimism concerning the direction of overall stock prices are likely in large part to balance sales triggered by exaggerated pessimism.

Although the interaction of dumb mistakes in real-world stock market transactions is much more complex, this simple example makes an important point: As long as the dumb mistakes are independent, they are likely to come close to offsetting each other. The critical word is *independent*. If dumb mistakes are *not independent*, they concentrate pressure in one direction or the other, driving stock prices much higher or much lower than is warranted. For example, suppose greed takes over to bring about extraordinary excesses in a bull market, or widespread fear works in the opposite direction to drive already depressed stock prices still lower in a bear market. Alternatively, investors in large groups may fall victim to the same silly rumors, widely circulated misinformation, or faulty interpretation of available facts. In any event, the resulting undervaluation or overvaluation may benefit the astute active manager who wisely takes the opposite side of the transaction.

For *independent* dumb mistakes, in contrast, the outcome is much like that for tossing a coin. As the coin is tossed, the outcome of the next toss does not depend in any way on the outcome of previous tosses. Since each toss is independent of the previous toss, the heads and tails are likely to come close to balancing each other, particularly as the number of tosses increases. Table 5-1 indicates the probability that heads rather than tails will show for each 100 tosses. Ninety-one percent of the time, heads will account for 42 to 58 of the 100 tosses, indicating the tendency for heads and tails to offset each other. The range, as a percentage of the number of tosses, would narrow as the number of tosses in each set increases, and, correspondingly, the range would widen for fewer tosses. Even when the number of tosses declines to 10, about 89% of the time the number of heads will still range from 3 to 7.

Table 5-1: Outcome of tossing coin 100 times.

Frequency	*Number of Heads*
81%	44–56
91	42–58
96	40–60

The coin tossing analogy holds for independent dumb mistakes. Only those dumb mistakes that do not offset each other foster mispricing, implying opportunity for active management. To the extent that dumb mistakes result in a balance between purchases and sales, the opportunities for the active investor disappear.

Gauging the Results of Active Investing

How severely does intense competition, together with the tendency for dumb mistakes to offset each other, limit opportunity for active investing? Let's examine the equity performance for the large, tax-exempt institutional investors, such as those that participated in the conference call with the management of Computer Associates. Performance of such institutional investors reflects the concentrated efforts of highly motivated, full-time specialists with many resources at their disposal. The costs that burden the performance data for such institutions, moreover, are lower than for the mutual fund averages, as summarized in Chapter 3. The performance data for such institutions, as for mutual funds, includes transaction costs but, unlike those for mutual funds, excludes costs of management, marketing, and other expenses. To report the same performance, mutual funds would have to achieve even greater success in active investing than the tax-exempt institutions (without allowance, as shown in Chapter 3, for the further burden on returns resulting from sales loads, redemption fees, or income taxes).

Getting a Better Look

Over the past two or three decades, increasingly thorough performance analysis has gradually reshaped the institutional view of active investment management. Many studies have appeared in academic journals or other specialized publications, and consultants serving the financial institutions have also provided much useful data.

Growing access to the power of the computer, beginning in the 1960s, has opened the way for major improvements in the study and calculation of performance data. Routine application of statistical risk measures has focused attention on the sensitivity of portfolio prices to up and down markets. If a portfolio performs well in an up market, is it also more vulnerable to loss in a down market? Statistical tools have also defined more precisely the value of diversification. When is a 30-stock portfolio no better diversified than a 20-stock portfolio?

Since the 1980s, performance measures have increasingly allowed for differences in portfolio objectives. A manager focusing on small-capitalization, high-growth stocks, for example, would ideally measure performance against an appropriate index of such stocks. Meanwhile, an influential industry group, the **Association for Investment Management and Research,** has progressively raised standards for performance measurement. As such standards have evolved, institutional investors have had to recognize that successful active investing is much more difficult than claimed by traditional proponents of active investing.

Sending the Message to Individual Investors

The evidence that has become familiar to institutional investors over the past decade or two is beginning to receive more attention in widely circulated newspapers and magazines. For example, *Fortune* magazine, in a cover story, concluded, *"Overall, money managers have done a dismal job."*[3] To support this gloomy assessment, the article included data from a leading pension consultant, Performance Analytics, as shown in Table 5-2. The record covers 2700 equity managers and 800 fixed income managers over periods ranging from six months to ten years. The median equity manager failed to match the return of the S&P 500 in each of the four periods measured. Similarly, the median fixed income manager also reported a lower return in each period than did the Merrill Lynch master bond index.

While the sample in the *Fortune* article is limited to a particular set of managers during a particular ten-year period, it is broadly consistent with the finding of more comprehensive academic research over the past several decades. By way of example, Burton Malkiel, then dean of the Yale School of Organization and Management, made the following observation in a book published in 1985 (about the beginning of the ten-year period covered by the data in the *Fortune* article):

Table 5-2: Equity returns for institutional portfolio managers compared with returns for the S&P 500.

Period Ending June 1994	*6 Months*	*3 Years*	*5 Years*	*10 Years*
Equity Managers				
Median (% return)	−4.8	8.7	9.6	14.1
S&P 500 (% return)	−3.4	9.3	10.3	15.1
Difference (percentage points)	−1.4	−0.6	−0.7	−1.0
Better than index (%)	29	34	37	26
Fixed Income Managers				
Median (% return)	−4.4	8.4	8.3	10.5
ML master bond index (% return)	−4.1	8.5	8.5	11.5
Difference (percentage points)	−0.3	−0.1	−0.2	−1.0
Better than index (%)	40	48	44	16

---

[3]Kathleen C. Smyth, "The Coming Investor Revolt," *Fortune*, October 31, 1994, p. 68. Copyright © 1994 Time Inc. All rights reserved.

> But while I believe in the possibility of superior professional invest-
> ment performance, I must emphasize that the evidence that we have
> thus far does not support the view that such competence exists; ... It is
> clear that if there are exceptional financial managers, they are very
> rare. This is a fact of life with which both individual and institutional
> investors have to deal.[4]

In the light of such evidence, you have good reason to consider a
key role for indexing in the investment process. Indexing provides
the framework in which active investing operates. It also serves as
the benchmark against which active investing is measured.

Foreign Markets

While our examination of the challenges confronting active management looks primarily to domestic stocks, the broad conclusions
also extend to the foreign stock markets. As in the domestic stock
market, the active manager of a foreign stock portfolio aims to
achieve performance superior to that of the competing index. To do
so, however, requires a higher standard than simply "superior forecasting." The forecasting skill needs to be sufficiently superior to
do more than overcome the differential in costs between active
management and indexing. The index fund cost advantage in foreign markets, moreover, is likely to average significantly higher
than in the domestic market. We estimate that it will compare more
closely with that for domestic m/s-cap stocks than for domestic
large-cap stocks (see Table 3-9).

How easy has it been for an actively managed foreign portfolio
to achieve favorable performance as measured against the relevant
index? At best, the evidence is mixed. Comparisons of the median
return for actively managed foreign stock portfolios with the MSCI
Europe, Australasia, and the Far East (EAFE) index have benefited
in recent years from the collapse of the Japanese stock market. The
Nikkei index of Japanese stocks experienced a net decline of more
than 50% from the 1989 peak to the end of 1996. At the beginning
of the bear market, moreover, Japanese stocks accounted for more
than 50% of the weight in the EAFE index (compared with about

---

[4]Burton G. Malkiel, *A Random Walk Down Wall Street*, 4th Edition, W. W. Norton & Co.,
New York, © 1985, p. 182. Professor Malkiel, now Chemical Bank Chairman's Professor of
Economics, Princeton University, also includes the quotation in the 6th edition, © 1996, p.
192.

30% early in 1997). Reluctance to hold such a large proportion of
the foreign stock portfolio in the issues of one country as well as
judgments concerning overvaluation of Japanese stocks influenced
portfolio decisions of active managers. Whether reflecting diversification restrictions or forecasting skill—or perhaps a combination
of both—underweighting of Japanese stocks so far in the 1990s has
bolstered performance of foreign stock portfolios relative to the
EAFE index. We caution, nevertheless, against mechanically projecting recent results into the future. In every market, foreign as
well as domestic, the median return of an actively managed portfolio will exceed that of the competing index in some years and lag
it in other years. The issue, as we have shown in our review of domestic markets, concerns the probabilities over an extended period. The accumulating evidence over many years and in many areas
of the world, including Europe and the emerging markets, underscores the difficulty of identifying in advance the actively managed
portfolio that will achieve superior future performance. In response to such evidence, more and more institutional investors
have introduced a role for indexing in their foreign stock portfolios,
and, increasingly, individual investors are beginning to follow their
lead.

Explaining the Paradox

At this point, many readers may feel that they are confronted by
two dramatically different—and contradictory—views of investing:

- The evidence presented so far in this chapter supports a narrow
  view of the opportunities available to active investing. It shows
  many highly motivated investment specialists competing fiercely with each other in highly liquid, publicly traded financial markets where relevant information is freely available. Although
  dumb mistakes translate into market transactions, they create
  opportunity for active investing only to the extent they reinforce
  each other. Because the competition is so intense and the independence of dumb mistakes renders them largely offsetting, active investing becomes a daunting challenge even for the highly
  qualified specialists.

- In contrast to our cautious assessment of active investing, you are likely to encounter a much more inspiring view from a wide range of sources. Mutual funds and a vast array of investment advisors point with pride to records that make active management look easy, at least for those who can claim such records. Vendors of investment products and services exude confidence in describing how they will achieve superior results. Newspapers and magazines turn the spotlight on investment champions, both to dramatize their accomplishments and to relay their secrets of success. Often, the prescription for success is deceptively simple—so simple that anyone with a little effort and ordinary common sense should succeed.

How do we reconcile the two very different points of view? There are several reasons individual investors, lacking rigorous performance measurement, may view active investing through a distorted lens:

- They too often fail to recognize the degree to which chance—both good luck and bad luck—explains the way portfolios perform.

- The numbers that they encounter, although perhaps accurate, may still serve to support misleading comparisons.

- They may overlook the power of wishful thinking, particularly when abetted by effective marketing. Investors would like to believe that they can secure the sizable rewards of successful active investing, and vendors of investment products or services understandably encourage such belief.

Understanding the Role of Chance

Several equity mutual funds have demonstrated superior performance on a highly consistent basis. Of the 300 funds with records extending ten years, 4 achieved results better than the group median in nine of the ten years. Another 13 recorded superior performance in eight of the ten years. Have these funds proven, by virtue of their outstanding records over an extended period of years, truly exceptional skill in active investing? Before answering this question, we turn to a coin tossing experiment.

Everyone is familiar with tossing a coin to determine whether it will land with heads or tails facing upward. Since each toss of the coin is unrelated to the previous toss, the outcome is purely a matter of chance. On the next toss, the odds of showing either heads or tails are equal—50%. With only two possible outcomes, each equally likely, the odds are easy to calculate for any combination of heads and tails over a series of tosses of any length.

Suppose we wanted to determine who in a college sophomore class could show the best results when calling the toss of a coin. For this purpose, we assemble the entire 300 members of the class in the campus auditorium. (Note that the number of students just equals the number of mutual funds in our sample.) An accommodating professor stands on the stage to toss a coin in the air 10 times. Three judges, made up of the top officers of the student government, observe the results of the successive coin tosses in order to record the outcomes. For each coin toss, each of the 300 students records on a special form his or her guess concerning the outcome, either heads or tails. The students then pass these forms along to staff assistants who oversee the tabulation of results. For the purposes of this example, we assume that the results in this coin tossing exercise conform to the most likely outcome based on the laws of probability.

The most likely pattern of success for the college students in calling the ten successive tosses of a coin is remarkably similar to the performance of the mutual funds over the past ten years. Table 5-3 compares the actual results for the mutual funds with the most likely outcome for the series of coin tosses. Figure 5-2 shows how the plots of the two series almost coincide. In an actual experiment, the outcome of the coin tossing may vary from the most likely estimates shown in the table. Similarly, over another ten-year period, the mutual funds would be unlikely to replicate the exact distribution shown for the past period. The patterns for the two series, nevertheless, are almost certain to look very similar.

The results of the coin tossing experiment raise interesting questions. No one would claim that the 16 students who correctly call the coin toss 8 or 9 times out of 10 display extraordinary forecasting skill. We know that success in this example is purely the result of chance. Why not apply similar skepticism in reacting to the records of the 17 mutual funds that reported superior performance in 8 or 9 years? The coin tossing experiment demonstrates that su-

Table 5-3: Coin tossing experiment compared with mutual fund performance.

No. Years (or Correct Calls)	No. Funds (in Top 50%)	No. Students (Correct Calls)
10	0	0
9	4	3
8	13	13
7	30	35
6	66	62
5	78	74
4	60	62
3	29	35
2	17	13
1	3	3
0	0	0
	300	300

Source: Morningstar Principia for Mutual Funds, January 1997, Morningstar, Inc., Chicago, IL, © 1997.

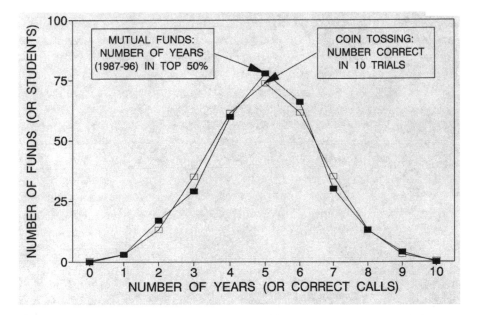

Figure 5-2: 300 DOMESTIC EQUITY MUTUAL FUNDS (PERFORMANCE COMPARED TO COIN TOSSING). Results of coin tossing and performance of mutual funds, as illustrated by data for the decade 1987–1996, are strikingly similar. (*Source: Morningstar Principia for Mutual Funds, January 1997*, Morningstar, Inc., Chicago, IL, © 1997.)

perior investment performance in 8 or 9 or more years out of the last 10 may simply reflect the workings of chance. How do we know, then, when a record of highly favorable performance—even over a period as long as ten years—measures extraordinary skill and when it measures extraordinary good luck? The answer is clear. To rely on the past record as a guide to future investment performance risks confusing good luck with skill.

By way of further example, let's compare mutual fund returns over two consecutive five-year periods. Figure 5-3 focuses on the same 300 funds, as cited previously, with performance data for the ten years ended 1996. For each of the funds, we first calculated the difference between the compound annual rate of return over the five years 1987–91 and the median return for the entire group of funds over the same period. Panel A ranks the funds by this measure of relative performance, with the most favorable at the far left. The best performing fund in this period achieved a compound annual rate of return 14 percentage points better than the median. At the other extreme, to the far right, the return for the fund with the least favorable performance lagged the median by an annual rate of 12 percentage points. Panel B displays the same performance measure for the subsequent five years, 1992–96, with the data for each fund displayed directly below that for the earlier five years. Of the 150 funds that achieved superior performance in the first five-year period, 62 (41%) also achieved superior performance in the second five-year period. Compared to the group with the initially superior performance, the 150 funds with lagging performance over the first five years actually experienced a moderately better mix of favorable and unfavorable performance in the subsequent five years. Over 1992–96, 88 (59%) of these funds reported superior performance. These results underscore the difficulty of assessing future prospects based on the past record.

How Honest Numbers Support Misleading Comparisons

A trap commonly waiting to ensnare busy investors consists of accurate numbers arranged to support misleading comparisons. Let's start with the assumption that most of the individual performance numbers that you encounter, at least those from reputable printed

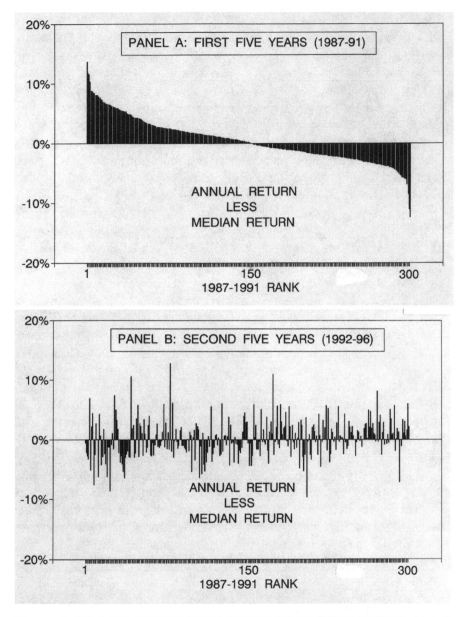

Figure 5-3: RELATIVE PERFORMANCE (300 DOMESTIC EQUITY FUNDS). Mutual fund performance over a five-year period provides little guidance for projecting the subsequent five years. (*Source: Morningstar Principia for Mutual Funds, January 1997*, Morningstar, Inc., Chicago, IL, © 1997.)

sources, are accurate. A certain amount of skullduggery, including outright misstatement of facts, takes place in the investment business—as it does elsewhere. However, investors who take the trouble to read the printed material published by reputable sources will likely see individual numbers compiled with an extremely high degree of accuracy. The degree of accurate disclosure on such important issues as investment performance is exceptionally high for two reasons: (1) government regulation of the investment business provides severe penalties for outright misrepresentation of material facts; and (2) most of the people who expect to make a long-term career in the investment business place a high value on a reputation for integrity.

So our concern here is not very much with the misrepresentation of material facts. Rather, we direct attention to the misinterpretation of performance numbers that, as stated, are individually accurate. Too often, the comparison of one accurate number with another accurate number misleads. Perhaps the comparison is offered with the best of intentions and little recognition of the flaw that distorts its message. Or it may simply reflect an effort on the part of the fund manager "to put the best foot forward" within a framework of completely accurate individual numbers.

Survivorship Bias.   To explain how survivorship bias distorts data, we assume that a mutual fund company initially offered five funds. As shown in Table 5-4, the fund company reviewed performance for the funds at the end of 1996, compiling data for each fund over the previous five years. Each number in the table reflects the difference between the compound annual rate of return for the fund and that of its benchmark over the period. For the five years ended 1996, the compound annual rate of return of the five funds, each measured against its respective benchmark, averaged a *negative* 1%. While two funds achieved better performance than the benchmark, three did not.

After the end of 1996, the fund company sold Fund B to another company operating a fund with a similar style. Since the fund company no longer operates Fund B, it now, very accurately, includes only the *surviving* four funds in the record of total performance. The revised company performance, as shown on the bottom line of the table, now amounts to a *positive 1%*. Through the miracle of survivorship bias, the fund group has converted a negative performance into a positive performance.

Table 5-4: Annual rate of return (1992–96) relative to designated benchmark for five mutual funds.

Fund	A	B	C	D	E	Avg.
Initially reported	−2	−10	+6	−2	+3	−1
Revised	−2	—	+6	−2	+3	+1

In order to achieve the benefits of survivorship bias, the fund company does not necessarily have to separate itself completely from the operations of Fund B, as indicated in our example. It may merge Fund B into Fund C, if the objectives of the two funds are sufficiently close to secure the approval of the shareholders. Since Fund C is the survivor, its record, rather than that of Fund B (or a combination for the records of Funds B and C), becomes the record to include in the average.

Burton G. Malkiel provides a dramatic example of survivorship bias over the ten years ended 1991. Data presented by Professor Malkiel, as shown in Table 5-5, highlights all general equity mutual funds (bottom line) and five groups of funds within this overall category.[5] The first column identifies the average annual rate of return for the funds in existence each year, including those discontinued before the end of the period. The second column, in contrast, lists comparable data only for those funds that survived through the end of the period (1991). The differences between columns 1 and 2, as shown in the third column, underscore the pervasive influence of survivorship bias. For each group, the surviving funds showed superior annual rates of return, and the weighted average for all general equity funds amounted to 1.4 percentage points.

Putting the Best Foot Forward.   Understandably, vendors of investment products and services—such as mutual funds, brokerage firms, and publishers of financial newspapers and magazines—strive vigorously to secure new business as well as maintain existing business. To this end, they do what other businesses do—they present their records in ways that put their efforts in a favorable light. With active investing, they need to identify evidence of success in anticipating the course of the financial markets. For the most

---

[5]Burton G. Malkiel, "Returns from Investing in Equity Mutual Funds 1971 to 1991," *The Journal of Finance*, Vol. L No. 2, June 1995.

Table 5-5: Survivorship bias for equity mutual funds over 1982–91.

Mutual Fund Group	All Mutual Funds in Existence Each Year	Funds in Existence 1982 through 1991	Difference
Capital Appreciation	16.32%	18.08%	1.76%
Growth	15.81	17.89	2.08
Small Company Growth	13.46	14.03	0.57
Growth and Income	15.97	16.41	0.44
Equity Income	15.66	16.90	1.24
All General Equity	**15.69**	**17.09**	**1.40**

part, their numbers are accurate, and they almost always can point with pride to specific accomplishments. Even accurate data presented by honest people, however, does not necessarily lead to unbiased conclusions.

Consider, for example, the hypothetical mutual fund company that is the subject of Table 5-4. Of the five funds that the company managed over the five years ended 1996, Fund C turned in a particularly favorable performance. Even though the average results for the five funds could not demonstrate overall skill in active investing, the company could legitimately mount an aggressive campaign to promote the highly favorable record of Fund C during a particular five-year period. A year from now, if Fund C encounters a period of poor performance that drags down its average, the company's primary marketing efforts may turn to another fund, one that is experiencing better results at that time.

Another approach to "putting the best foot forward" concerns a method of preparing a new fund for market that is known as *incubation.* Edward Wyatt, writing in *The New York Times,* describes the practice:

> To give the start-ups a booster shot, a growing number of fund companies are following an old strategy that allows a new fund to build a performance record even before it starts to solicit money from the public...
>
> ...Seeded with a few hundred thousand dollars from a fund company and its insiders, and operated initially out of the view of its performance-hungry investors, a small new mutual fund might be able to generate returns that will shoot it to the top of the performance rankings. Those returns can be artificially high because an incubating fund generally does not allow redemptions by shareholders. Fund companies are then able to market that performance to the public, stepping through a loophole in Government regulations that restrict similar actions by private investment pools....

...The incredibly strong gains of the stock market over the last two years have provided the perfect environment for the fertilization and incubation of hot performing new funds, said A. Michael Lipper, president of Lipper Analytical Services, a fund tracking company. "Incubation tends to be a bull market phenomenon, and you tend to see them in good markets for initial public offerings (I.P.O.'s)."

Big fund companies enjoy an advantage in such a market because they have the buying power to get scarce shares in hot I.P.O.'s. If a company allocates those shares to a small fund, they can have a big impact on performance....

...For investors, then, incubators pose a special hazard. While an incubated fund's total return may be accurate, sustaining such a performance may be difficult when there is a deluge of new money or when investors are free to redeem their shares at will.[6]

Recognizing the Power of Wishful Thinking

Perhaps the influence that most distorts the contribution of active investing is the power of wishful thinking. In the absence of rigorous performance measurement, investors—sharing a common human characteristic—are vulnerable to reshaping a view of the past as they would like to see it. Since we want to believe that we have made wise investments, we look for evidence to support our belief. We sometimes welcome too uncritically the broker or the mutual fund that reassures us concerning the wisdom of our past investment decisions. If investors cannot remember precisely how well their investments have performed, they are likely to conclude that their portfolios have achieved better returns than has actually been the case.

Active Investing in "Smart" Financial Markets

What are the implications of "smart" financial markets for active investing? The evidence does not close the door on active investing but, rather, reshapes the way you make use of it. Chapters 3 and 4 identify the index fund cost advantage. Chapter 5 addresses the difficulty of anticipating the course of the financial markets. Taken

---

[6]Edward Wyatt, "It's a Fund! Bringing Up Baby Mutuals," *The New York Times*, March 16, 1997, p. F-1. Copyright © 1997 by The New York Times Co. Reprinted by permission.

together, these three chapters argue in favor of a central role for indexing in the investment process. Nevertheless, there are three good reasons to maintain a continuing role for active investing:

1. Active Judgments Are Required by Indexing. Even the most dedicated proponents of indexing cannot, in practice, completely eliminate active decision making. As a starting point for an index fund portfolio, you must decide which indexes to target and how much to allocate to each index fund. The choices depend on assumptions concerning the future. Will the assumptions conform strictly to projections of the past record? If so, which historical period provides the appropriate version of the past record? Or should you modify the assumptions derived from the past record in the light of the changing context in which investors now operate?

In day-to-day operations, moreover, investors in index funds must make judgments concerning timing. Do you buy immediately the targeted amounts, or do you spread purchases over a significant time interval? As differing returns for the various holdings of index funds reshape asset mix, when should rebalancing take place?

Finally, investors cannot escape active judgments as new risks and opportunities develop in the investment environment. By way of a simple example, what if *major changes* develop in the outlook for inflation and interest rates? How should you react as evidence mounts, contrary to your view of history, that "this time is different?"

2. Active Investing and Indexing Complement Each Other. Just as active investing benefits from operation within an index fund framework, indexing benefits from coordination with active investing:

- For active management, the role of indexing in the development of the portfolio plan establishes hurdles that active investing must overcome. The broadening perspective provided by an index fund framework refocuses efforts both to control risk and to identify the exceptional opportunity. Investors who attempt to bar all active judgments from entering the front door will likely see them creep in the back door. Because such judgments have not been considered in an orderly decision process, they are less likely to be well reasoned than if they were subjected to the discipline of active investing.

- For indexing, coordination with active investing assigned to a designated portion of the portfolio also provides significant benefits. With such coordination, the investor is better able to hold index fund investments to a steady course. Active judgments that might otherwise hobble the indexing effort remain separate as they receive systematic scrutiny within the guidelines established for active investing.

3. Take Advantage of Exceptional Skill. Investors who believe that they have exceptional skill (or access to it) will want to benefit from it. We applaud both skill and ambition; the purpose of this book is not to discourage either positive quality. Rather, our goal is to encourage greater discrimination in the use of active investing within the risk control provided by an index fund framework.

The Rule of 1-2-3

The rule of 1-2-3 provides broad perspective on how "smart" actively managed funds have to be in order to overcome the index fund cost advantage. It takes into account expenses included in the expense ratio, transaction costs, sales loads, and personal income taxes. This rule, subject to the qualifications listed below, can be stated as follows: *In order to equal the return of the benchmark index fund, the actively managed mutual fund must invest in issues that average a significantly higher annual rate of return: about 1% for bonds, 2% for large-cap stocks, and 3% for m/s-cap stocks.*

Table 5-6, including both taxable and tax-deferred accounts, supports the rule of 1-2-3. The first column lists the index fund cost advantage in relation to ten groups of actively managed funds as shown in previous chapters (Tables 3-9 and 4-4). The assumption concerning the holding period is 20 years. The second column identifies the incremental return that the issues in the actively managed fund would have to achieve in order for the actively managed fund to equal the return for the benchmark index fund. For tax-deferred accounts, the figures in the two columns are identical. For taxable accounts, the actively managed fund encounters a greater challenge. The additional return shown in column 2 exceeds the cost advantage shown in column 1 in order to allow for the additional income taxes that accompany the additional returns.

Table 5-6: To break even, the actively managed mutual fund requires holdings that average significantly higher returns than for the benchmark index fund.

20-Year Holding Period:	Index Fund Advantage	Actively Managed Additional Returns
Large-Cap		
5% Front-End Load, Taxable	1.8%	2.2%
No Load, Taxable	1.6	1.9
5% Front-End Load, Tax Deferred	1.8	1.8
No Load, Tax Deferred	1.5	1.5
Large-Cap Average		**1.9%**
M/S-Cap		
5% Front-End Load, Taxable	2.7%	3.4%
No Load, Taxable	2.5	3.0
5% Front-End Load, Tax Deferred	2.8	2.8
No Load, Tax Deferred	2.5	2.5
M/S-Cap Average		**2.9%**
Bonds		
4% Front-End Load, Tax Deferred	1.2%	1.2%
No Load, Tax Deferred	0.9	0.9
Bond Average		**1.1%**

While the rule of 1-2-3 underscores a significant point, it clearly does not apply in an equal way to every actively managed mutual fund. As indicated by Table 5-6, the overall average for large-cap equity funds of approximately 2% represents a range for the four component groups that extends about 0.4 percentage point in either direction. Variations for the individual funds within each component group are even wider. In a similar way, the averages for the bond funds (1%) and m/s-cap funds (about 3%) also represent wide ranges. Changes in personal income taxes (ordinary or capital gains) will modify comparisons for the taxable accounts. Despite these necessary qualifications, the rule of 1-2-3 serves an important purpose. It provides a broad measure of the handicap carried by actively managed mutual funds as they compete with the index funds in "smart" financial markets.

PART 3

INVESTING IN AN UNCERTAIN WORLD

chapter six

DEVELOPING THE PORTFOLIO PLAN

Balancing Risk and Reward

As the initial step in portfolio building, Chapter 6 looks to three distinctly different groups of securities. *Common stocks* constitute the most dynamic group, opening the way to both extraordinary opportunities and special risks. At the other extreme, *cash*—invested temporarily in money market funds or other short-term, high-quality instruments—provides limited returns in exchange for little or no risk. *Bonds* occupy an intermediate position. They are less risky—and likely to be less rewarding—than stocks. At the same time, they are more risky, but hold forth the likelihood of higher returns, than cash. In large measure, apportionment of financial assets among these three groups determines the portfolio balance between risk and expected return. Accordingly, this chapter addresses asset mix. *What balance of these three very different asset groups is most appropriate for a particular investor at a particular point in time?*

Adjusting to Individual Circumstances

No standard set of answers applies across the broad range of investors. Mutual fund brochures and various publications outlining advice to the individual investor often provide model portfolios based on age. They may show the young adult with 90% of the portfolio committed to common stocks while the retiree holds 30%

in stocks. Such advice may be just right for certain investors, but does not take into account a wide variety of other factors that clearly bear on the decision, for example:

- How secure is the investor's employment and how favorable are prospects for future increases in income?
- How much allowance should be made for the separate income of a spouse or prospects for an inheritance?
- On the other side of the balance sheet, what are the investor's obligations?
- Do such obligations include raising and educating children? If so, what are the children's ages?
- Is the investor saving to buy a home, or, for a homeowner, how big is the mortgage?
- How large are other debts, ranging from credit card balances to installment loans?

Just as important as resources and obligations is the investor's temperament. Even if the numbers support a 90% commitment to stocks, a young investor may not want to consider the possibility that the value of his or her hard-earned savings could suddenly decline by 30% or more in a bear market. Conversely, a senior citizen living within the income provided by a pension may willingly accept such risks with the aim of expanding contributions to charity or the legacy to heirs.

Chapter 6 presents a straightforward method for developing individually tailored answers to the basic question concerning asset mix. There are two advantages to this do-it-yourself approach. Initially, you have the opportunity to shape the portfolio plan to your special circumstances. Custom design takes the place of the cookie-cutter approach, where one plan applies to every member of the same broad category. Subsequently—as changing circumstances call for adjustment—your understanding of the reasons for the initial decision provides perspective that works to keep your plan on track.

Simplification of Portfolio Planning

For the purpose of this chapter, we define each asset group in terms of a representative measure:

1. For stocks, the choice is the S&P 500. This index accounts for most stocks in investor portfolios, since it makes up about 70% of the market value of all stocks publicly traded in the United States.

2. For bonds, let's use five-year Treasury notes. They serve as a useful proxy for the weighted average of all outstanding Treasury securities with maturities ranging from 1 to 30 years. Treasury securities, although their returns do not move in lockstep with those of other fixed income securities, provide a broad indicator of changing patterns for other high-quality fixed income markets.

3. For cash investments, one-month Treasury bills serve our purpose. Guaranteed by the full faith and credit of the United States and carrying a very short maturity, they represent the highest-quality fixed income instrument with minimal risk.

Limiting this chapter to three principal asset groups greatly simplifies portfolio planning. Large institutional investors may use eight or ten asset groups for this purpose—but at the cost of increasing complexity. For the individual investor with limited time and resources at his or her disposal, the simpler approach outlined here accomplishes much the same objective with a great deal less effort. To handle a greater number of asset groups would require sophisticated computer programming as well as a great deal more specialized inputs. The three-asset approach, in contrast, is easy to understand and avoids the need for complicated quantitative tools. As shown in Chapter 7, you can readily adjust this approach to accommodate additional asset groups.

Asset Mix in an Index Fund Framework

Planning asset mix depends on the same principle that underlies the use of index funds. As explained in Chapter 5, you are likely to find it hard to identify active investing that will provide results better than can be explained by chance. Let's therefore plan asset mix in an index fund framework, temporarily excluding reliance on active investing. After the asset-mix plan has been completed, there is then the opportunity for active investing in a segment of the portfolio. The purpose is twofold: (1) to control the risks of active investing in the event that, this time, it turns out badly; and (2) to

improve the likelihood of success of active investing through a selection process that measures active decision making against the
index fund alternative.

To the extent portfolio planning initially excludes active investing,
diversification assumes increasing importance. Consider first the opposite approach. If you rely entirely on active investing to come up
with the right answer, diversification logically gives way to concentration on the asset group that you believe is best situated to produce
favorable returns. You hold stocks when they appear attractive, but
switch to bonds or cash when the active decision process so indicates. Similarly, within each asset group, you would select a few particularly attractive issues rather than seek broad diversification.

Planning asset mix in the absence of active decision making provides a sharp contrast. Active investing can play a role in the investment process, but first let's see what we can accomplish without it. To this end we diversify—both among asset groups and
within asset groups.

Diversification—because it limits portfolio risk without limiting expected return—is sometimes described as the nearest thing in investing to a "free lunch." Table 6-1 presents a simple example. Two risky
assets, A and B, each provide an expected annual return of 10%. Portfolio assets are evenly divided between A and B, so the expected annual return for the overall portfolio also amounts to 10%. For either
asset A or B, suppose there is one chance in ten that the return could
fall below negative 10% in any one year. For the portfolio, however,
the downside risk at the 1-in-10 level of probability is negative 7%—
a lower level of risk than indicated for either asset individually.

Portfolio risk diminishes when the two assets are combined, reflecting differing patterns of returns. When the return on one asset
declines sharply, chances are the return for the other asset will not
decline as much—or it may even increase. Extreme declines in re-

Table 6-1: How diversification limits risk.

| | Annual Rate of Return | |
Asset	*Expected*	*1 Chance in 10*
A	10%	−10%
B	10	−10
Portfolio	10%	−7%

turns for both assets at the same time, although possible, are much less likely than for either asset individually. While diversification does not always produce risk reduction as pronounced as that indicated in this example, the general principle holds, in varying degrees, for any combination of risky assets where returns are not perfectly correlated.

Identifying the Marker Portfolios

This chapter provides you with three alternative *marker* portfolios to use as guideposts in portfolio planning. Each of these portfolios represents a very different relationship between risk and return, ranging from those with low risk, low-expected return to those with high risk and high expected return.

Figure 6-1 identifies the three marker portfolios. Each consists of the same asset categories but in sharply differing proportions. The most important difference in the portfolios is the percentage of common stocks, represented by the S&P 500. The range extends from 75% for the most aggressive portfolio to 25% for the most con-

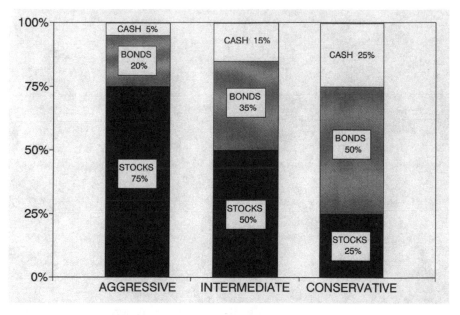

Figure 6-1: MARKER PORTFOLIOS, ASSET ALLOCATION. Three marker portfolios reflect varying mix of stocks, bonds, and cash.

servative. The bond category, represented by five-year Treasury notes, accounts for the second largest group in each portfolio. It varies from 20% to 50% of the total. The remainder consists of cash equivalents. While money market funds provide a common alternative, our marker portfolios use one-month Treasury bills ranging from 5% to 25% of the total.

Four-Step Process

The three alternative portfolios will serve you as a tool in determining the asset mix that best meets your objectives. You may choose one of the standard marker portfolios, and, if necessary, fine tune overall risk and expected return in the light of your special requirements. For example, you may include in your comparisons a portfolio halfway between the intermediate and the aggressive marker portfolios. Averaging the estimates for risk and expected return for the two standard portfolios identifies in an approximate way the corresponding measures for the in-between portfolio. The ultimate selection of asset mix depends on a process that consists of four steps:

1. View each of the marker portfolios in the light of your particular circumstances. This chapter focuses on both the expected return for each portfolio and the risk of other outcomes. With this information, you can arrive at your own decision concerning the balance of risk and expected return appropriate to your purposes. You won't have to accept a portfolio plan simply because a magazine article or mutual fund brochure presents a sweeping generalization applied to an entire category of investors.

2. In the interests of fine tuning, adjust the assets in the selected marker portfolio. To return to the previous example, suppose the aggressive portfolio appears too risky but the intermediate portfolio does not qualify as sufficiently dynamic. Table 6-2 displays two possible adjustments, each with risk and return characteristics about halfway between those of the two marker portfolios. Other adjustments could move the risk/return profile more closely in line with either the aggressive or intermediate marker portfolio.

3. Translate the marker portfolio into the benchmark portfolio plan. Chapter 7 explains how to do this. The benchmark portfolio plan identifies a combination of index mutual funds with the

Table 6-2: Fine tuning of the marker portfolios.

	Marker Portfolio		Adjusted Portfolio	
	Aggressive	*Intermediate*	*Alternative 1*	*Alternative 2*
Stocks	75%	50%	65%	60%
Bonds	20	35	25	30
Cash	5	15	10	10
Total	100%	100%	100%	100%

same percentages of stocks, bonds, and cash as the marker port-folio. In doing so, it also broadens representation in both the stock and fixed income markets. The goal of your benchmark portfolio plan is to secure the benefits of improved diversification without substantially altering exposure to the overall risk represented by the marker portfolio.

4. Introduce active investing into your portfolio plan. Chapter 8 shows how to seek incremental returns through active investing without an unacceptable increase in overall portfolio risk.

Periodic Rebalancing

Periodic rebalancing of your marker portfolio drives corresponding adjustments in your benchmark portfolio plan. At inception of the investment program, the marker portfolio represents the percentages of stocks, bonds, and cash that you have selected to meet your particular requirements. Over the succeeding year, differing rates of market price change and reinvestment of dividend or interest income will gradually modify the asset mix. You therefore allow for rebalancing at the end of the year to restore the initial percentages for both the marker portfolio and the benchmark portfolio plan. Subsequent chapters discuss how the benchmark portfolio plan guides the actual portfolio.

How Much Return?

The starting point for assessing the likely return and risk for each of the three marker portfolios is the historical record. We underscore *starting point*. The raw historical data does not automatically provide the projections that drive asset-mix decisions. Rather, these projections derive from analysis of the historical record.

To gauge the average historical returns of the financial markets, studies often begin by consulting the record of investments in the U.S. financial markets since 1926. The necessary data on stocks, bonds, and cash over that extended period is more comprehensive than for earlier periods—and readily accessible. Historical data incorporated in the planning of asset mix seldom extends to periods earlier than 1926 because of dramatic changes in the workings of the economy and the operations of the financial markets since that time. Table 6-3 lists the compound rates of return for the three assets over 1926–96.

Figure 6-2 compares the average annual compound rate of return for the three marker portfolios over 71 years, 1926–96. To calculate these rates, we assume that each of the three marker portfolios began on January 1, 1926 with the asset mix specified in Figure 6-1. At the end of each month, each portfolio reinvested all income—for stocks, dividend income; and for bonds and cash, interest income. At the end of each year, rebalancing restored the initial asset mix. Suppose, for example, stocks increased as a percent of total assets in a particular year because they provided a higher return than either bonds or cash. To restore the designated asset mix would require an appropriate transfer from stocks to one or both of the other asset groups.

Even if we were certain that past returns would serve as a highly reliable guide to the future, we would still need to address two issues in estimating expected returns. The first concerns *adjustment for the changing value of the dollar*. To this end, we focus on returns

Table 6-3: Compound rates of return for three major asset classes, 1926–96.

Asset	*Annual Rate of Return*
S&P 500	10.7%
5-Year Treasury Notes	5.2
1-Month Treasury Bills	3.7

Source: Stocks, Bonds, Bills & Inflation 1997 Yearbook™, Ibbotson Associates, Chicago, IL (annually updates work by Roger G. Ibbotson and Rex A. Sinquefield). Used with permission. All rights reserved.

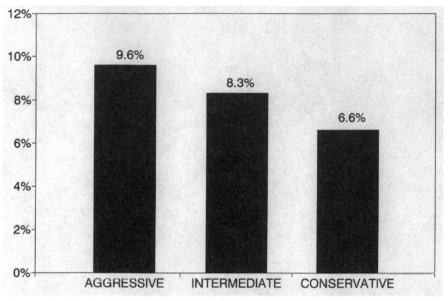

Figure 6-2: COMPARISON OF MARKER PORTFOLIOS. Compound annual rates of return for three marker portfolios, 1926–96. (*Sources:* Computed using data from *Stocks, Bonds, Bills & Inflation 1997 Yearbook*™, Ibbotson Associates, Chicago, IL [annually updates work by Roger G. Ibbotson and Rex A. Sinquefield.] Used with permission. All rights reserved.)

after allowance for the changing level of the Consumer Price Index. The second issue concerns identification of *the boundaries of the relevant past.* Average returns for each of the three key portfolio components—stocks, bonds, and cash—have varied significantly with the choice of time period. Looking backward from the vantage point of a long bull market provides a very different perspective than the view from the trough of a severe bear market.

Adjusting for Inflation

Adjustment of historical returns for inflation recognizes the longer-term influence of the changing value of the dollar on investment returns. Figure 6-3 compares the data shown in Figure 6-2 with the same data adjusted for the average annual compound rate of change in the Consumer Price Index. Over the 71 years of financial market history, the real value of the dollar (measured in terms of its purchasing power) declined by 89%. The equivalent compound *annual* rate of increase for the CPI, as shown in Figure 6-3, is 3.1%.

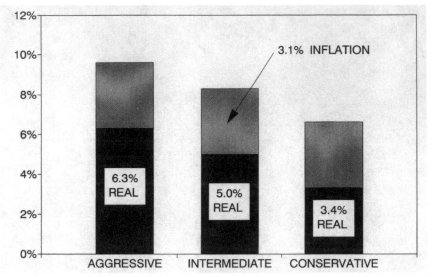

Figure 6-3: MARKER PORTFOLIOS (ANNUAL RETURNS, 1926-96). Real returns are adjusted for inflation. (*Source*: Computed using data from *Stocks, Bonds, Bills & Inflation 1997 Yearbook™*, Ibbotson Associates, Chicago, IL [annually updates work by Roger G. Ibbotson and Rex A. Sinquefield.] Used with permission. All rights reserved.)

Defining the Relevant Past

Because the environment in which the financial markets operate has changed so much over the 71-year period, many observers (including the authors of this book) also look separately at the record of more recent decades. To this end, let's divide the period in half, permitting separate focus on the 35 years ended 1996. While the beginning year, 1962, is an arbitrary choice, the period since that time better represents the conditions that bear on current investment decisions than does the earlier period. Two events that seem far removed from the current investment horizon dominated the 1926–61 period: the Depression of the 1930s and World War II. For the period 1962–96, the challenges confronting the financial markets took a new turn. The rebuilding of the war-torn industrial world gradually resulted in increased competition as well as new opportunities for American business. With the escalation of hostilities in Vietnam, inflation, rather than depression, surfaced as the primary threat to the health of the financial markets. While inflation has settled back over the past decade to approximately the long-term average rate, the possibility of a renewed upsurge—with adverse market implications for stocks as well as bonds—remains a continuing concern.

Estimating the Most Likely Returns

Figure 6-4 graphically displays the estimates of expected return that we apply to the three marker portfolios. We base these estimates on the record for the 1962–96 period, and, to translate nominal returns into real returns, we adjust for inflation. Over the most recent 35 years—as compared with the last 71—real returns were moderately to slightly lower for each of the three portfolios. Table 6-4 compares real returns for the most recent 35 years with those for the entire 71 years beginning 1926. Because of the effects of compounding, the nominal rate of return exceeds the sum of the real rate and the rate of inflation. Appendix 6-1 presents the data on stocks, bonds, and bills required to calculate the returns shown in Table 6-4.

How Much Risk?

Planning asset mix recognizes that economic visibility does not extend very far into the future. By way of illustration, Table 6-5 identifies three points in the past when stock market valuations reflected pessimistic or optimistic extremes that underwent dramatic change in subsequent years.

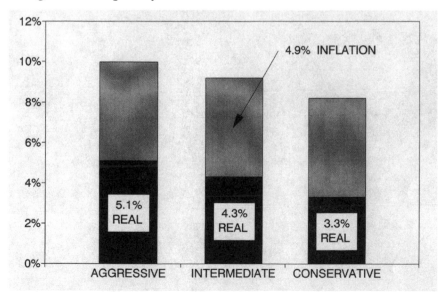

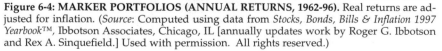

Figure 6-4: MARKER PORTFOLIOS (ANNUAL RETURNS, 1962-96). Real returns are adjusted for inflation. (*Source:* Computed using data from *Stocks, Bonds, Bills & Inflation 1997 Yearbook*™, Ibbotson Associates, Chicago, IL [annually updates work by Roger G. Ibbotson and Rex A. Sinquefield.] Used with permission. All rights reserved.)

Table 6-4: Marker portfolio returns for last 35 years in longer-range perspective.

Annual Rate	1926–96	1962–96	Difference
Aggressive			
Real Return	6.3%	5.1%	–1.2%
Inflation	3.1	4.9	+1.8
Nominal Return	9.6	10.3	+0.7
Intermediate			
Real Return	5.0%	4.3%	–0.7%
Inflation	3.1	4.9	+1.8
Nominal Return	8.3	9.4	+1.1
Conservative			
Real Return	3.4%	3.3%	–0.1%
Inflation	3.1	4.9	+1.8
Nominal Return	6.6	8.3	+1.7

Source: Computed using data from *Stocks, Bonds, Bills & Inflation 1997 Yearbook™*, Ibbotson Associates, Chicago, IL (annually updates the work of Roger G. Ibbotson and Rex A. Sinquefield.) Used with permission. All rights reserved.

Guarding against the Unexpected

The historical data listed in Table 6-5 underscores the need to guard against the unexpected. Let's take a closer look at each of three periods:

Dynamic Bull Market. In the early years after World War II, few observers foresaw the tremendous postwar prosperity that lay ahead. At the end of 1949, the S&P 500 sold at 7 times trailing

Table 6-5: Changing economic visibility as reflected in price-earnings ratios (P/E) and dividend yields.

Year End	S&P 500			Treasury Yields	
	Price	P/E	Yield	20-Yr. Bond	1-Mo. Bill
1949	17	7.2	8.8%	2.1%	1.1%
1961	72	22.4	3.0	4.2	2.6
1974	69	7.7	5.4	7.6	8.0
1996	741	18.9	2.0	6.7	5.2

Source: Computed using data from *Stocks, Bonds, Bills & Inflation 1997 Yearbook™*, Ibbotson Associates, Chicago, IL (annually updates the work of Roger G. Ibbotson and Rex A. Sinquefield.) Used with permission. All rights reserved. Also, Standard & Poor's, New York, NY, a Division of the McGraw-Hill Companies.

earnings. Dividends to be paid in the year ahead provided a yield of almost 9% (compared with yields for Treasury bills and other short-term, high-quality fixed income investments of about 1%). The extremely low valuation reflected both short- and long-term concerns. Economists and investment advisors broadly agreed, not only that postwar prosperity would be short-lived, but also that longer-term growth in the market value of common stocks was, at best, highly uncertain. As events proved otherwise over subsequent years, investors dramatically revalued stocks upward.

Extended Bear Market. By 1961, the S&P 500 sold at 22 times trailing earnings and yielded 3%. Creeping inflation, as viewed then, gradually eroded the value of bonds but contributed to the value of stocks. Accordingly, the outlook for continuing inflation became a reason for owning stocks rather than a reason not to own them. Institutional investors began to worry, as they did periodically in the 1960s, that expanding demand for stocks from rapidly growing pension funds would create a long-term shortage. Optimism concerning the long-term outlook for stock prices flourished, probably to a greater extent than at any time since the late 1920s. Yet in 1962 stock prices suffered a sharp setback, and, at year end 1974—more than 13 years later—the S&P 500 hovered around the level at year end 1961.

Another Surprise. Although escalating inflation surprised the financial markets in the second half of the 1960s, few investors anticipated the damage that inflation would do to market values of both stocks and bonds in the 1970s. By the end of 1974, stock valuations had returned to approximately the 1949 levels, and yields for 20-year Treasury bonds had risen to almost 9% from less than 5% a decade earlier. The gloom concerning investment prospects persisted into the early 1980s, setting the stage for a renewed upward revaluation for both stocks and bonds in the ensuing years.

Two Contradictory Goals

As you can see from this brief look at financial market history, risk is a critical factor in planning asset mix. Making choices among the three marker portfolios depends not only on expected return, but also on the risk that the actual return will fall short of target. You want to increase return, but you also want to limit risk. Since these two goals are contradictory, planning asset mix always involves compromise. The mix of assets represents a tradeoff between "How much can I expect to gain?" and "How much could I lose?" The aggressive marker portfolio, which offers the highest expected return in the group, also entails the greatest risk. At the other extreme, the conservative marker portfolio greatly reduces risk—but at the expense of expected return.

To place the current stock market in historical perspective, we have included recent market measures in Table 6-5. By the end of 1996, stocks again were valued much as they were at year end 1961. The price-earnings ratio was not quite so high, but the dividend yield was significantly lower. Although bond yields have declined sharply from the record levels of the early 1980s, they remain well above those at year end 1961.

Measuring Risk

To compare alternative portfolios, you need a simple way of envisioning risk as well as identifying expected return. For the three marker portfolios, expected return takes the form of a single figure, stated in real terms and supported by inflation-adjusted historical experience. Risk lacks an equally straightforward measure, since it deals not only with what is expected, but also with a wide range of other possibilities. Institutional investors use statistical measures to gauge risk, but these mathematical tools do not readily adapt to the needs of the individual investor.

Absence of a simple benchmark for visualizing risk hampers investment in several ways. For many investors, an exaggerated fear of risk may unnecessarily limit opportunities for gain. For other investors, unwarranted complacency concerning risk may expose the portfolio to unacceptable losses. Changing trends for the financial markets, moreover, foster exaggerated swings in the investor perception of risk. The investor may pay too little attention to risk under favorable market conditions and give it too much weight after market prices plunge.

Defining the Longer Term

To identify a way of looking at risk that is both simple to understand and easy to remember, let's focus on how the investor view of the longer term changes as market conditions change.

Increasing optimism in the financial markets and expanding economic visibility reinforce each other. As optimism grows, investors are likely to envision the future, perhaps even the next 30 or 40 years, with growing clarity. Under such circumstances, they regard future setbacks in the financial markets as temporary annoyances on the road to dazzling longer-term rewards. Accordingly, the prospective rewards of long-term investing, looming ever larger as they compound over an expanding time horizon, dwarf the interim risks.

An unfavorable turn in the financial markets, in sharp contrast, reshapes the investor view. As portfolio losses materialize, the longer term suddenly begins to shrink, often at an alarming pace. The investor, reflecting the mounting fears in the financial marketplace, is no longer so sure that the current setback in the financial markets is simply a temporary pause along the road to ever greater riches.

So how long is the longer term? Since the investor view of the longer term responds to conditions in the financial markets, we take this principle into account in examining the relationship of risk to expected return. For an investor losing money, a year turns out to be a very long time—and five years may define the outer limits of the longer term. We therefore establish five years as the time horizon over which we measure risk.

Least Favorable Five-Year Returns

To identify a single-figure gauge of risk, let's look at the least favorable five-year returns, inflation adjusted, during the period 1962–96. Figure 6-5 identifies and compares this risk measure for the three marker portfolios. It addresses a key question that the investor, in planning asset mix, would like to have answered: *How much could I lose if the future repeats the worst experience of the relevant past?*

The tie-in with actual market history also provides perspective on the likelihood of recurrence. The least favorable five-year returns, by definition, would have occurred only once in the 31 peri-

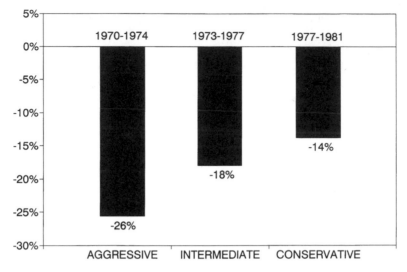

Figure 6-5: MARKER PORTFOLIOS (LEAST FAVORABLE 5-YEAR REAL RETURNS, 1962-96). Adjusted for inflation. (*Source*: Computed using data from *Stocks, Bonds, Bills & Inflation 1997 Yearbook*™, Ibbotson Associates, Chicago, IL [annually updates work by Roger G. Ibbotson and Rex A. Sinquefield.] Used with permission. All rights reserved.)

ods of this length beginning 1962. One chance in 31, if taken by the investor as a broad (albeit imperfect) indication of risk, would represent a probability of about 3%. A more complex statistical approach used by institutional investors in planning asset mix provides similar estimates. As explained in Appendix 6-2, the probabilities calculated in this manner range from 3% for the aggressive marker portfolio to 5% for the conservative version. To provide a single, easily remembered figure applicable to the three marker portfolios, we assign a probability of 4% to each measure of risk. The 4% probability—1 chance in 25—refers to the likelihood of recurrence over the coming five years of the least favorable return reported for any five-year period included in the years 1962–96.

Choosing the Right Portfolio

Measures of expected return and risk for the three marker portfolios, as identified in Table 6-6, provide you with the data needed to

Table 6-6: Comparison of expected cumulative return over the next five years with most and least favorable five-year returns 1962–96 (both inflation adjusted).

		Marker Portfolio			
	S&P 500	Aggr.	Interm.	Cons.	T-bills
Expected Return	33%	28%	23%	18%	7%
Most Favorable	111	101	89	76	29
Least Favorable	−36	−26	−18	−14	−8

Source: Computed using data from *Stocks, Bonds, Bills & Inflation 1997 Yearbook*™, Ibbotson Associates, Chicago IL (annually updates work by Roger G. Ibbotson and Rex A. Sinquefield.) Used with permission. All rights reserved.

make a choice. By way of perspective, comparable data are also included for the S&P 500 and one-month Treasury bills. Note that the expected return does not forecast a specific outcome at the end of the next five years. Reflecting the compound rate of real return over 1962–96, the expected return represents a single-figure estimate of probable returns, with about equal chance of either a higher or lower outcome. The least favorable figure serves as an example of how low returns might plunge over the next five years under extremely adverse circumstances. It becomes useful only when coupled with an estimate of probability, which we designate as approximately 1 in 25 (or 4%). To devise a simple rule of thumb, we apply the same estimate to the three marker portfolios, the S&P 500, and one-month Treasury bills. For perspective, Table 6-6 also shows the most favorable five-year returns for each series during the period.

Figure 6-6 represents graphically the measures shown in Table 6-6. The bar for each of the marker portfolios and the two asset groups identifies the range of five-year returns for 31 periods over 1962–96. The horizontal line intersecting each bar indicates the expected return over the next five years. While the lower extreme of each bar represents the least favorable five-year return 1962–96, the upper end marks the most favorable five-year return during the same period. Using historical volatility as a guide, the probability is about nine chances out of ten that returns for each portfolio or asset group, inflation adjusted, will fall within the limits of the designated bar.

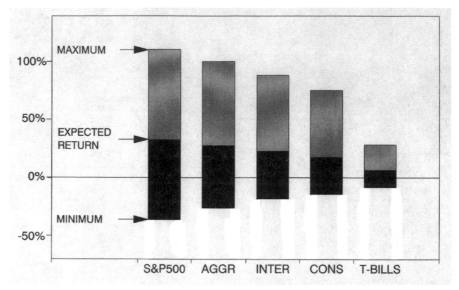

Figure 6-6: RANGE OF REAL RETURNS (5-YEAR PERIODS ENDING 1966-96). Comparison of expected return over the next five years with the range of five-year returns since 1961 (both adjusted for inflation). (*Source:* Computed using data from *Stocks, Bonds, Bills & Inflation 1997 Yearbook*™, Ibbotson Associates, Chicago, IL [annually updates work by Roger G. Ibbotson and Rex A. Sinquefield.] Used with permission. All rights reserved.)

Starting in the Middle

In planning asset mix, the intermediate marker portfolio provides a useful starting point. The information summarized in Table 6-6 permits you to consider how this portfolio would meet your special circumstances. The expected five-year return, after adjusting for inflation, amounts to 23%. Since this projection reflects historical experience over the past 35 years, it completely ignores efforts to adjust for contemporary conditions. It does not adjust the expected return downward because valuations are currently so high by many long-standing benchmarks, especially book value and dividends, but also the price-earnings ratio. Nor does it adjust the expected return upward to allow for the much better returns recorded since the early 1980s. The odds are about even that the return could fall short of this target, with about 1 chance in 25 that the return over the next five years will fall as low as negative 18%. The choice of the intermediate portfolio depends on balancing the *likelihood* of a gain of about 23% against the *risks* of much less favorable results.

In evaluating the risks, you should keep in mind how different risk looks when losses materialize over an extended period. If the returns over five years were to fall to the least favorable level, they would almost certainly appear even worse during an interim period. Figure 6-7 traces the year-end values for the three marker portfolios during 1973–77, which coincided with the least favorable five-year results for the intermediate portfolio. Over the entire five years, the value of the intermediate portfolio declined by 18% but, during the first two years, the decline reached 30%. (For the other two marker portfolios, similar patterns emerged.)

As the investors live through a period of depressed returns, they have no way of knowing how soon the financial markets will take a turn for the better. *"This time is different"* is the chilling phrase that arises in every bear market. Perhaps this time really will be different! Whatever the eventual outcome, portfolio losses that persist for several years—or longer—severely test investor confidence and patience. Unfortunately, vigorous assurances by economists and investment experts do not provide reason for lowering the odds on risk. Severe bear markets, especially for stocks, begin with widespread optimism.

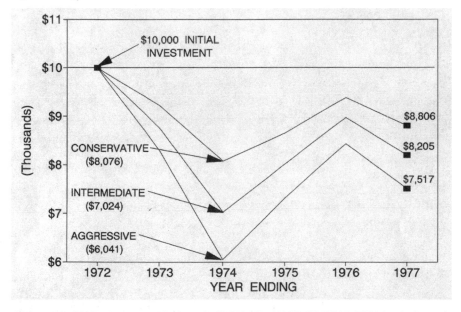

Figure 6-7: MARKER PORTFOLIOS (YEARLY CHANGE IN REAL WEALTH). Annual changes in dollar value (adjusted for inflation) of the three marker portfolios over 1973–77.

Exploring Alternatives

The next step, after considering the intermediate marker portfolio, is to explore the possibility of either a more aggressive or a more conservative marker portfolio. You repeat the approach applied to the intermediate marker portfolio with either alternative. Shifting to the aggressive portfolio increases the five-year expected return by 5 percentage points—but the risk measure will increase by 8 points. Moving in the other direction—to the conservative portfolio—reduces expected return by 5 percentage points while the reduction in risk amounts to 4 points.

The data in Table 6-6 discourage commitment of your entire portfolio to either stocks or cash equivalents. The S&P 500 achieves a higher expected return than the aggressive marker portfolio, but, lacking diversification among asset groups, shows a disproportionately large increase in risk. The portfolio of T-bills comes closest to representing a risk-free asset but is not completely without risk. Compare returns for the Treasury-bill portfolio with those for the conservative portfolio. Reflecting the advantages of diversification, the conservative portfolio shows an 11-percentage-point advantage in expected return but only 6 points difference in terms of the risk measure.

One of the three marker portfolios will best suit the individual requirements of most investors. Where fine tuning seems appropriate, you may adjust asset mix to plan a portfolio partway between the aggressive and the intermediate or partway between the intermediate and the conservative. Earlier in the chapter, Table 6-2 provided an example dealing with the aggressive and intermediate portfolios. As a general rule, you may develop a new portfolio midway between either pair of marker portfolios by averaging the percentage allocations for each of the three component asset groups. The expected return and risk measures for the new portfolio will then approximately reflect the respective averages of these measures for the two marker portfolios.

Building on the Marker Portfolio

The choice of the marker portfolio is a critical step in the investment process because it determines how much risk and expected return will be incorporated in your investment program. It does not, however, determine the specific composition of the portfolio. Accomplishing this task is the goal of the next two chapters. Chapter 7 focuses on diversification within the three broad asset groups and the specific index funds designated to accomplish diversification. Chapter 8 addresses active investing. It shows how active investing operates within the index fund framework.

Appendix 6-1: Underlying Data for Stocks, Bonds, and Bills

Returns calculated for the three marker portfolios, as shown in Table 6-4, reflect the data for stocks, bonds, and bills listed in Table 6-7. To facilitate comparison, Table 6-7 follows the same format as Table 6-4.

Table 6-7: Returns for stocks, bonds, and bills over the last 35 years, in longer-range perspective.

Annual Rate	1926–96	1962–96	Difference
S&P 500			
Real Return	7.4%	5.8%	−1.6%
Inflation	3.1	4.9	+1.8
Nominal Return	10.7	10.9	+0.2
5-Year Treasury Notes			
Real Return	2.0%	2.6%	+0.6%
Inflation	3.1	4.9	+1.8
Nominal Return	5.2	7.6	+2.4
1-Month Treasury Bills			
Real Return	0.6%	1.3%	+0.7%
Inflation	3.1	4.9	+1.8
Nominal Return	3.7	6.3	+2.6

Source: Stocks, Bonds, Bills & Inflation 1997 Yearbook™, Ibbotson Associates, Chicago, IL (annually updates the work of Roger G. Ibbotson and Rex A. Sinquefield.) Used with permission. All rights reserved.

Appendix 6-2: Risk Calculation

The approach to estimating risk used in Chapter 6 serves as a simple substitute for a statistical measure widely used by institutional investors. The statistical approach looks at the historical variability of returns in order to calculate the *standard deviation of return*. This measurement of variability provides a basis for projecting the probability of future returns. Based on calculation of standard deviation, the bottom line of Table 6-8 displays the probability that the least favorable five-year return over 1962–96 will recur over the next five years. These probability estimates for the three marker portfolios, the S&P 500, and one-month Treasury bills agree, in an approximate way, with the simple rule-of-thumb estimate of 1 chance in 25 (or 4%) used in Chapter 6.

Table 6-8: Probability estimates based on standard deviation of inflation-adjusted returns approximate the rule-of-thumb estimates employed in Chapter 6.

	S&P 500	Marker Portfolio Aggr.	Inter.	Cons.	T-bills
5-Year Least Favorable Return	−36%	−26%	−18%	−14%	−8%
Probability of Recurrence within Next Five Years					
Rule of Thumb (1 chance in 25)	4%	4%	4%	4%	4%
Based on Standard Deviation	2	3	4	5	6

Source: Computed using data from *Stocks, Bonds, Bills & Inflation 1997 Yearbook*™, Ibbotson Associates, Chicago, IL (annually updates work by Roger G. Ibbotson and Rex A. Sinquefield.) Used with permission. All rights reserved.

chapter seven

PUTTING INDEX FUNDS TO WORK

Implementing the Marker Portfolio

The marker portfolios, as explained in Chapter 6, offer a choice between differing combinations of risk and expected return. By making a choice, you identify the balance of risk and expected return that best meets your circumstances. Too much risk opens the door to the likelihood, sooner or later, of financial disaster. Too little risk, in contrast, closes the door unnecessarily to opportunity. Unwary investors, lacking the tools to define risk and expected return, may stumble into excessive risk. Perhaps more often, they miss out on high returns as a result of exaggerated caution. The marker portfolios provide a tool to identify the appropriate compromise between the two extremes.

Identifying the Building Blocks

The purpose of Chapter 7 is to identify the mix of index mutual funds that will take the place of the indexes that make up the selected marker portfolios. You don't invest in an *index*, since it merely represents a calculation of the changing values of the issues that comprise it. It is the *index mutual fund* that serves as an actual investment. As such, it entails the various costs identified in Chapters 3 and 4. Although these costs almost always are much less than for actively managed mutual funds, they subtract marginally from returns.

In planning the mix of index mutual funds, you accomplish two primary goals:

1. You *enhance diversification.* By way of illustration, the S&P 500 is the only index to represent common stocks in the marker portfolios. Replacement of the S&P 500 with a combination of domestic- and foreign-stock index mutual funds increases diversification, thus improving the relationship between expected return and risk.

2. You *establish a benchmark* for active management. The measure of active investing is how well it performs relative to the index fund that it replaces. The role of index funds in planning asset mix does not preclude active investing but, rather, presents a formidable alternative.

Establishing Criteria

The choice of an index mutual fund to represent a designated segment of the financial markets depends on both tracking and client service. Tracking reflects: (1) the match of the issues in the fund with the index, and (2) the costs that routinely subtract from fund returns. Client services encompass the many conveniences that facilitate dealing with the fund.

Most index mutual funds, at least those sponsored by the leading fund families, qualify as acceptable as measured by *index match and client services.* Where there are no significant concerns relating to these areas, differences in the *index fund cost advantage* logically become the most important factor in making a choice.

Index Match.   Since the purpose of an index fund is to track a designated index, the match between the fund and the targeted index has to be the initial consideration. A poor match negates the reason for indexing. As a result of luck, mismatch may add to, as well as subtract from, fund returns. The danger is that a poor match, no matter how favorable the performance last time, may cause an unacceptably large shortfall next time. Reflecting wide accessibility of the necessary technology, most index funds have been able to demonstrate adequate matching, through either replication of the entire index or a carefully planned program of sampling.

While all index funds encounter varying degrees of mismatch, the resulting chance fluctuations tend to offset each other over time. However, you should watch out for obvious danger signs. Suppose, for example, the tracking error falls significantly outside the range for competing index funds, even after allowance for differences in expenses and transaction costs. Alternatively, poor acceptance to date of an index fund—especially if it is part of a weak fund family—raises questions concerning the future. An index mutual fund unable to attract sufficient assets may be more vulnerable than are larger funds to excessive mismatch, particularly during periods of unusual stress in the financial markets.

Client Service.   For each investor, individual preferences and personal convenience shape the appraisal of client service. Because client service represents a key element in marketing, mutual fund families strive mightily to provide much the same array of services. By comparing fund prospectuses, you may identify differences that could matter in your particular circumstances. For example, many fund families wire dividends directly to the shareholder's bank account; others do not. Practices may differ concerning routine reporting of data on average costs or other information of special interest to a particular investor.

To many mutual fund shareholders, a key measure of client service is the convenience of dealing with a single fund family—or at least no greater number of fund families than necessary. If you already own funds administered by one fund family, you may prefer to add index funds offered by the same group. In a similar way, your views concerning future needs may influence current choice. Suppose you are currently seeking to purchase an S&P 500 index fund and you also plan to add other index funds in the future. Under such circumstances, the fund family that can best meet both your current and future requirements may have special appeal.

Cost Advantage.   Assuming both tracking and client service meet acceptable standards, differences in costs become the primary consideration in choosing among competing index funds. For any targeted index, the index funds with the lowest costs hold forth the likelihood of the highest returns. The fund prospectus provides the data necessary to identify expense ratios, turnover rates, and sales loads. It also shows whether the fund sponsor currently absorbs a portion of the expense ratio. If so, the expense ratio may rise significantly when the subsidy ends. Although the prospectus does not specifically report transaction costs, Chapters 3 and 4 suggest how the turnover rate, together with an estimate of the cost per transaction, provides useful guidance. To focus attention on the wide differences in index fund costs, Appendix 7-1 displays selected data from the January 1997 Morningstar report. As shown in Chapters 3 and 4, the index fund cost advantage depends heavily on a low expense ratio combined with a low turnover rate and the avoidance of sales load, either front end or deferred.

Defining a Specific Portfolio

To plan for a specific portfolio of index funds, let's start with the following three assumptions. Subsequently, we show how you may vary the assumptions to meet your particular circumstances, making adjustments as necessary in the portfolio plan.

Tax Status.   With individually managed tax-deferred accounts growing rapidly, let's first turn our attention to the asset mix for a tax-deferred portfolio. Growth of both individual retirement accounts (IRAs) and employer-sponsored retirement plans, such as 401(k)s, is contributing to the uptrend. For such portfolios, no taxes become due until the investor withdraws funds, usually on retirement.

We expect that index funds will become increasingly available in tax-deferred accounts. In establishing an IRA, the investor may select a mutual fund family that specifically offers index funds. Fund families, recognizing the limitations on annual contributions and aiming to accommodate new investors in tax-deferred accounts, usually reduce the initial minimum-purchase requirement. Employer-sponsored plans, such as 401(k)s, may limit the choice of mutual funds to a particular fund family. Several of the leading fund families with an especially strong presence in 401(k)s and similar plans already offer index funds. For competitive reasons, an increasing number of other fund families seem certain to follow. Where the investor, as an employee, is a captive of a particular plan that does not offer index funds, he or she may have the opportunity to suggest to management the need for expanded options. The current fund family serving investors in the plan may add index funds in response to client interest, or perhaps management will keep in mind employee interest in index funds the next time it considers competing bids.

Marker Portfolio. Our initial example focuses on the intermediate marker portfolio. As this chapter examines the three broad asset categories—stocks, bonds, and cash equivalents—we define the index mutual funds needed to fulfill the portfolio requirements. The goal is to achieve a diversification plan that depends on index mutual funds to the extent possible. Where necessary—as for tax-exempt bond funds—we use the nearest equivalent, identified as *near-index funds.* Characteristics of this alternative to a standard index fund include broad diversification of the designated market segment, low expense ratio, low turnover, and no sales load. We then demonstrate the advantages of the recommended diversification, comparing the more completely diversified portfolio with the marker portfolio.

Market Value. We focus on an initial portfolio value of $100,000, recognizing that your portfolio may range from a small fraction of this amount to many times more. Since major differences in dollar value may call for adjustments in diversification, we subsequently turn our attention to both smaller portfolios and those much larger, even in the multimillion-dollar range.

Diversifying with Index Mutual Funds

Opportunities to invest in index mutual funds are growing rapidly. Although institutional investors have led the way toward indexing, individual investors are now beginning to shift assets in the same direction. Index mutual funds marketed to institutional investors ordinarily require large initial investments—often $100,000 and even as much as $10,000,000. To identify index mutual funds oriented to individual investors, let's focus on those with a minimum initial investment of $5000 or less. Currently, about half these funds track the S&P 500, but offerings tied to other areas of

Table 7-1: Index mutual funds requiring initial investment of no more than $5000.

| Year end | Stock Funds | | | Bond Funds | Other Funds* | Total |
	Large-Cap	M/S-Cap	Foreign			
1996	35	12	8**	7	9	71
1991	9	4	2	1	—	16
1986	2	—	—	1	—	3

Source: *Morningstar Principia for Mutual Funds, January 1997,* Morningstar, Inc., Chicago, IL © 1997.

*Includes index funds that target the total stock market, specialty stock groups, and balanced funds (stocks and bonds).

**Includes Vanguard Total International Portfolio, which holds shares of three other Vanguard foreign-stock index funds.

the stock market seem certain to increase rapidly in response to growing demand. Table 7-1 traces the growth over the past decade in opportunities for individual investment in index mutual funds.

Common Stock Funds

While the S&P 500 represents a major share of the domestic stock market, it offers something less than optimal diversification. As shown by Table 7-2, the market value of publicly traded stocks in principal world markets at year-end 1996 amounted to about $19 trillion. The S&P 500 accounted for about 30% of the world total,

Table 7-2: World stock market at year end 1996.

	$ (trillions)		Percent	
S&P 500	$5.6		30%	
Wilshire 4500	2.5		13	
Total Domestic		$ 8.1		43%
Europe	$5.3		28%	
Pacific	4.1		22	
Emerging Markets	1.4		7	
Total Foreign		10.8		57
World Total		$18.9		100%

Source: Standard & Poor's, New York, NY, a division of The McGraw-Hill Companies; Wilshire Associates, Santa Monica, CA; and Morgan Stanley Capital International (MSCI), Morgan Stanley & Company, Inc., New York, NY.

and other domestic issues (m/s-cap stocks, as represented by the Wilshire 4500) accounted for an additional 13%. We draw on indexes compiled by Morgan Stanley Capital International (MSCI) to represent the foreign stock markets. The Europe, Australasia, and Far East Index (EAFE) consists of two major segments, Europe and the Pacific. To allow for emerging markets, we make use of an MSCI index that represents stocks of companies domiciled in 26 countries with less developed economies. At year end 1996, foreign stocks represented by the combined indexes accounted for 57% of the total world market value compared with 43% for domestic stocks.

Highlighting the Differences

The major stock groups that make up the world market index differ significantly from each other in industry diversification. To identify these differences, we compare data for the five Vanguard index mutual funds that target these indexes. Table 7-3 lists data for two domestic index mutual funds (Vanguard 500 and Extended Market portfolios) and three foreign funds [Vanguard European, Pacific (Free), and Select Emerging Markets (Free) portfolios]. The designation *Free* reflects a version of the underlying MSCI index that excludes issues unavailable for purchase by foreigners. The *Select* version of the MSCI EMF modifies the index to limit representation to 14 key countries, as explained in Appendix 1-6.

Boldface type in Table 7-3, based on the weightings in the Vanguard index funds, identifies the index with the highest percentage for each sector. The S&P 500 displays higher percentages of consumer staples and energy stocks than do the other indexes. The Wilshire 4500 exhibits the largest proportion of market value in technology and ranks a close second in services. It also leads in the percentage of retail stocks, although only by a small margin. While the Europe index ranks first in percentage of market value accounted for by health stocks, it also includes heavy weightings in the financial and industrial cyclical sectors. By wide margins, the Pacific index leads in the percentages represented by the industrial cyclical and consumer durable goods sectors. The Select EMF index ranks highest in financial, service, and utility stocks but displays very small weightings in retail, health, and technology.

Table 7-3: Sector weightings as a percentage of market value, December 31, 1996.

Index (Vanguard Fund)	S&P 500 (500)	Wilshire 4500 (Ext. Mkt.)	Europe (Eur. Port)	Pacific (Pac. Free)	Emerg. Mkt (Sel. EMF)
Utilities	3.4%	5.4%	4.3%	4.8%	**10.3%**
Energy	**9.3**	4.6	8.9	1.5	4.4
Financial	15.1	21.1	21.8	29.1	**31.7**
Cyclical	16.5	12.9	15.3	**24.8**	17.0
Durable Goods	4.0	3.6	6.0	**13.6**	6.7
Staple	**11.2**	4.1	10.5	3.8	7.5
Service	12.4	17.5	11.9	10.1	**18.0**
Retail	5.2	**5.8**	5.6	4.3	1.8
Health	10.7	9.9	**11.3**	2.8	0.6
Technology	12.4	**15.2**	4.6	5.1	1.9
Total	100.0%	100.0%	100.0%	100.0%	100.0%

Source: *Morningstar Principia for Mutual Funds, January 1997,* Morningstar, Inc., Chicago, IL, © 1997.

Within the domestic segment, the S&P 500 generally represents much larger companies than the Wilshire 4500. Again, we use the Vanguard index funds as a basis for comparison. For the S&P 500, the median capitalization at the beginning of 1997 was $18.4 billion compared with $1.0 billion for the Wilshire 4500. The median capitalizations on the same date for the foreign stocks represented by the two EAFE ndexes were $15.7 (Europe) and $12.0 [Pacific (Free)], each smaller than for the S&P 500 but considerably larger than for the Wilshire 4500. The comparable figure for the stocks in the Select EMF index was $4.0 billion.

Geography differentiates the two EAFE indexes from the domestic stock indexes. The companies represented by EAFE are domiciled abroad, primarily in the leading industrialized countries. Table 7-4 shows a breakdown of market values for the stocks in the Vanguard European and Pacific (Free) portfolios at the beginning of 1997.

In comparison with EAFE, EMF offers greater opportunities as well as greater risks. The Vanguard Select EMF portfolio represents issues in 14 less developed countries spread across five continents. At the end of 1996, as shown in Table 7-5, seven countries accounted for almost 80% of the market value of the fund.

Table 7-4: EAFE (market value $9.4 trillion at year end 1996) reflects the combined market values of stocks traded in Europe and the Far East.

Europe	$ (trillions)	Percent	Pacific	$ (trillions)	Percent
United Kingdom	$1.9	35%	Japan	$3.0	73%
Germany	0.7	14	Hong Kong	0.4	9
France	0.6	12	Australia	0.3	7
Switzerland	0.5	10	Malaysia	0.2	6
Netherlands	0.4	8	Singapore	0.2	4
Other	1.2	21	Other	0.0	1
Total	$5.3	100.0%	Total	$4.1	100.0%

Source: The Vanguard Group of Investment Companies, Valley Forge, PA.

Smoothing Fluctuations in Domestic-Stock Returns

Within the domestic market, our diversification goal is to hold index funds representing the S&P 500 and the Wilshire 4500 in proportion to their respective market capitalizations. In this way, the portfolio secures the average return for all holders of domestic stocks. Extending diversification to the entire domestic stock market, meanwhile, helps to control risk. Diversification tends to smooth fluctuations to the extent returns for major segments of the market—as well as for individual issues—move along differing paths.

The record of recent years demonstrates the benefits of diversification. Over the three years 1991–93, total investment return for the S&P 500 amounted to 55% compared with 84% for the Wilshire 4500. During the subsequent three years—1994–96—the return for the S&P 500 increased to 71% while that for the Wilshire 4500 slipped to 52%.

Table 7-5: Composition of the Vanguard Select EMF at year end 1996.

Emerging Market	% Assets
Malaysia	18.6%
Brazil	13.8
Hong Kong	13.6
South Africa	12.2
Mexico	9.0
Singapore	6.3
Indonesia	6.1
Other	20.3
Total	100%

Source: The Vanguard Group of Investment Companies, Valley Forge, PA.

Addressing Special Costs and Risks in Foreign Markets

If the differing patterns of returns were the only consideration, foreign stocks would also merit representation in the index fund portfolio in relation to their respective market values. The argument for adding foreign stocks to a domestic portfolio starts out in the same way as for diversification within the domestic category. In either case, diversification benefits from bringing together the divergent patterns of return for different stock groups. Divergence between returns of foreign stocks and domestic stocks, moreover, tends to be greater than the divergence between those for m/s-cap stocks and an S&P 500 index fund.

Nevertheless, special costs and risks relating to indexing abroad limit the role of foreign stocks in the index fund portfolio plan. Mutual funds that index foreign stock markets are almost certain to incur higher transaction costs and management fees than do comparable domestic index funds. At the same time, the investor located in the United States encounters special risks in foreign markets, including the changing value of the American dollar in foreign exchange markets. A rapidly rising dollar, as in the early 1980s, could significantly depress the dollar value of foreign holdings, even where returns in local currencies are favorable. Conversely, a sharp decline in the value of the dollar, such as in the several years subsequent to 1985, would enhance the dollar-denominated returns from foreign investments. A further problem for tax-deferred accounts is the withholding of a portion of taxes by many foreign countries. While a taxable account may recover such taxes through offsetting reduction in U. S. taxes, this option is not available to the tax-deferred account.

Identifying the Global Equity Mix

In view of the special costs and risks associated with foreign investing, diversification planning looks to foreign-stock holdings of pension plans for perspective. Pension funds operate from the vantage point of an informed domestic investor. For more than a decade, they have persistently added to the percentage of equities committed to foreign stocks, but their aggregate holdings remain well below the percentage in the world market. At the beginning of 1997, foreign stocks accounted for approximately 12% of the equity holdings of the 200 largest pension funds..

With the example of the private pension plans in view, our equity diversification for the intermediate index fund portfolio commits 20% of the equity holdings to the MSCI index of foreign stocks (EAFE and EMF). This percentage, while higher than the average for large pension funds, takes into account the continuing rapid growth of pension fund investment in foreign markets. At the same time, our 20% target compares with 57% for foreign stocks as a proportion of the total world market value of equities. We divide the remaining 80% between the two broad segments of the domestic equity market. Weighting the S&P 500 and Wilshire 4500 to reflect the market values that they represent (70% and 30%, respectively), we show the overall equity diversification in Table 7-6.

Adding Bonds to the Portfolio

To define the bond segment of the marker portfolio, let's focus on broad diversification within the domestic market. For the intermediate marker portfolio with total assets of $100,000, bonds account for $35,000 (35%). Assuming the portfolio is tax deferred, the goal is to commit this sum to an index mutual fund that represents the broad spectrum of taxable fixed income securities. Such a fund would track the Lehman Aggregate Bond Index (Aggregate Bond Index), which includes almost all outstanding taxable notes and bonds.

Table 7-6: Equity diversification for a $100,000 intermediate portfolio (50% equities).

	Market Value	
	$ (thousands)	% Equities
S&P 500	$28	56%
Wilshire 4500	12	24
MSCI (EAFE plus EMF)	10	20
Total	$50	100%

For the marker portfolios, five-year Treasury notes represent the bond market for two reasons. First, data for this Treasury series are readily available for the period extending back to 1926. Tracing the returns of the series over more than seven decades offers a useful perspective concerning risks under a wide range of market conditions. Second, the five-year Treasury notes provide much the same combination of risk and expected return as the Lehman Aggregate Bond Index (Aggregate Bond Index) as presently constituted.

Figure 7-1 compares the returns for the five-year Treasury notes with those for the Aggregate Bond Index. By including longer maturities and varying degrees of quality, the Aggregate Bond Index benefits from a small advantage in expected return. Although the issues in the Aggregate Bond Index are individually more risky, on average, than are those in the Treasury index, the broad diversification helps to control risk. Over the ten years ended 1996, the returns of the two series have moved rather closely together. The Aggregate Bond Index reported a compound annual rate of return of 8.5% compared with 7.8% for the Treasury notes. Reflecting the ad-

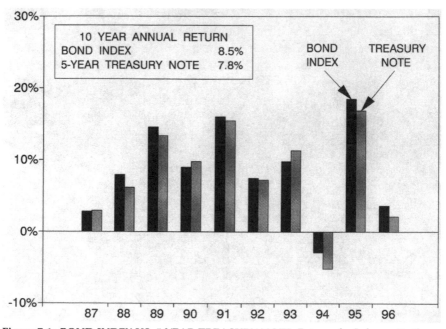

Figure 7-1: BOND INDEX VS. 5-YEAR TREASURY NOTE. Returns for Lehman Brothers Aggregate Bond Index and five-year Treasury notes. (*Sources: Morningstar Principia for Mutual Funds, January 1997 Yearbook*, Morningstar, Inc., Chicago, IL, © 1997; and *Stocks, Bonds, Bills & Inflation 1997 Yearbook*™ [annually updates work by Roger G. Ibbotson and Rex A. Sinquefield]. Used with permission. All rights reserved.)

vantages of more complete diversification, the Aggregate Bond Index demonstrated slightly less variability in returns than the Treasury notes. (Variability is widely accepted by institutional investors as a measure—albeit less than perfect—of risk.)

Representing Cash in the Portfolio

In the absence of an index to represent the cash portion of the index fund portfolio, we look to the performance of money market funds. A wide choice is available. Since money market funds stress safety of principal, they ordinarily confine investments to a well-diversified mix of high-quality, fixed income issues with very short maturities. To a considerable extent, differences in yields reflect differences in the expenses that subtract from the shareholder's return.

The Vanguard Prime Money Market Portfolio serves as a proxy for an index of cash equivalents. As shown in Figure 7-2, the returns of the money market fund, after absorbing expenses and

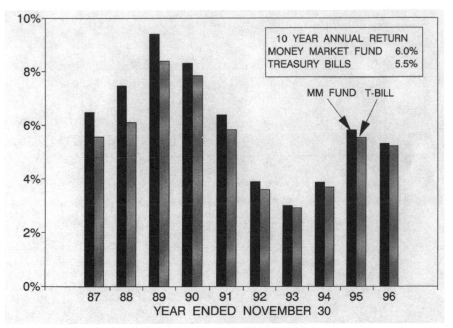

Figure 7-2: MONEY MARKET FUND VS. TREASURY BILLS. Example of how returns for a money market fund (Vanguard Prime Portfolio) compare with those of one-month Treasury bills. (*Sources*: Computed using data from *Stocks, Bonds, Bills & Inflation 1997 Yearbook*™, Ibbotson Associates, Chicago, IL [annually updates work by Roger G. Ibbotson and Rex A. Sinquefield]. Used with permission. All rights reserved. Also, The Vanguard Group of Investment Companies, Valley Forge, PA.)

transaction costs, recorded a small advantage (6.0% compared with 5.5%) over those for the Treasury bills during the ten years 1987–96. Since Treasury securities benefit from the backing of the U.S. government, they enjoy a higher credit rating than any other investment, including money market funds. Despite differences in quality and risk, money market funds have generally produced returns, over their history to date, that have rather closely paralleled those of short-term Treasury bills.

Planning with Index Mutual Funds

Table 7-7 summarizes how the intermediate marker portfolio translates into a portfolio consisting of index mutual funds plus a money market fund. The Vanguard mutual funds, as identified in the following list, are used to illustrate the implementation of the marker portfolio. To provide perspective on tracking, Appendix 7-2 compares the returns for each of the stock and bond index mutual funds with those of its respective index.

- *The 500 Portfolio* matches approximately the stocks included in the S&P 500.

- *Extended Market Portfolio* targets the combined performance of the thousands of publicly traded domestic stocks not included in the S&P 500 (Wilshire 4500).

- *Total International Portfolio* represents combined MSCI Indexes [European and Pacific (Free) components of the EAFE Index together with the emerging markets stocks in Select EMF].

- *Total Bond Market Portfolio* tracks the Lehman Brothers Aggregate Bond Index.

Table 7-7: Putting index funds to work in a $100,000 intermediate marker portfolio (tax deferred).

	Marker Portfolio		*Vanguard Funds*	
Stocks	S&P 500	50%	500 Portfolio	28%
			Extended Market	12
			Total International	10
Bonds	5-Year Treas. Notes	35	Total Bond Market	35
Cash	3-month Treas. Bills	15	Prime Money Market	15
Total		100%		100%

- *The Prime Money Market Portfolio* serves the cash portion of the portfolio plan.

Since we do not recommend specific mutual funds, our listing of examples serves only for purposes of illustration. With explosive growth underway in the offerings of index mutual funds to individual investors, the available choices seem certain to widen. Our standard advice is therefore to consult the updated information, including the fund prospectus, at the time you invest.

Tracking the Marker Portfolio

How reliable is the marker portfolio as a measure of return in the corresponding mutual fund portfolio? Management expenses and transaction costs, which are excluded from the return calculations for the indexes that comprise the marker portfolio, subtract from the performance of the mutual fund portfolio. Despite this difference, the mutual fund portfolio closely tracks the performance of the marker portfolio. Figure 7-3 compares the returns for the intermediate mutual fund portfolio with those for the corresponding marker portfolio over the six years ended 1996. As explained in Chapter 6, each series is rebalanced annually to restore at the beginning of each year the initial percentages of stocks, bonds, and cash. The compound annual rate of return over this period for the mutual fund portfolio (11.9%) closely approximated that of the marker portfolio (12.3%). Calculations for both portfolios reflect annual rebalancing.

Adjusting the Plan

So far, we have focused on a tax-deferred, intermediate marker portfolio with a value of $100,000. We now vary these characteristics to address the range of circumstances that you may encounter: *changes in the tax status of the portfolio, other choices of marker portfolio, and larger or smaller market value of portfolio assets.* Let's begin with the tax status, examining first the taxable portfolio. We then consider adjustments that become advantageous, if, as frequently happens, you hold both tax-deferred and taxable portfolios.

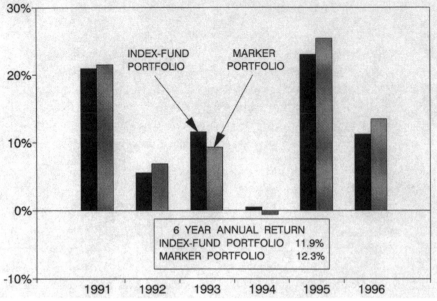

Figure 7-3: **INTERMEDIATE PORTFOLIO RETURNS.** Comparison of returns for the intermediate index-fund portfolio with the corresponding marker portfolio. (*Source:* Computed using data from *Stocks, Bonds, Bills & Inflation 1997 Yearbook*™, Ibbotson Associates, Chicago, IL [annually updates work by Roger G. Ibbotson and Rex A. Sinquefield. Used with permission. All rights reserved.] and *Principia for Mutual Funds, January 1997*, Morningstar, Inc., Chicago, IL, © 1997)

Changing the Tax Status

Restatement of the tax status of the portfolio calls for a reconsideration of the asset mix. In contrast to the tax-deferred portfolio, the taxable portfolio looks to after-tax returns as the measure of investment performance. Although state and local income taxes may apply, the examples that we present here do not take them into account. Federal taxes represent by far the larger subtraction from returns, and the tax exemption that applies to federal taxes does not necessarily extend to state taxes. In assessing a particular tax-exempt alternative, you should also allow for adjustment in after-tax returns due to state and local income taxes.

Where you hold only one investment portfolio—*either* taxable or tax deferred—the plan for *equity* diversification reflects the same mix of index mutual funds. Stocks in general provide a partial tax shelter, since the portion of total return represented by capital gains does not become subject to taxes until the capital gains are realized. Equity index mutual funds, meanwhile, shield you from capital gains taxes better than do most actively managed mutual funds. The reason, as explained in Chapter 3, is the policy of index mutual funds concerning capital gains. Absent pressure to switch from "unattractive" stocks to "more attractive" issues, index mutual funds ordinarily realize extremely low levels of capital gains.

The bond and cash segments of the taxable portfolio, in contrast to the equity portion, may benefit significantly from the use of tax-exempt alternatives. Table 7-8 presents two sets of mutual funds. The Vanguard Intermediate-Term Municipal Bond Portfolio, exempt from federal taxes, is compared with the Vanguard Total Bond Market Portfolio, a taxable index fund. Two Vanguard money market funds, one taxable and one tax exempt, provide a similar comparison. As demonstrated by the after-tax yield calculations, the return advantage for the tax-exempt fund depends on your marginal tax rate together with the yields currently available in the marketplace. Reflecting the exemption from federal taxes, the yields offered by the two municipal bond funds—intermediate term and money market—are significantly lower than for the comparable taxable funds. If your tax rate is sufficiently high, however, the tax-exempt funds provide the superior after-tax return. In the light of comparisons shown in Table 7-8, you have reason to consider the tax-exempt funds if your marginal federal tax rate exceeds 31%.

In shifting from a taxable to a tax-exempt fund, the goal is to secure an advantage in after-tax returns without a significant change

Table 7-8: Comparison of yields before and after federal taxes on January 31, 1997, for taxable (T) and tax-exempt (E) mutual funds.

Vanguard Funds	*Average Maturity*	*Yield Bef. Tax*	*Aft. Tax-Yield (Marg. Tax Rate)*		
			(15%)	*(31%)*	*(39.6%)*
Bond Funds					
Total Bond Market (T)	6.8 yr.	6.59%	5.60%	4.54%	3.98
Municipal Bond— Intermediate (E)	7.2 yr.	4.64	4.64	4.64	4.64
Money Market Funds					
Prime Money Market (T)	54 days	5.18%	4.40%	3.57%	3.13%
Municipal Bond— Money Market (E)	55 days	3.37	3.37	3.37	3.37

Source: The Vanguard Group of Investment Companies, Valley Forge, PA.

in risk. To this end, we seek to maintain average maturities and average quality ratings at about the same level. As illustrated by the examples presented in Table 7-8, the taxable bond fund reports average maturity at 6.8 years while the figure for the tax-exempt fund is 7.2. Both funds rank high in average quality, as indicated by ratings assigned by independent rating organizations to the individual issues in each fund. In a similar way, the two money market funds report very similar average maturities (very short) and quality ratings (very high).

Comparisons over the past ten years provide perspective on differences in returns for taxable and tax-exempt bond funds with similar maturities. Figure 7-4 presents data for the period 1987–96. Although the returns clearly do not move in lockstep, they trace sufficiently similar patterns to allow the tax-exempt fund to substitute for the taxable fund where the former provides an advantage in after-tax yield. The same conclusion applies to the two versions of money market funds, one taxable and the other tax exempt.

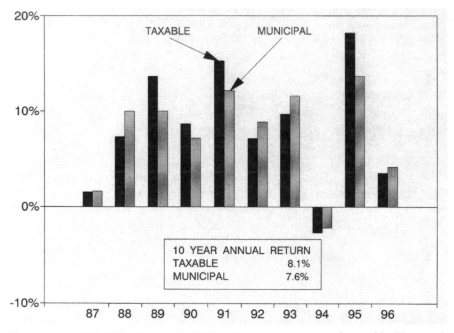

Figure 7-4: BOND FUNDS: TAXABLE VS. MUNICIPAL. Returns for taxable (Vanguard Total Bond Market Portfolio) and tax-exempt (Vanguard Municipal Intermediate-Term Portfolio) bond funds with similar average maturity and quality ratings trace similar patterns. *(Source: Morningstar Principia for Mutual Funds, January 1997, Morningstar, Inc. Chicago, IL © 1997)*

Table 7-9: Putting index funds to work in a $100,000 intermediate marker portfolio (taxable).

	Marker Portfolio		*Vanguard Funds*	
Stocks	S&P 500	50%	500 Portfolio	28%
			Extended Market	12
			Total International	10
Bonds	5-Year Treas. Notes	35	Municipal Bond– Intermediate	35
Cash	1-month Treas. Bills	15	Municipal Bond– Money Market	15
Total		100%		100%

Table 7-9 shows a revision of Table 7-7 to provide for the use of tax-exempt funds. This time we assume that the portfolio is taxable and the investor's marginal income tax rate permits a significant return advantage for the tax-exempt funds. The other assumptions remain the same. The marker portfolio is the intermediate alternative, and portfolio assets amount to $100,000.

Coordinating Tax-Deferred and Taxable Portfolios

So far in this chapter, we have assumed that you hold either a tax-exempt or taxable portfolio—but not both. For many investors, such is the case. Lacking a choice, these investors do not have to decide how to allocate financial assets between two portfolios with differing tax status. More and more investors, nevertheless, face the challenge of coordinating investments between tax-exempt and taxable portfolios. They may contribute to a tax-deferred retirement plan, such as an individual IRA or employer-sponsored 401(k) plan. At the same time, they build assets in taxable portfolios through savings from cash income, exercise of stock options, sale of appreciated property, or perhaps through gifts or inheritance.

In general, the diversification for the combined portfolios should take precedence over that for each portfolio viewed separately. For the most part, it is the total investment performance that matters rather than the specific return for each portfolio. By way of example, Table 7-10 shows total assets of $100,000, with $50,000 held in a tax-deferred portfolio and $50,000 in a taxable portfolio. The first

pair of columns outlines the diversification for the combined portfolio, identifying the mutual funds weighted to represent the investor's choice of the intermediate-term marker portfolio. The second pair of columns indicates very different diversification for the
tax-deferred portfolio, while the third pair presents a complemen-
tary pattern for the taxable portfolio.

How can you determine the distribution of your mutual fund investments between the two portfolios? Your primary goal is to improve the net return after taxes, including allowance for future liability for deferred capital gains taxes. Since no sweeping
generalization applies to every situation, we offer the following
checklist. It first summarizes reasons in favor of equities in the taxable account, as shown in Table 7-10. A second section suggests reasons for doing the opposite. Careful examination of your circumstances in the light of the checklist will help you decide.

Table 7-10: Diversification of the combined portfolio takes precedence.

	(1) Combined		(2) Tax-Deferred		(3) Taxable	
	$ (thou-sands)	%	$ (thou-sands)	%	$ (thou-sands)	%
500 Portfolio	$ 28	28%			$28	56%
Extended Market	12	12			12	24
Total International	10	10			10	10
Total Bond Market	35	35	$35	70%		
Prime Money Market	15	15	15	30		
	$100	100%	$50	100%	$50	100%

Equities in the Taxable Account

Absent offsetting considerations, several factors are likely to favor
placing your stock funds in the taxable portfolio and fixed income
securities in the tax-deferred portfolio.

- Equity funds benefit from the opportunity to defer tax liability on
  capital gains until they are realized. For common stocks—in contrast to fixed income funds—most of the investment return is expected to result from market price appreciation. Indexing of equity funds magnifies the benefit of deferral of capital gains taxes,
  since equity index funds ordinarily realize a much smaller portion
  of capital gains from year to year than do actively managed funds.

- Under unfavorable market conditions, sale of shares in a stock fund—perhaps to switch to shares of another fund—may present an opportunity to realize a tax loss. Holding the fund in a tax-deferred account precludes such opportunity.

- With tax rates for ordinary income higher than for capital gains, there is a further reason to concentrate equity funds in the taxable account. For a tax-deferred account, market price appreciation (which in a taxable account could benefit from the lower long-term capital gains rate) translates into ordinary income at the time of withdrawal.

- Capital gains taxes, if deferred, may be paid later at a lower rate. After retirement, your tax rate may decline. Donation of the stock fund to a philanthropic institution can provide opportunity to eliminate the tax liability. Holding an appreciated asset until it passes into your estate can accomplish the same goal.

- For foreign equity funds held in a taxable account, taxes withheld by the government of the country in which a foreign company is domiciled may be used as a tax deduction or a tax credit when filing U.S. income taxes. Holding the foreign equities in a tax-deferred account precludes making use of such tax deductions or tax credits.

Equities in the Tax-Deferred Account

Putting stock in the taxable portfolio and fixed-income securities in the tax-deferred account is not always the right approach. Depending on your personal circumstances, you may have good reason to distribute assets differently between the two portfolios.

- Variation in the time horizon between the two portfolios may warrant overriding tax considerations. How soon will you need to withdraw cash? A much shorter time horizon for the taxable portfolio than for the tax-exempt portfolio provides reason for concentrating highly liquid, low-risk investments, such as a money market fund, in the taxable portfolio.

- If your tax rates are sufficiently high, use of tax-exempt municipal bonds or money market funds may offset a portion of the disadvantage of shifting fixed income securities to the taxable portfolio.

- Where both portfolios are small, the tax-deferred portfolio provides greater flexibility in implementing diversification. As discussed earlier in this chapter, mutual funds usually maintain smaller minimum initial purchase requirements for tax-deferred portfolios. The investor may therefore implement in a tax-deferred portfolio a portion of the diversification plan that could not be accomplished in a taxable portfolio of the same value.

> *Although we raise investment issues relating to taxes, we caution the reader that this book is not intended to provide specific tax advice. Tax laws change frequently and may apply differently to differing situations. Your personal circumstances, including the level of taxable income, may change. When in doubt, consult a qualified tax specialist familiar with your particular circumstances.*

Choosing Other Marker Portfolios

Other things equal, choice of the marker portfolio serves to define the mix of mutual funds. As shown in Table 7-11, the weighting of each of the mutual funds adjusts to the diversification of the marker portfolio. The left-hand columns of Table 7-11 list the proportion of stocks, bonds, and cash in each of three marker portfolios. The right-hand columns indicate the mix of Vanguard mutual funds corresponding to the specified marker portfolio. Table 7-11, which again assumes a portfolio market value of $100,000, applies to both tax-deferred and taxable portfolios. For the bond and cash segments of a taxable portfolio, it lists in each case a tax-exempt alternative.

How Market Value Shapes Portfolio Diversification

Opportunities for diversification depend to a degree on the market value of portfolio assets. So far, our examples have focused on a portfolio value of $100,000. Let's see what happens to the mix of index funds when adjustment is made for different market values.

Table 7-11: Putting index funds to work in a $100,000 marker portfolio, with adjustments for differing objectives and differing tax status.

Marker Portfolios				Vanguard Mutual Funds			
	Cons.	Inter.	Aggr.		Cons.	Inter.	Aggr.
S&P 500	25%	50%	75%	500 Portfolio	14%	28%	42%
				Extended Market	6	12	18
				Total International	5	10	15
5-Year Treas. Notes	50	35	20	Total Bond Market *or* Mun. Bond– Intermediate	50	35	20
3-Mo. Treas. Bills	25	15	5	Prime Mon. Mkt. *or* Mun. Bond– Money Mkt.	25	15	5
	100%	100%	100%		100%	100%	100%

If you are just starting to accumulate savings for an investment program, minimum initial purchase requirements serve as a constraint on diversification. The minimums vary widely among funds, but are usually less for IRAs and other tax-exempt portfolios. Even in a taxable account, however, many funds will accept an initial investment of $1000 or even less. Vanguard sets the minimum initial investment for the index funds cited as examples in Chapter 7 at $3000, but lowers the requirement to $500 for IRAs.

The investor with limited assets may begin the investment program as soon as assets are sufficient to purchase a single mutual fund. What kind of fund qualifies for the first purchase? The four broad options are stocks, bonds, cash (probably a money market fund) or balanced fund (which includes both stocks and bonds). The choice depends on the selection of the marker portfolio, as explained in Chapter 6. Table 7-12 indicates how the choice of the marker portfolio corresponds with the investment category represented by the mutual fund.

Your initial purchase may represent a temporary investment. Because of initial minimum purchase requirements, you may not be able to buy the shares identified as most suitable for long-term investment. For example, suppose you would like to buy a particular S&P 500 index fund, but the minimum initial purchase requirement exceeds your assets currently available for investment. As an alternative, you may purchase a broadly diversified common stock fund with similar characteristics to the S&P 500 as long as it does not

Table 7-12: For a start-up portfolio, marker portfolio guides initial mutual fund purchase.

Marker Portfolio	Mutual Fund Category
Aggressive	Stocks
Intermediate	Balanced
Conservative	Bonds or Money Market

have a sales load. You may then consider switching to a better situated fund after assets have grown sufficiently to meet initial purchase requirements. As your assets increase, adding other funds can gradually bring the mix of mutual funds close to the diversification of the targeted marker portfolio. Table 7-13 addresses taxable portfolios with smaller market values. It outlines distribution of assets among the previously discussed Vanguard mutual funds for each of the three marker portfolios and three differing market values.

As your portfolio increases in value beyond $100,000, the door opens to additional opportunities. Other things equal, the plan for diversification among index and other mutual funds, whether taxable or tax exempt, may remain the same as the portfolio grows to $1 million or even much more. With the increase in portfolio value, however, reasons for adjustments within the framework of the

Table 7-13: Mix of index funds adjusted to market value of portfolio assets.

Assets (000)	Conservative			Intermediate			Aggressive		
	$100	$50	$25	$100	$50	$25	$100	$50	$25
500 Portfolio	14%	13%	13%	28%	28%	26%	42%	42%	42%
Extended Mkt.	6	6	12	12	12	12	18	18	18
Tot. International	5	6	—	10	10	12	15	15	15
Tot. Bond Mkt. Municipal Bond–Intermediate	50	50	50	35	35	35	20	19	13
Prime Money Market Municipal Bond–Money Market	25	25	25	15	15	15	5	6	12
	100%	100%	100%	100%	100%	100%	100%	100%	100%

basic diversification plan are likely to become more compelling. To cite the Vanguard funds as an example, substitution of the three component portfolios [Europe, Pacific (Free) and Select EMF] for the Total International Portfolio offers greater flexibility to depart from the index fund portfolio plan as well as possible tax advantages. How the characteristics of any fund apply to your situation requires a careful reading of the fund prospectus in the light of your particular circumstances. In Chapter 8, we specifically address active investing in an index fund framework.

Appendix 7-1: Index Funds Available to the Individual Investor

Of the 7746 mutual funds listed by Morningstar at year end 1996, 71 qualify as index funds broadly available to the individual investor. As evidence of the rapid increase in the interest of individual investors in indexing, fund families have introduced 55 of these funds since the beginning of 1992. Table 7-14 ranks the funds by net assets within major segments of the financial markets. Excluded from this list are enhanced index funds, which combine indexing with active management, and funds requiring an initial purchase of more than $5000. Also omitted are funds restricted to institutional use, such as a 401(k) plan. If you are a participant in a 401(k) plan with access to index funds other than those included on our list, you will receive the necessary information from your employer.

We once again urge you to consult the fund prospectus prior to investing. *The information included in Table 7-14 (or elsewhere in this book) is not intended to serve as a recommendation for purchase or sale of a specific fund.* The brief summary data for each fund provided by Table 7-14 is necessarily incomplete. By way of example, the table makes no attempt to identify fund management or how well past performance has met fund objectives. The expense-ratio column does not signal which funds currently waive part or all of expenses. The minimum initial purchase requirement does not specify other, more lenient terms that may apply to tax-deferred accounts such as IRAs. To request a fund prospectus that more fully discusses objectives, costs, and risks, as well as other important information, investors may call the toll-free phone number listed for each fund.

Table 7-14: Index mutual funds in major categories, ranked by net assets, December 31, 1996.

Index Fund	Target Index	Assets $ (millions)	Load or 12b-1*	Exp. Ratio	Turn-over	Incep. Date	Min. Initial. Purchase	Phone Number
Domestic—Large Cap								
Vanguard Index 500	S&P 500	$30,312		0.20	4	76-08	$3,000	800-662-7447
Schwab 1000	Schwab 1000	$ 1,751		0.49	2	91-04	$1,000	800-526-8600
Fidelity Market Index	S&P 500	$ 1,574		0.45	5	90-03	$2,500	800-544-8888
Vanguard Index Value	S&P/BARRA VALUE	$ 1,003	M	0.20	27	92-11	$3,000	800-662-7447
Seven Seas S&P 500 Index	S&P 500	$ 877		0.18	29	92-12	$1,000	800-647-7327
T. Rowe Price Equity Index	S&P 500	$ 819		0.45	1	90-03	$2,500	800-638-5660
Vanguard Index Growth	S&P/BARRA GROWTH	$ 783		0.20	24	92-11	$3,000	800-662-7447
Dreyfus S&P 500 Index	S&P 500	$ 653		0.55	4	90-01	$2,500	800-645-6561
BT Investment Equity 500 Idx	S&P 500	$ 448		0.25	6	92-12	$2,500	800-730-1313
Stagecoach Corporate Stock A	S&P 500	$ 407	M	1.01	6	84-01	$1,000	800-222-8222
Galaxy II Large Co Index Ret	S&P 500	$ 353		0.40	7	90-10	$2,500	800-628-0414
Norwest Advant Index I	S&P 500	$ 335		0.50	14	94-11	$2,000	800-338-1348
Victory Stock Index	S&P 500	$ 306	F	0.55	12	93-12	$ 500	800-539-3863
Schwab S&P 500 Inv	S&P 500	$ 244		0.00	0	96-05	$1,000	800-526-8600
MainStay Equity Index A	S&P 500	$ 225	F,M	1.10	4	90-12	$1,000	800-522-4202
USAA S&P 500 Index	S&P 500	$ 174		0.00	0	96-05	$3,000	800-382-8722
Citizens Index	S&P 500	$ 165	M	1.82	6	95-03	$2,500	800-223-7010
Domini Social Equity	Domini Social Index	$ 111	M	0.98	5	91-06	$1,000	800-762-6814
One Group Equity Index B	S&P 500	$ 78	D,M	1.30	9	94-01	$1,000	800-338-4345
One Group Equity Index A	S&P 500	$ 53	F,M	0.55	9	92-02	$1,000	800-338-4345
California Invmt S&P 500 Idx	S&P 500	$ 53		0.20	2	92-04	$5000	800-225-8778
Portico Equity Index Ret	S&P 500	$ 44	F,M	0.66	4	95-01	$ 100	800-228-1024
Munder Index 500 A	S&P 500	$ 39	F,M	0.36	8	92-12	$1,000	800-438-5789
Munder Index 500 B	S&P 500	$ 30	D,M	0.71	0	95-11	$1,000	800-438-5789
Biltmore Equity Index A	S&P 500	$ 18	F	0.48	60	93-05	$ 250	800-994-4414
Wilshire Target Lrg Gr Invmt	Wilshire Lrg Co Grth	$ 18	M	0.93	44	92-09	$2,500	888-200-6796
Wilshire Target Lrg Val Inv	Wilshire Lrg Co Val	$ 15	M	0.89	56	92-09	$2,500	888-200-6796
Compass Index Equity Inv A	S&P 500	$ 14	F,M	0.61	18	92-06	$ 500	888-426-6727
ASM	DJIA	$ 12		3.01	340	91-03	$1,000	800-445-2763
Transamerica Prem Index Inv	S&P 500	$ 10	M	0.25	0	95-10	$1,000	800-892-7587
Kent Index Equity Invmt	S&P 500	$ 10	F,M	0.80	3	92-12	$1,000	800-633-5368
First American Equity Indx B	S&P 500	$ 10	D,M	1.35	9	94-08	$1,000	800-637-2548
First American Equity Indx A	S&P 500	$ 7	F,M	0.57	9	92-12	$1,000	800-637-2548
Devcap Shared Return	Domini Social Index	$ 1	M	0.00	0	95-10	$1,000	800-371-2655
Harris Ins Index A	S&P 500	$ 0	F,M	0.00	0	96-04	$1,000	800-982-8782

*F=Front-end sales load, D=Deferred sales load, M=12b-1 distribution and marketing expenses (included in expense ratio).

183

Table 7-14 *(continued)*

Index Fund	Target Index	Assets $ (millions)	Load or 12b-1*	Exp. Ratio	Turn-over	Incep. Date	Min. Initial. Purchase	Phone Number
Domestic—Medium/Small-Cap								
Vanguard Index Extended Mkt	Wilshire 4500	$2083		0.25	15	87–12	$3000	800-662-7447
Vanguard Index Small Cap Stk	Russell 2000	$1647		0.25	28	60–10**	$3000	800-662-7447
Galaxy II Small Co Index Ret	Russell Spec Small Co	$ 326		0.40	10	90–10	$2500	800-628-0414
Schwab Small Cap Index	Schwab Small Cap Index	$ 221		0.68	24	93–12	$1000	800-526-8600
Composite Northwest A	S&P MidCap 400	$ 188	F,M	1.10	11	86–11	$1000	800-543-8072
Dreyfus MidCap Index	S&P MidCap 400	$ 184		0.50	20	91–06	$2500	800-645-6561
California Invmt S&P MidCap	S&P MidCap 400	$ 37		0.40	18	92–04	$5000	800-225-8778
Composite Northwest B	S&P MidCap 400	$ 16	D,M	1.95	11	94–03	$1000	800-543-8072
Wilshire Target Sm Gr Invmt	Wilshire Sm Co Growth	$ 16	M	1.01	87	92–10	$2500	888-200-6796
Wilshire Target Sm Val Invmt	Wilshire Sm Co Value	$ 15	M	0.88	81	92–09	$2500	888-200-6796
Gateway Small-Cap Index	Wilshire 250 Index	$ 11		1.68	20	93–06	$1000	800-354-6339
Gateway Mid-Cap Index	S&P MidCap 400	$ 6		1.98	18	92–09	$1000	800-354-6339
Domestic—Total Stock Market								
Vanguard Index Total Stk Mkt	Wilshire 5000	$3495		0.25	3	92–04	$3000	800-662-7447
Foreign Stocks								
Vanguard Intl Eqty European	MSCI-Europe	$1542		0.35	2	90–06	$3000	800-662-7447
Vanguard Intl Eqty Pacific	MSCI-Pacific Free	$1023		0.35	1	90–06	$3000	800-662-7447
Vanguard Intl Eqty Emerg Mkt	MSCI-Emerg Mkt Free	$ 622		0.60	3	94–05	$3000	800-662-7447
Schwab Intl Index	Schwab Int'l Index	$ 260		0.85	0	93–09	$1000	800-526-8600
One Group Intl Eqty Idx A	MSCI-EAFE	$ 11	F,M	1.22	6	93–04	$1000	800-338-4345
One Group Intl Eqty Idx B	MSCI-EAFE	$ 7	D,M	1.97	6	94–01	$1000	800-338-4345
STI Classic Intl Eqty IdxInv	MSCI-EAFE	$ 6	F,M	1.45	30	94–06	$2000	800-428-6970
Vanguard Tot. Intl Eqty Port.	MSCI	***		***	***	96–05	$3000	800-662-7447

*F=Front-end sales load, D=Deferred sales load, M=12b-1 distribution and marketing expenses (included in expense ratio).

**Converted to an index fund 89–10.

***Vanguard Total International (Equity) Portfolio is a market-value weighted composite of three Vanguard foreign-stock funds—European, Pacific (Free), and Select EMF portfolios. Assets of $280 million at year end 1996 are included in the asset totals for the component funds.

Table 7-14 (continued)

Index Fund	Target Index	Assets $ (millions)	Load cr 12b-1*	Exp. Ratio	Turn-over	Incep. Date	Min. Initial. Purchase	Phone Number
Specialty Stocks								
American Cent Global Gold	Ft-Se Gold Mine Index	$ 433		0.61	28	88-08	$1000	800-331-8331
Vanguard Special REIT Index	Morgan Stanley REIT Index	$ 326		0.00	0	96-05	$3000	800-662-7447
American Gas Index	Amer Gas Assoc Index	$ 233		0.85	10	89-05	$2500	800-343-3355
American Cent Global Nat Res	DJWSI Energy Basic Mat	$ 66		0.76	39	94-09	$1000	800-331-8331
Galaxy II Utility Index Ret	Russell 1000 Utility Index	$ 51		0.40	5	93-01	$2500	800-628-0414
Principal Pres PSE Tech 100	PSE Technology Index	$ 6	F,M	0.00	0	96-06	$1000	800-826-4600
GrandView REIT Index	GrandView REIT Index	$ 0	F	1.05	0	95-06	$5000	800-525-3863
Domestic Bonds								
Vanguard Bond Idx Total	LB Aggregate Bond	$2953		0.20	36	86-12	$3000	800-662-7447
Vanguard Bond Idx Intrm-Term	LB Intermediate-Term Bond	$ 457		0.20	71	94-03	$3000	800-662-7447
Vanguard Bond Idx Short-Term	LB Short-Term Bond	$ 327		0.20	65	94-03	$3000	800-662-7447
Galaxy II U.S. Treas Idx Ret	Salomon Bros. US Treas Index	$ 114		0.40	50	91-06	$2500	800-628-0414
Portico Short-Term Bond Ret	LB Short-Term Bond	$ 60	F,M	0.69	101	95-01	$ 100	800-228-1024
Vanguard Bond Idx Long-Term	LB Long-Term Bond	$ 44		0.20	45	94-03	$3000	800-662-7447
Dreyfus Bond Market Idx Inv	LB Aggregate Bond	$ 0	M	0.65	40	94-04	$2500	800-645-6561
Stocks & Bonds								
Vanguard Balanced Index	W 5000 + LB Agg Bond	$ 808		0.20	16	92-09	$3000	800-662-7447

*F=Front-end sales load, D=Deferred sales load, M=12b-1 distribution and marketing expenses (included in expense ratio).

Source: *Morningstar Principia for Mutual Funds, January 1997*, Morningstar, Inc., Chicago, IL, © 1997.

Appendix 7-2: Index Fund Tracking Error

Table 7-15 shows how well five Vanguard index mutual funds track their respective indexes. Three of these funds—the S&P 500, Extended Market, and Total Bond Market—serve as benchmark funds in the index fund portfolio plan. Another benchmark fund, The Total International Portfolio, consists of three component funds. The table displays records for the two major components, European and Pacific (Free) portfolios. The record of the other component, the Select EMF, is too short (only two full calendar years) to be included.

The table presents an analysis of six years of data. Column 1 displays the compound annual rate of return for the index funds over 1991–96, while column 2 shows the comparable data for the respective indexes. Columns 3 and 4 identify the largest and smallest annual tracking errors for each fund over the six-year period. Average tracking errors, as shown in column 5, reflect partially offsetting errors from year to year.

As indicated by the range of annual tracking errors for each fund, average tracking errors will almost certainly differ by varying degrees over future periods. Returns for three funds [Extended Market, Europe, and Pacific (Free)] exceeded respective returns for the targeted indexes over the past six years. Since expenses and transaction costs subtract from returns, there

Table 7-15: Tracking errors for five index mutual funds over six years ended 1996.

Vanguard Index Fund	Return (Annual Rate)		Annual Tracking Error		
	Fund	Index	Largest	Smallest	Average
S&P 500	17.46%	17.62%	−0.26%	−0.08%	−0.16%
Extended Market	18.89	18.69	−1.60	−0.05	+0.20
Europe	13.34	13.15	+1.39	−0.15	+0.19
Pacific	4.67	4.56	+0.76	−0.03	+0.11
Total Bond Market	8.30	8.48	−0.75	−0.05	−0.18

Source: Morningstar Principia for Mutual Funds, January 1997, Morningstar, Inc., Chicago, IL, © 1997.

is little reason to project such favorable results into the long-range future.

The bar graphs on pages 188-190 underscore the very close correlation of the returns of the benchmark funds with those of their respective indexes. Figure 7-5 focuses on the two domestic equity index funds, while Figure 7-6 examines the tracking records of the two foreign equity funds. Figure 7-7 summarizes the record of the Total Bond Market Portfolio.

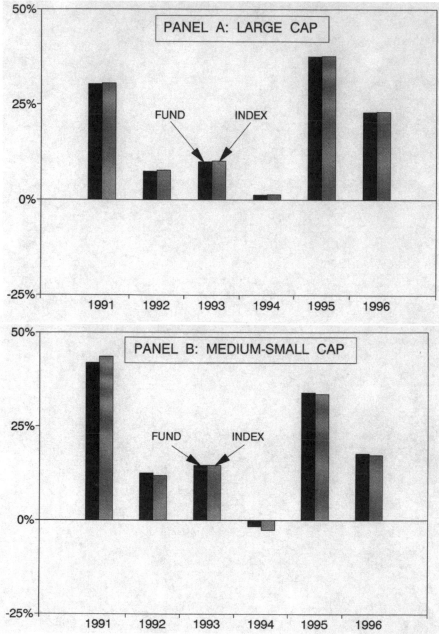

Figure 7-5: DOMESTIC STOCKS. Comparison of annual rates of return over six years 1991-96: Panel A, Vanguard 500 Portfolio versus S&P 500 Index; Panel B, Vanguard Extended Market Portfolio versus Wilshire 4500 Index. *(Source: Morningstar Principia for Mutual Funds, January 1997, Morningstar, Inc., Chicago, IL © 1997)*

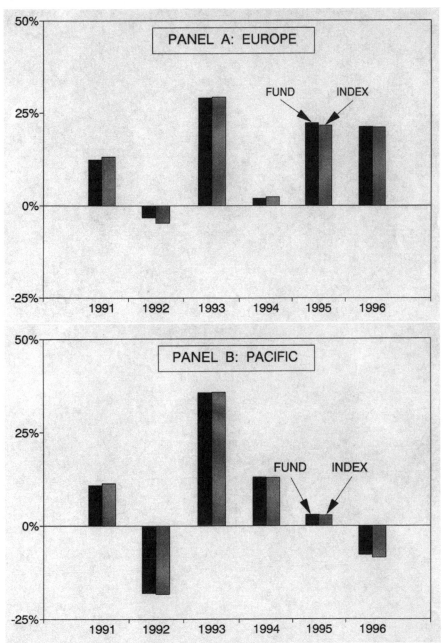

Figure 7-6: FOREIGN STOCKS. Comparison of annual rates of return over six years 1991-96: Panel A, Vanguard European Portfolio versus MSCI Europe Index; Panel B, Vanguard Pacific Portfolio versus MSCI Pacific Index. *(Source: Morningstar Principia for Mutual Funds, January 1997, Morningstar, Inc., Chicago, IL © 1997)*

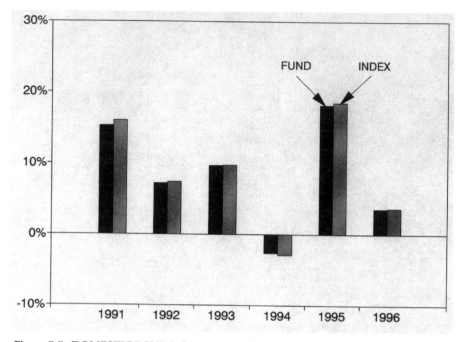

Figure 7-7: DOMESTIC BONDS. Comparison of annual rates of return over six years 1991-96: Vanguard Total Bond Market Portfolio versus Lehman Brothers Aggregate Bond Index. *(Source: Morningstar Principia for Mutual Funds, January 1997,* Morningstar, Inc., Chicago, IL © 1997)

OUTSMARTING THE INDEXES

Departing from the Index Fund Portfolio Plan

Active investing calls for departure from the index fund portfolio plan. As explained in Chapters 6 and 7, the mix of index funds that matches your choice of marker portfolio defines your neutral position. This is the portfolio that you would hold in the absence of superior forecasting skill. Accordingly, departing from the index fund plan implies superior insight into the outlook for the financial markets. For the active investor, the challenge is to outsmart the financial markets by a margin more than sufficient to overcome the index fund advantage relating to costs and taxes.

Active investing may take the form of either investor action or, in the face of portfolio change that you do not initiate, lack of action. Examples of investor action to implement an active decision are commonplace. Reacting to perceived mispricing in the financial markets, you may sell existing holdings or acquire new holdings. The result may be much the same, however, if you accept revisions that occur for other reasons. Variations in the rate of return for the asset groups that make up the index fund plan are likely to modify the asset mix. Dividend payments—or additions and withdrawals from the portfolio for other reasons unrelated to investment strategy—will also alter the portfolio balance. When such changes take place, you may routinely take steps to correct them or, by leaving them uncorrected, translate the change into active strategy.

Chapter 8 examines active investing from three different vantage points:

1. Alternative ways of implementation, with particular emphasis on the growing opportunities provided by indexing
2. Control of risk through establishment of ranges in which active investing may operate
3. Assessment of benefits for active investing and indexing as a result of coordination with each other

Exploring Alternatives

Within the index fund framework, the definition of active investing broadens to include strategic applications of indexing. Traditionally, active investing has focused on the selection of the superior actively managed mutual fund or the identification of the prospective winners among individual issues. Table 8-1 adds two categories to this list. One consists of the index funds already in place that make up the index fund portfolio plan. The other category comprises the index funds that target more specialized segments of the financial markets.

Revising Index Fund Weightings

For the benchmark index funds that make up your portfolio plan, overweighting and underweighting offer substantial opportunity to apply active investment strategy. Overweighting means that assets committed to a particular benchmark index fund exceed the level specified in the index fund portfolio plan. Conversely, underweighting describes a holding that falls short of the percentage established by the index fund portfolio plan. Suppose, for example, your plan calls for 10% of portfolio assets to be held in the Total In-

Table 8-1: Four approaches to active investing.

1. Delegation to actively managed funds
2. Selection of individual issues
3. Over- and underweighting of index funds already in place
4. Introduction of other index funds

ternational Portfolio. Because you are particularly bullish on foreign stocks, you decide to increase the holdings of this fund to 15%. To accomplish this change, you may direct cash to this fund, withdraw cash from other portfolio holdings, or refrain from correcting a percentage increase resulting from market price changes.

Opportunities for timely revision in the weightings of the benchmark index funds depend on how much their returns vary from each other from year to year. Figure 8-1 summarizes annual data for the indexes that underlie the five benchmark funds identified in Chapter 7. As shown in Panel A, the returns for these indexes have varied widely, not only from year to year but also from each other during the same year. Panel B directs attention to differences between the most favorable and least favorable returns each year. The largest difference was recorded in 1986, when the 65% rise in MSCI Index (representing the EAFE plus the EMF Index) compared with 4% for Treasury bills (serving as a proxy for money market funds). Even in 1994, the year with the smallest difference, the MSCI Index produced a return of 7% compared with a *negative* return of 4% for the Lehman Brothers Aggregate Bond Index.

Adding Other Index Funds

Index funds targeted to specialized segments of the financial markets provide further opportunity to implement active strategies. Suppose, for example, that you conclude that not only are common stocks particularly attractive, but smaller capitalization issues are especially well situated. You could increase the weightings for the equity index funds already in the portfolio. Adding to the large-cap index fund would let you participate in the favorable prospects for the stock market. An overweighting for the m/s-cap index fund would be even better, enabling you to participate more specifically in prospective gains for smaller capitalization stocks. A third option would be the addition of an equity index fund with median market capitalization much smaller than for the m/s-cap segment of the portfolio. In a similar way, addition of an emerging market fund (focusing on less developed economies) serves as an alternative to an overall increase in the foreign segment of the portfolio.

Figure 8-2 displays the variability of returns for six indexes, each of which offers opportunity to overweight more narrowly defined

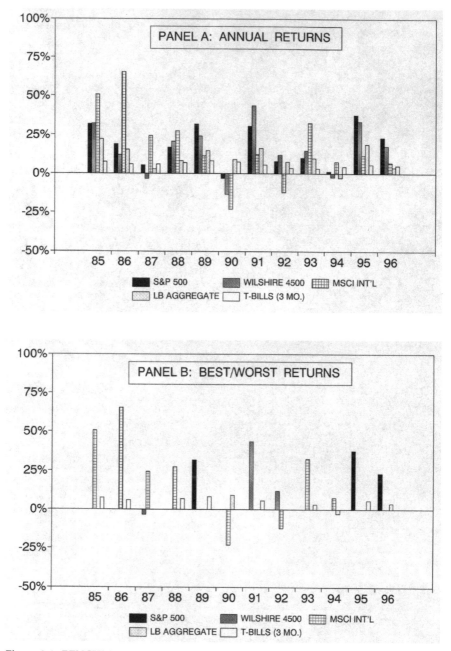

Figure 8-1: BENCHMARK INDEXES. Variations in returns of benchmark index funds provide opportunity for active investing. *(Source: Morningstar Principia for Mutual Funds, January 1997*, Morningstar, Inc., Chicago, IL © 1997)

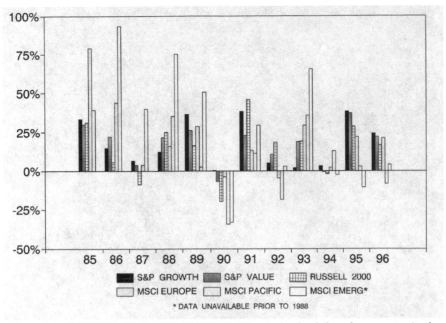

Figure 8-2: RETURNS OF OTHER INDEXES. Other index funds broaden opportunity for active investing. (*Source: Morningstar Principia for Mutual Funds, January 1997*, Morningstar, Inc., Chicago, IL © 1997)

segments of the equity markets. Small-cap stocks are represented by the Russell 2000 Index (with median capitalization at year end 1996 of $555 million). Foreign stock funds track separately three components of the MSCI Index—Europe, Pacific (Free), and Select EMF. In the large-cap area, the S&P BARRA Value Index and the S&P BARRA Growth Index constitute two segments of the S&P 500. As indicated in Table 7-14, at least one mutual fund tracks each of these indexes, and we expect more to become available over the next year or two.

Controlling Risk

Risk control depends on controlling departures from the index portfolio plan. The asset mix for your index fund portfolio plan reflects your choice of a marker portfolio, representing the tradeoff of expected return and risk that you selected as appropriate for your circumstances. When you switch part of a normal holding in your index fund portfolio plan to another investment, your goal is to add incrementally to return. You expect that your actual portfolio will now perform better than your index fund portfolio plan—but what if this time your decision is just plain wrong? The way to control the risk of lagging the returns of the portfolio plan is to regulate the extent of the departure from the plan.

Establishing Ranges

To delineate the area in which active investing may operate, the portfolio plan establishes upper and lower limits around the normal percentage for each asset group. As shown in Table 8-2, the normal percentages define the mix of index mutual funds for a tax-deferred portfolio designed to match the intermediate marker portfolio. The ranges indicate the maximum deviation from normal. You would maintain the asset mix approximately in line with normal if you had no reason to expect active investing to achieve a more favorable outcome. As your view of the financial markets changes, the ranges serve two purposes:

- They provide latitude for you to translate your convictions into action (through revisions in weightings).

- They limit the risk if, this time, the conviction turns out to be mistaken.

The ranges allow for a shift of up to 10% of the portfolio from one major asset group to another, with additional changes within the

Table 8-2: Active adjustments in asset mix for the intermediate marker portfolio.

Vanguard Mutual Fund	Normal	Range	Normal	Range
500 Portfolio	28%	±5%		
Extended Market	12	±5		
Total International	10	±5		
Total Stocks			50%	±10%
Total Bond Market			35	±10
Prime Money Market			15	±10
Total			100%	

various asset groups. You may add or subtract 5 percentage points to any one of the three stock groups as long as the total adjustment for stocks does not exceed 10 percentage points. Similarly, you may make adjustments of up to 10 percentage points to either of the other two major asset groups—bonds or cash—but only to one of them at a time.

Table 8-3 expands on Table 8-2 to allow for variations in portfolio objectives and tax status. It addresses the conservative and aggressive portfolios, as well as the intermediate portfolio presented in the previous table. To provide for both taxable and tax-exempt portfolios, the lower half of the table lists tax-exempt versions of the bond and money market funds. As explained in Chapter 7, you would choose the tax-exempt alternative when yield spreads and marginal personal tax rates indicate a sufficient advantage.

Although the ranges in which active investing operates are much the same for the three portfolios, the aggressive portfolio differs in three areas. It widens the ranges for both the 500 Portfolio and the Extended Market Portfolio to ±10 percentage points. At the same time, it limits downside flexibility for the money market funds to 5 points, since adjustment by this amount would reduce the holding to zero.

Making Other Portfolio Adjustments

The asset ranges identified in Table 8-3 also accommodate investments in other than the benchmark funds that make up the index fund portfolio plan. You may identify other funds—say, the ABC Fund—as particularly attractive. Your decision to acquire the ABC Fund may be guided by the recommendation of a trusted advisor or result from your own study or special knowledge of the area in which the fund invests. Your purpose may be to expand participation through an index fund in an area of investment that seems particularly promising, such as very small-capitalization domestic stocks or foreign stocks in emerging markets. Alternatively, you may aim to benefit from the special skill or the particular investment approach offered by an actively managed fund. Our concern here, however, is not your reason for the decision but, once the decision is made, how to coordinate active investing with indexing.

Table 8-3: Adjustments in asset mix for portfolios with varying objectives and tax status.

Vanguard Mutual Fd.	Aggressive		Intermediate		Conservative	
	Normal	Range	Normal	Range	Normal	Range
500 Portfolio	42%	±10%	28%	±5%	14%	±5%
Extended Market	18	±10	12	±5	6	±5
Total International	15	±5	10	±5	5	±5
Total Stocks	75%	±10%	50%	±10%	25%	±10%
Total Bond Market or Mun. Bd.–Inter.	20	±10	35	±10	50	±10
Prime Mon. Mkt. or Mun. Bd.–Mon. Mkt.	5	+10,–5	15	±10	25	+10
Total Portfolio	100%		100%		100%	

Where the ABC Fund fits in the portfolio depends on its normal composition. In Table 8-4, the column headed "ABC Fund" defines the fund characteristics that match it with the benchmark index funds in the next column. Consider the following examples:

- ABC is an actively managed, large-cap equity fund, with median cap in excess of $5 billion. You buy these shares because you expect them to achieve better returns than the large-cap index fund that targets the S&P 500. Otherwise, you would be better off holding the large-cap index fund.

- A *very-small*-cap equity index fund, with median cap of less than $5 billion, is paired with the benchmark m/s-cap equity index fund. The stocks in this small-cap fund constitute a selected portion of the broader population represented by the Extended Market Portfolio.

- In a similar way, the actively managed foreign fund takes the place of a portion of the Total International Portfolio, which aims to represent almost all the publicly traded markets outside the United States.

- For the fixed income markets, the actively managed funds are matched with the benchmark fund depending on two criteria: (1) whether the holdings are taxable or tax-exempt, and (2) whether the maturities are greater or less than two years.

Table 8-4: How ABC shares fit into the index fund portfolio plan.

ABC Fund	*Benchmark Index Fund*
Stocks	
Domestic	
Median-cap more than $5 billion	500 Portfolio
Median-cap less than $5 billion	Extended Market
Foreign	Total International
Fixed Income	
Maturity more than 2 years	
Taxable	Total Bond Market
Tax exempt	Municipal Bond–Intermediate
Maturity less than 2 years	
Taxable	Prime Money Market
Tax exempt	Municipal Bond–Money Market

Adding Actively Managed Funds

Let's take a look at a specific example of active investing within the index fund portfolio plan. Suppose, again, that the ABC shares represent an actively managed large-cap equity fund. Without changing holdings of any other funds, you may substitute ABC shares for benchmark large-cap shares equal to 5% of the portfolio. If you decide to revise asset mix—perhaps reducing money market holdings by 5 percentage points—the ABC shares may represent as much as 10% of the portfolio. Table 8-5 illustrates three alternative revisions in the intermediate portfolio shown in Table 8-2 to make room for the addition of the ABC Fund.

While revision of the three index fund portfolios may each incorporate several different versions of the ABC Fund—actively managed or index—the ranges control risk. Suppose you identify three funds, each of which gives promise of performance superior to that of the corresponding benchmark index fund:

- AM-SC identifies an actively managed small-cap fund.

- AM-LT Treas. focuses specifically on investments in the market for long Treasury bonds in the expectation that interest rates will decline.

- Index-EM permits the investor to overweight emerging market stocks in foreign markets.

Table 8-6 shows how these funds, when you consider them particularly attractive, might fit into each of the three standard index fund portfolios. Again, the boldface type identifies revisions in the

Table 8-5: Adding the actively managed large-cap ABC Fund to the intermediate portfolio.

Vanguard Mutual Fund	Normal	Range	Alt. #1	Alt. #2	Alt. #3
500 Portfolio	28%	±5%	**23%**	**23%**	28%
ABC Fund		+10	**5**	**10**	**5**
Extended Market	12	±5	12	12	12
Total International	10	±5	10	10	10
Total Stocks	50%	±10	50%	**55%**	**55%**
Total Bond Market	35	±10	35	35	**30**
Prime Money Market	15	±10	15	**10**	15
Total	100%		100%	100%	100%

Table 8-6: How active investing adds three mutual funds to the portfolio plan.

Mutual Fund	Aggressive			Intermediate			Conservative		
	Normal	Range	Alternative	Normal	Range	Alternative	Normal	Range	Alternative
500 Portfolio	42%	±10%	42%	28%	±5%	28%	14%	±5%	14%
Extended Market	18	±10	18	12	±5	12	6	±5	6
AM-SC		+10	**10**		+10	**10**		+10	**5**
Total International	15	±5	10	10	±5	10	5	±5	5
Index-EM		+10	**5**		+10	**10**		+10	**5**
Total Stocks	75%	±10%	85%	50%	±10%	60%	25%	±10%	35%
Total Bond *or* Mun. Bd.–Inter.	20	±10	10	35	±10	25	50	±10	40
AM-LT		+10	**5**		+10	**10**		+10	**10**
Prime Mon. Mkt. *or* Mun. Bd.–Mon. Mkt.	5	+10,–5	0	15	±10	5	25	±10	15
Total Portfolio.	100%		100%	100%		100%	100%		100%

portfolio structure to accommodate these funds. Note that despite the extensive revisions, each of the three portfolios continues to represent something close to the level of risk that you determined in initially selecting a marker portfolio. In the examples shown in Table 8-6, the three versions of the ABC Fund account for a total of 20% to 25% of portfolio assets, leaving 75% to 80% of the portfolio committed, as before, to the benchmark index funds.

Where the characteristics of the ABC Fund overlap those of two index funds, you may adjust the asset mix accordingly. If, for example, ABC is a domestic stock fund with median market capitalization of about $5 billion (shown in Table 8-4 as the boundary between large-cap and m/s-cap funds), it logically represents equal portions of the large-cap and m/s-cap stocks. You could reduce by 5 percentage points the holdings of each of the two index funds—large-cap and m/s-cap—in order to add a holding of the ABC Fund amounting to 10% of the portfolio. The same principle applies to fixed income funds. If ABC refers to a fixed income fund with average maturity of two years—in between that for bonds and money market funds—ABC could replace equal portions of the bond index fund and the money market fund.

Investing in Individual Securities

Even though you rely primarily on mutual funds for participation in the financial markets, you may also have reason to invest in individual securities. You may acquire the stock of the company for which you work through employee purchase plans, an employer matching program in a 401(k) retirement plan, or the exercise of stock options. You may inherit shares of particular stocks or receive them as gifts. You may invest in U.S. Treasury bonds or notes, attracted by the exemption from state income taxes as well as the credit standing of the issuer. You may identify certain issues as particularly attractive, reflecting either your own research or advice that you value.

The ranges shown in Table 8-3 accommodate individual securities as well as the many variations in mutual funds. Table 8-4, presented as a guide for the placement of mutual funds within the structure of the long-term portfolio plan, serves the same function for individual securities. For example, holders of such stocks as General Electric, Exxon, or AT&T (each with current market values well in excess of $5 billion) recognize them as large-cap stocks. Netscape Communications, Revco Drug Stores, and Red Lion Hotels provide examples of m/s-cap stocks. A five-year certificate of deposit (CD), as issued by banks, shares the same category as the total bond index, while a one-year CD is classified with money market funds.

Individual securities—particularly common stocks—demonstrate greater variability than diversified mutual funds representing the same market segment. The portfolio ranges, by limiting direct holdings of individual securities, control overall risk at an acceptable level. As illustrated by Table 8-3, direct holdings of both bonds and stocks may total as much as 30% of portfolio assets. This level of commitment, however, implies diversification among at least three different securities. Based on the ranges, no one security amounts to more than 10% of the portfolio, and no combination of two or more common stocks amounts to more than 20% of the portfolio. In addition to direct holdings of common stocks, an individual bond or note may account for an additional 10% of portfolio assets.

Direct holdings of several individual stocks in an index fund portfolio may provide special tax advantages. Equity mutual funds, reflecting the generally upward trend of the stock market, ordinarily realize net capital gains from year to year, with the tax liability passed along to the shareholder. For actively managed funds, the capital gains have significantly exceeded ordinary dividend income in many recent years. Index funds cannot entirely avoid capital gains but generally hold them to a much lower level. Although both actively managed funds and index funds are likely to experience capital losses in portions of their portfolios, they generally pass along to the shareholder a net balance of realized gains—and the corresponding tax liability.

In contrast, an investor holding several individual issues has the option of managing the liabilities for capital gains taxes. Suppose direct holdings of individual stocks within the permissible portfolio ranges number five issues. Issue A achieves a very large capital gain, issue B experiences a substantial capital loss, and market price changes for the other three stocks fall somewhere in between. Under these circumstances, you may have reason to sell the losing issue B, offsetting all or part of the capital gains tax liability generated by your mutual fund investments. Issue A—with the large unrealized capital gain—may serve as a charitable donation, permitting you to avoid the capital gains tax as well as receive the benefits of tax deduction for a charitable gift.

Implementing Change

Implementation of the various versions of active investing discussed in this chapter requires revision in two or more areas of your portfolio. To accomplish such changes, you logically look first to the alternative that entails the lowest penalties in terms of transaction costs and liability for capital gains taxes. Suppose your goal is to decrease the percentage of assets invested in large-cap equities in order to increase the weighting in m/s-cap equities. If you regularly add savings to your portfolio—perhaps on a monthly or quarterly basis—you may for a time direct the entire cash flow to m/s-cap stocks. To expedite the targeted change in asset mix, you may divert dividends—representing capital gains as well as ordinary income—from large-cap to m/s-cap stocks. Regular withdrawals from a portfolio, such as may be required from an IRA during retirement years, provide a similar opportunity in reverse. Without addition of new money to m/s-cap stocks, withdrawals from other portfolio holdings gradually achieve the planned percentage change in asset mix.

What if circumstances call for more rapid change in asset mix? Management of cash inflows and outflows or redirection of dividend or interest income may not provide sufficient funds quickly enough to take advantage of the present opportunity. Under such circumstances, examining your portfolio in light of the ranges identifies alternative candidates for offsetting sale. In choosing among alternatives, the primary consideration, as always, is the resulting asset mix. The secondary consideration, however, is the burden on returns of each alternative in terms of transaction costs or capital gains taxes. As underscored in Chapters 3 and 4, the accumulation of such charges over an extended period can substantially modify the results of the investment program.

Active Investing in an Index Fund Framework

In the face of the many compelling arguments that support indexing, the portfolio plan steadfastly includes a role for active investing. Understandably, investors are reluctant to pass up the potential rewards of superior forecasting skill if they believe that they have an opportunity to identify such skill in advance. The door therefore remains open for the enterprising investor to make use of active investing, but in a framework that carefully controls risk. Equally important, both active investing and indexing are likely to benefit from coordination of these two very different approaches to investing.

How Active Investing Benefits

The index fund framework raises the hurdle that active investing must overcome, encouraging greater selectivity. Designating the index fund as an alternative to active investing presents an unambiguous measure of investment performance. Active investing would have to achieve returns *superior* to that of the index fund that it replaces, even though indexing begins with a considerable advantage in terms of costs and taxes. As the index fund framework raises the performance standard, it also narrows the door that active investment must pass through. Because of the limits on active investing, the portfolio necessarily becomes more selective. If none of the current candidates seem clearly attractive, the index fund portfolio provides the luxury to wait until a better alternative becomes available.

Without the index fund framework, active investing will likely get by with more accommodating performance standards. If the performance of the active investment falls short relative to one standard, comparison with another may make it look better. Faced with a confusing array of statistics, many investors rely on vague impressions rather than the logical comparisons to gauge the performance of their active investments.

The index fund challenge places pressure on active investing, not only to narrow the index fund cost advantage, but also to follow a sharply different approach to diversification. Other things equal, the chances that active investing will add incrementally to performance improve to the extent that the index fund cost advantage narrows. Investors looking to add active investing to an index fund portfolio have good reason to avoid sales loads and other substantial marketing expenses. They also have a strong incentive to question expense ratios and turnover rates that appear excessive. Concentrating holdings in areas of particular attraction, meanwhile, offers opportunities to increase the payoff of forecasting skill without raising costs. Since the index funds that dominate the portfolio stress maximum diversification, active investing, occupying a limited area of the portfolio, is able to move in the opposite direction. It may focus on a limited number of individual issues or a mutual fund that concentrates on a narrowly defined area, such as technology stocks, very-small-cap stocks, or high-yield bonds. Overall, the combined portfolio remains highly diversified, while the actively managed portion of the portfolio leverages its skill with the goal of magnifying its contribution to incremental returns.

How Indexing Benefits

Indexing, in turn, can better fulfill its role when you dedicate an area of the portfolio to active investing. The key is to separate indexing and active investing so that each can operate independently. Without this separation, indexing, sooner or later, becomes highly vulnerable to the promise of huge rewards that active investing holds forth (but does not necessarily deliver). Pressure to abandon indexing operates over a wide range of market conditions. In a bull market, indexing limits participation in areas that achieve especially high returns. In a bear market, active investing may focus on avoiding large losses, while indexing commits the portfolio to continuing investment in areas where returns are dropping at a distressing rate.

The coexistence of indexing with active investing permits indexing to stay on track while opening the door—in a carefully controlled way—to active investing. If active investing succeeds, it will add incrementally to the returns of the index fund portfolio plan. Because of the discipline imposed by the ranges, however, about 70% or more of the index fund plan will continue to be implemented. If the active investing falls short of its goals, indexing limits the risk.

Keeping an Open Mind

Coordination of active investing with indexing contributes to perspective in both areas. Proponents of these two competing approaches have often viewed each other as adversaries, representing completely incompatible points of view. Active investing has often denounced indexing as mindless acceptance of the mediocre. Proponents of indexing, in turn, have sometimes dismissed *all* active investing as not only futile but as clearly counterproductive, reflecting unnecessary costs and risks. Yet both approaches coexist in day-to-day-investing. When active investors deny that indexing has merit, they overlook tremendous opportunities to reduce costs, defer taxes, and control risk. Total rejection of active investing, on the other hand, means that the active decision process does not receive systematic attention. The result is a haphazard version of active investing, with little chance of bringing the benefits of superior forecasting skill.

Keeping an open mind, in contrast, permits you to coordinate the contributions of both active investing and indexing to your overall investment effort. Unambiguous definition of the roles of indexing and active investing clears the way to let each approach serve its specialized function. You are able to call on active investing when the opportunity to benefit from superior forecasting appears sufficient to overcome the index fund advantage in terms of costs and taxes. Indexing, providing the framework for the investment portfolio, maintains the balance of risk and expected return at least close to the level previously determined in the light of your particular circumstances.

PART 4

RESPONDING TO CHANGE

chapter nine

GAUGING PERFORMANCE

Maintaining Perspective

Performance measurement provides the information you need to maintain a realistic perspective concerning the outcome of your investment strategy. In the absence of such information, wishful thinking is almost certain to take over. As investors, we want to believe that we have made smart investment decisions. A sound method of performance measurement, taking into account the relevant details, identifies what really happened.

Despite the critical role of performance measurement, pursuit of perfect accuracy can become counterproductive. When it is not readily accomplished, the misplaced emphasis may divert attention from helpful approximations more easily achievable. Where such factors as cash flows and liability for personal income taxes complicate the measurement process, you will likely find useful the shortcut adjustments illustrated in this chapter. Although falling short of perfect accuracy, they enable you to keep track of the approximate outcome of strategy without an unacceptable burden of calculation.

Dangers of Wishful Thinking

Even a little wishful thinking may turn out, over an extended period of managing investments, to be very costly. Psychologists have shown how wishful thinking may distort consumers' assessments of their purchases or employees' attitudes toward their jobs. A recent study dramatically illustrates the power of wishful thinking as it applies to investors in mutual funds. Published in *The Journal of Financial Research,* the article concludes "that investor recollections of past performance are consistently biased above actual past performance."[1] Data on two samples of investors covered in the article indicated that overestimation of performance averaged more than 3 percentage points for one group and over 6 percentage points for the other.

Although the overestimation of mutual fund performance in this study refers to only a single year, investing extends over a span of many years. A modest one-year difference in return projected into the longer term compounds to a very large difference in market value. Figure 9-1 provides three examples of the growth of an initial investment of $10,000 in a tax-exempt account over a 20-year time horizon:

- The first of the three bars indicates the market value of an actively managed equity mutual fund that grows at a compound annual rate (with dividends reinvested) of 8%.

- The second bar represents the more rapid increase in market value that would occur if, as the investor erroneously believes, the total return were 3 percentage points higher, or 11%.

- The third bar identifies the market value of an index fund alternative. For purposes of this example, let's assume that the aggregate return of the index fund holdings before all costs and expenses is exactly the same as for the actively managed funds. Because of the index fund cost advantage, however, the growth of its market value compounds at a 10% annual rate.

Longer-term comparisons underscore the need for realistic measurement of investment returns. Over a one-year period, the investor's perception of the return for the actively managed fund implies a gain of $100 over that for the index fund. The actual return, in contrast, lags that of the index fund by $200. By the end of five years, the compounding has significantly widened the shortfall. Over 20 years—as represented by the bar graph—the differences

---

[1]William N. Goetzmann and Nadav Peles, "Cognitive Dissonance and Mutual Fund Investors," *The Journal of Financial Research,* Vol. XX, No. 2, Summer 1997, p. 146.

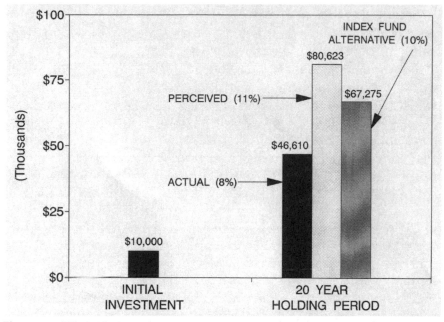

Figure 9-1: PENALTY OF WISHFUL THINKING. How biased perception of performance can divert attention from a more profitable alternative (percentages refer to annual rate of return).

become much more pronounced. An initial investment of $10,000 in the index fund, reflecting a compound annual rate of return of 10%, has grown to more than $67,000. If the actively managed fund were actually to achieve an annual rate of return of 11%—reflecting an average annual overestimation of 3 percentage points—the market value would have risen to almost $81,000. With the return of only 8% annually, however, the market value of the actively managed fund at the end of 20 years amounts to less than $47,000.

By investing in an index fund, the investor could expect to achieve a return that comes close to matching that of the stock market. In this example, the investor settles for a lower return (by 2 percentage points) under the mistaken impression that the actively managed fund provides a higher return. The 20-year cost of wishful thinking—the $20,000 difference between $67,000 and $47,000—amounts to double the initial investment. For other investors, the cost may be greater or less—and on occasion the difference will favor the actively managed fund. But, in the absence of unbiased performance measurement, how will you ever know?

How Fluctuating Returns Add to Confusion

An uneven pattern of fluctuating investment returns can add to the confusion. Even with identification of the appropriate benchmark, changing relationships between mutual fund and benchmark returns from year to year leave plenty of room for mistaken impressions. Table 9-1, focusing on the five years 1992–96, presents an example. In the absence of careful performance comparisons, the shareholder may be well pleased with the performance of the mutual fund. The average compound rate of return of 13.4% means that the market value of the mutual fund held in a tax-exempt account has almost doubled in just five years. The returns for the mutual fund, moreover, have exceeded those of the S&P 500 in three of the past five years. The average of the five individual yearly returns, moreover, is higher for the mutual fund than for the benchmark. Yet the mutual fund, as shown by comparison of the average annual compound rates of return over the five years, registered a significant shortfall in return. On a $10,000 initial investment, the mutual fund grew to $18,714. If the fund return had equaled that of the benchmark, the market value would have amounted to $20,282—a difference of $1568.

Bridging the Gap between Hope and Reality

How closely you monitor investment performance is up to you.

Table 9-1: Wide swings in investment return may produce misleading impressions.

Year	Mutual Fund	S&P 500	Difference
1996	43.3%	23.0%	20.3%
1995	51.9	37.4	14.5
1994	(19.5)	1.3	(20.8)
1993	25.5	10.0	15.5
1992	(14.9)	7.7	(22.6)
Average	17.3%	15.9%	1.4%
Compound Annual Rate	13.4%	15.2%	(1.8)%
Initial Investment	$10,000	$10,000	—
Ending Market Value	18,714	20,282	($1,568)

- You may continue the practice that so many investors routinely follow: accepting vague impressions of how their investments are performing. Such impressions, often shaped by wishful thinking and almost always wide of the mark, are likely sooner or later to prove costly.

- If you have the time and the patience, you could establish a completely accurate method of performance measurement, comparable to that of the large financial institutions. Such a goal is feasible under certain circumstances, but few individual investors will undertake the commitment required to keep the program up to date.

- You could look for a compromise between the two extremes. The critical ingredient is not complete accuracy but, rather, control of bias. Efforts to develop highly detailed measures of performance are worse than useless if bias drives the conclusions. In contrast, very simple methods to keep track of performance, if wisely chosen, may well accomplish their purpose.

This chapter shows you how to implement the third alternative. It is a workable compromise that provides you with feedback on the success of your investment portfolio without requiring an unacceptable input of time and effort. First, you'll see how to apply the measurement process to the assessment of total portfolio performance. A simple comparison of two numbers, one for the benchmark portfolio and the other for the investor's portfolio, gauges overall results. The next section considers the sources of success or failure. It examines returns within each broad asset category, as well as those attributable to variations in asset mix. A final section addresses liability for personal income taxes. Although tax advice is beyond the scope of this book, this chapter highlights two issues that you need to take into account in considering total investment return in a taxable account.

Measuring Total Portfolio Performance

The ultimate goal of performance measurement is the comparison of total return for your portfolio with that of the appropriate benchmark portfolio. In the absence of personal income taxes, total investment return consists of two parts. Income, whether dividends from stocks or interest payments from debt instruments, ordinarily provides the more stable component. Change in capital value, the other component, is much less predictable from one period to the next.

The total investment return for the *benchmark portfolio* depends on the mix of index funds selected to meet your particular objectives. Since the benchmark portfolio represents the index funds that you would hold in the absence of superior forecasting skill, it serves as your neutral position.

Investor Strategy Contribution

The *investor portfolio,* although guided by the broad structure of the benchmark portfolio, may differ significantly from benchmark normal. Departures from the benchmark portfolio reflect investor strategy that aims to achieve better returns than the benchmark portfolio. As pointed out in Chapter 8, investor strategy may take the form of direct action or, in the face of portfolio change for other reasons, lack of corrective action to return the portfolio to benchmark normal.

Table 9-2 illustrates how subtracting the benchmark rate of return from the investor rate of return provides a single, unambiguous measure of investment performance. We initially ignore personal income taxes, focusing on pretax performance, not only for tax-deferred accounts, but also for taxable portfolios. The difference in pretax returns for the two portfolios is the contribution of investor strategy, either positive or negative, to total portfolio return. For this example, the return for the investor portfolio (14.5%) exceeded that of the benchmark portfolio (11.3%) by 3.2 percentage points.

Table 9-2: Contribution of investor strategy reflects the difference in total rates of return for two competing portfolios.

	Rate of Return
Investor Portfolio	14.5%
Less Benchmark Portfolio	11.3
Contribution of Investor Strategy	+3.2%

Identifying the Benchmark Return

The rate of return for the benchmark portfolio reflects the weighted average of the funds that are included in it. The example shown in Table 9-3 incorporates fund returns for 1996 for the intermediate benchmark portfolio. The necessary information is readily available in the financial press (*Wall Street Journal, Barrons,* and the financial sections of many daily newspapers), as well as from such services as Morningstar. The first column, patterned after the combination of Vanguard funds presented in Chapter 7, shows the weighting of each component of the intermediate portfolio plan. The next column lists the total investment return for each of these funds. The third column, reflecting the return for each fund multiplied by its weighting, indicates the contribution of each fund to the total portfolio return. The sum of the percentages listed in column 3 determines the benchmark rate of return for 1996.

Calculating Investor Return

In the absence of net cash flow either in or out of the portfolio, the rate of return for the investor portfolio is even simpler to calculate than the rate for the benchmark portfolio. As shown in Table 9-4, the total investment return (in dollars) equals the difference between the ending market value and the beginning market value. This difference, divided by the beginning market value, indicates the rate of return for the investor portfolio.

Table 9-3: Total rate of return for intermediate benchmark portfolio for 1996.

Index Mutual Fund	Weighting	Fund Return	Portfolio Return
500 Portfolio	28%	22.9%	6.4%
Extended Market	12	17.6	2.1
Total International	10	7.5*	0.8
Total Bond Market	35	3.6	1.2
Prime Money Market	15	5.3**	0.8
Total	100%		11.3%

Source: The Vanguard Group of Investment Companies, Valley Forge, PA.

*Includes 4 months (January–April) when the fund operated as a private account with the same objectives, policies, and limitations.

**12 months ended November.

Table 9-4: Rate of return for investor portfolio for 1996 (absent net cash flow).

	$ (thousands)
Ending Market Value	$114.5
Less Beginning Market Value	100.0
Total Return	$ 14.5
Rate of Return (Total Return/Beginning Market Value)	**14.5%**

Adjusting for Cash Flows

While the concept of total investment return is simple, cash flows greatly complicate the calculation. Most portfolios, individual and institutional alike, experience over the year flows of cash in or out—or perhaps a combination of both. Large institutional investors, managing hundreds of millions or even many billions of dollars, routinely call on outside consultants to provide performance measurement that precisely adjusts for cash flows. Since these calculations require more time and effort than most investors want to dedicate to performance measurement, we offer a simpler alternative. It works well where the net cash flow during the measuring period amounts to less than 10% of the value of the portfolio. Even where net cash flow is significantly larger, it provides estimates that can help to keep performance in perspective.

Cash flows may arise for a number of reasons. Table 9-5 lists transactions that may either add to or subtract from the portfolio over the year. This example allows for an overall portfolio divided between a tax-deferred account represented by a 401(k) plan and a taxable account. In addition to the cash flows in and out of the taxable account, the table lists monthly additions to the 401(k) plan.

Tabulation of cash flows requires an accurate method of keeping track, since omissions, depending on their dollar value, may significantly distort the adjustment. One method establishes a separate checking account to handle routine household expenses on a day-to-day basis. Balances in the checking account are included in the investment portfolio only when they are transferred to the money market fund. Accordingly, additions to and withdrawals from the investment portfolio (including a money market fund) represent only larger transactions. An alternative method makes

Table 9-5: Example of cash flows in and out of the investor portfolio.

Date	Purpose	Withdrawals	Additions
January 31	Savings		$ 1,500
	401(k) plan		750
February 28	Savings		1,300
	401(k) plan		750
March 31	Savings		1,200
	401(k) plan		750
April 6	Dental bills	$ 600	
April 19	Birthday present		1,000
April 30	Savings		2,200
	401(k) plan		750
May 15	Income tax refund		1,200
May 31	Savings		1,600
	401(k) plan		750
June 30	Savings		2,100
	401(k) plan		750
July 31	Savings		1,600
	401(k) plan		750
August 20	College tuition	10,000	
August 31	Savings		1,400
	401(k) plan		750
September 15	House painting	5,000	
September 30	Savings		1,200
	401(k) plan		750
October 31	Savings		1,200
	401(k) plan		750
November 12	Vacation expenses	5,200	
November 30	Savings		1,000
	401(k) plan		750
December 4	Holiday presents	1,700	
December 31	Year-end bonus		5,000
	401(k) plan		750
Total		$22,500	$32,500

use of check-writing software, such as Intuit's *Quicken* or Microsoft's *Money*. These programs routinely provide a record with the necessary information. For this example, the net additions amount to $10,000 ($32,500 less $22,500).

Revision of the data for the investor portfolio underscores the importance of adjusting for even small cash flows. The initial version of 1996 performance, as shown in Table 9-4 and reproduced in the "Not Adjusted" columns of Table 9-6, makes no allowance for cash flows in or out of the portfolio during the year. As a result, the

Table 9-6: Revision in performance calculation to allow for net cash flow into the investor portfolio.

	Not Adjusted		Adjusted	
	(000)	*(000)*	*(000)*	*(000)*
Ending Market Value	$114.5		$114.5	
Less 1/2 Net Cash Flow	—		5.0	
Adjusted Ending Market Value		$114.5		$109.5
Beginning Market Value	$100.0		$100.0	
Plus 1/2 Net Cash Flow	—		5.0	
Adjusted Beginning Market Value		100.0		105.0
Total Return		$ 14.5		$ 4.5
Rate of Return		**14.5%**		**4.3%**
(Total Return/Adj. Beginning Mkt. Value)				

investor strategy contributed a positive 3.2 percentage points to portfolio performance. Suppose, however, that the net cash flow into the portfolio over the year had amounted to $10,000, as indicated in Table 9-5. To measure more accurately investor performance under these circumstances, columns 3 and 4 show a short-cut method of adjusting for net cash flow. Subtract one-half of the net cash flow from the ending market value and add one-half to the beginning market value. As a result, the total investment return amounts to $4500. When this figure is divided by the adjusted beginning market value of $105,000, the investor rate of return amounts to 4.3%. The adjustment restates performance (investor portfolio return less benchmark return of 11.3%) from distinctly *positive* 3.2% to significantly *negative* 7.0%.

How accurate is this simple adjustment for net cash flow? It will be highly accurate if, for example, cash flows evenly into the portfolio over the year and, each time, is invested in proportion to the market value of each holding. Since cash flows seldom conform to such regular patterns, the adjustment is less than perfect. Where the net cash flows are moderate in proportion to the market value of the portfolio, however, the resulting distortion is limited. In any event, adjusting for cash flow as outlined here will provide a much smaller error than failure to adjust at all. For representative examples, adjustment for net cash flow reduces the unadjusted error by at least 90%—and usually much more. For a 10% net cash flow over the year, adjustment error is likely to amount to considerably less than 1 percentage point of overall portfolio return. It is possible for such adjustment error to exceed 1 percentage point—but only with the convergence of unlikely circumstances. Such large and unlikely errors would reflect wild swings in the financial markets together with particularly perverse timing of the cash flows. For net cash flow amounting to 20% of beginning market value, the error, other things equal, would approximately double.

Identifying Sources of Positive and Negative Returns

In addition to assessing the investment returns of the overall portfolio, performance measurement also examines the contribution of the various portfolio strategies. As described in Chapter 8, your portfolio may include actively managed mutual funds, other-than-benchmark index funds, or holdings of individual stocks or bonds. A review of the performance of the individual holdings addresses two questions:

- Has the overweighting or underweighting of major asset groups, such as large-cap stocks, m/s-cap stocks, or cash equivalents, helped or hindered performance?

- How successful has been the selection of particular funds or issues to implement the overweighting or underweighting within the various asset groups?

To illustrate our response to these two questions, let's return to the investor portfolio considered earlier in this chapter. As shown in Table 9-2, the investor portfolio return exceeded that of the designated benchmark portfolio by 3.2 percentage points. The total return of the investor portfolio, as calculated in Table 9-4, reflected the absence of cash flows into or out of the portfolio during the measuring period. The next two sections identify the sources of the positive performance for this sample portfolio.

Evaluating Asset Allocation Strategy

To measure the outcome of asset allocation strategy, you first identify overweighting or underweighting of major asset groups. To illustrate, Table 9-7 lists the mutual funds that make up the investor portfolio and its designated benchmark. In this example, as before, the intermediate index fund portfolio serves as benchmark. Italics designate funds that appear only in the investor portfolio, while the prefix "AM" identifies the fund as actively managed. The first pair of columns displays the weighting of each fund in the benchmark portfolio at the beginning of 1996 together with the weighting of each major asset category. The second pair of columns shows the comparable data for the investor portfolio. The far right-hand column highlights the areas where the major asset groups are overweighted (+) or underweighted (−).

The next step is to identify the success of strategy in the three areas of overweighting or underweighting. To this end, Table 9-8 compares the major asset groups that are overweighted with those

Table 9-7: How the investor portfolio differs from the benchmark portfolio.

	Benchmark Portfolio		Investor Portfolio		Overweighting/ Underweighting
Stock Funds					
500 Portfolio	28%		28%		
Large-Cap Stocks		28%		28%	
Extended Market	12%		12%		
AM Small-Cap			5		
M/S-Cap Stocks		12		17	+5%
Total International	10%		10%		
Index-Emerg. Mkt.			5		
Foreign Stocks		10		15	+5
Bond Funds					
Total Bond Market	35%		25%		
AM-Long-Treas.			10		
Bonds		35		35	
Money Market					
Prime Money Market	15%		5%		
Cash Equivalents		15		5	−10
Total		100%		100%	

Table 9-8: Rate of return attributable to asset allocation strategy.

Major Asset Group	Benchmark Return	Return Advantage	Over/Under Weighting	Contribution to Portfolio Return
M/S-Cap Stocks	17.6%	12.3%	+5%	0.6%
Cash Equivalents	5.3			
Foreign Stocks	7.5%	2.2	+5	0.1
Cash Equivalents	5.3			
Total				**0.7%**

that are underweighted. At far left, we pair the two overweightings (m/s-cap stocks and foreign stocks) with the offsetting under-weightings (in both examples, cash equivalents).

- Column 1 indicates the return for each of these major groups in the benchmark portfolio. For this purpose, it draws on 1996 returns for the Vanguard funds serving as benchmarks for the designated groups.

- Column 2 reflects the difference in return for each pair of asset groups, one overweighted and the other underweighted. Over-weighting of the m/s-cap stocks produced a return advantage of 12.3%, while that for foreign stocks amounted to 2.2%.

- Column 3 specifies the percentage of the portfolio market value committed to the strategy. For m/s-cap stocks and foreign stocks, each category reflected overweighting of 5 percentage points.

- Column 4, showing the result of multiplying the return advantage in column 2 by the overweighting in column 3, identifies the contribution of asset allocation strategy to total portfolio return. As aggregated in the bottom line of column 4, asset allocation strategy added 0.7% to total portfolio return in 1995.

Selecting Vehicles to Implement Asset Allocation

The second issue relating to investment strategy concerns the selection of the *specific* investment vehicles to implement the asset allocation strategy. If, in the foregoing example, the investor had used the benchmark index funds to implement asset allocation

strategy, the net contribution to portfolio return would equal the
0.7 percentage point shown in Table 9-8. Often, however, the portfolio holds actively managed funds, index funds other than benchmark funds, or individual stocks or bonds. How much of the contribution to total portfolio return results from the selection of
particular funds (or issues) rather than overweighting or underweighting of major asset groups?

By way of responding to this question, Table 9-9 again addresses
the investor portfolio shown in Table 9-7. Instead of examining
overweightings and underweightings of major asset groups, Table
9-9 directs attention to selection of specific vehicles within their respective asset categories:

- The groupings at the far left pair the strategic holding (identified
  by italics) with the asset group that it represents. Column 1 lists
  the total investment return for each.

- Column 2 lists the difference in returns between the strategic
  holding and the asset group.

- Column 3 identifies the weighting of the strategic holding in the
  overall portfolio.

- As shown in column 4, contribution of each strategic holding to
  overall portfolio return reflects multiplication of the figure in column 2 times that in column 3.

The bottom line of column 4 indicates that fund selection accounted for an additional 2.5 percentage points increase in total
portfolio return. Together, asset allocation strategy (0.7 percentage

Table 9-9: Rate of return due to fund selection within the major asset
groups.

Strategic Holding vs. Asset Group	Total Return	Return Advantage	Weighting (Strat. Hold.)	Contribution to Portfolio Return
M/S-Cap Stocks	17.6			
AM-Small-Cap	47.6%	30.0%	+5%	1.5%
Foreign Stocks	7.5			
Index-Emerg. Mkt.	15.8%	8.3	+5	0.4
Total Bond Market	3.6			
AM-High-Yield Corp.	9.5	5.9	+10	0.6
Total				**2.5%**

points) and the selection of funds to implement asset allocation strategy added 3.2 percentage points to total portfolio return.

Meeting the Consistency Test

As outlined here, performance measurement for the sources of portfolio performance relaxes one of the standards that applies to overall portfolio return. Assessment of overall portfolio performance includes adjustment for cash flows. Measurement of the components of portfolio performance dispenses with the cash-flow adjustment in order to limit the amount of routine accounting. Measurement of component returns, nevertheless, can still provide useful clues concerning strategy successes and failures. In any event, they must meet the test of consistency with the measure of overall portfolio performance adjusted for net cash flow. Substantial disparity between the estimates provided by the two approaches raises a red flag for the investor. Under such circumstances, the investor is in a position to reexamine the comparisons of component returns to identify significant distortion.

What to Do about Taxes

For a taxable account, personal income taxes add a further dimension to performance measurement. You cannot ignore taxes, since they directly reduce your investment return. At the same time, the allowance for taxes depends not only on your current situation, but also on your assumptions concerning a future that is not yet fully visible. Variables in the current situation include the tax rates applicable to your particular circumstances, the division between ordinary income and long-term capital gains, and the proportion of realized capital gains. Estimates of the tax consequences of unrealized capital gains—often an important component in rate of return—reflect assumptions concerning future tax rates as well as the anticipated holding period of the investment.

Even if we were in the business of offering tax advice—*which we are not*—we could not anticipate the many variables that relate to each investor's particular situation as circumstances change. Accordingly, detailed guidance concerning tax adjustments to performance measurement is beyond the scope of this book. Where you require such information on taxes, consult with a qualified tax advisor. As background for reviewing performance of taxable accounts, there are two items in particular that warrant attention.

Tax-Exempt Securities

Comparison of securities that are exempt from certain taxes with those that are not requires special care. Suppose, for example, a municipal bond fund exempt from federal taxes in a particular investor portfolio is compared with a fully taxable bond fund in the benchmark portfolio. Under such circumstances, performance comparisons logically must allow for the tax difference. In a similar way, comparison of Treasury securities that are exempt from state taxes with a fully taxable bond fund warrants review of the difference in tax burden.

Capital Gains Taxes

Overlooking the way capital gains taxes work can distort the impressions of portfolio performance. Differing policies concerning realization of capital gains can significantly modify the effective rate of return after allowance for both current and prospective taxes. Other things equal, such differences frequently add up to a significant sum over time. They are sensitive to the holding period as well as to assumptions relating to stock market returns, the cost characteristics of the fund, and the tax bracket of the shareholder. For the representative funds that we use as examples in Chapter 3, the annual index fund advantage attributable to deferral of capital gains taxes ranges from 0.1 percentage point for 5 years to 0.5 percentage point for 30 years.

chapter ten

MAKING IT HAPPEN

How to Get Started

The starting point for effective management of your investment program is planning and scheduling. To this end, Table 10-1 provides a six-item checklist. Accompanying each item is the number of the chapter (in parentheses) that discusses it and a target date for its completion.

The first four items on the checklist, to be repeated each year, serve as the basic agenda. Except for item 3, which concerns active investing, demands on investor time are limited. Since active investing is optional, you may shape the outlay of time to your individual circumstances.

The last two items address obstacles that can get in the way. At the inception of the investment program, they may appear very re-

Table 10-1: Agenda for portfolio management.

Item (Chapter)	Action
1. Choose your risk level (6)	At inception
2. Identify/implement your index fund portfolio (7)	Usually next 3–12 months
3. Open the door to active investing (8)	Opportunistically
4. Keep track of your performance (9)	Year end
5. Don't let capital gains taxes stop you (10)	When restructuring
6. Be ready for "This time is different!" (10)	When least expected

mote—if they come into view at all. Sooner or later, however, they threaten to disrupt even the most carefully planned investment program. This chapter explains how they weigh on your investment decisions and what to do about them.

Addressing the Key Decisions

The first four agenda items address the key decisions that make up the foundation of your investment program. No matter how large your assets grow, each of these items will again require attention in each subsequent year.

1. Choose Your Risk Level with Great Care

When starting (or reviewing) your investment program, make sure you select the marker portfolio that meets your particular needs. The choice is critical, because it determines how much risk you are willing to accept in exchange for opportunity to expand future returns.

To identify the portfolio that best reflects your risk tolerance, set aside an hour or two for introspection. Chapter 6 narrows the choice to three principal alternatives—conservative, intermediate, and aggressive versions of the marker portfolio. Selected data included in this chapter provide you with the perspective needed to make a decision. Looking to history for guidance rather than to a particular forecast in the marketplace, the choice depends on comparison of the likely range of outcomes over a five-year time horizon.

Rather than accept a broad generalization concerning your age group, you should develop your portfolio plan in light of your particular circumstances. If none of the three model marker portfolios exactly meets your requirements, Chapter 6 shows you how to make necessary adjustments.

Repetition of this first step at least once each year serves two purposes:

- It reminds you why you made the choice in the first place. After many months of a continuing bull market, the role of risk in determining the initial choice may gradually fade from memory. Similarly, a painful bear market may exaggerate future risk, diverting attention from the developing opportunities. In either event, the review helps keep you on the course established in light of the historical perspective.

- Review of the marker portfolio also provides occasion to respond, in a carefully considered, systematic way, to change in your circumstances. For example, your need for near-term liquidity may have increased or decreased, your income may be higher or lower, or your financial obligations may have risen or diminished. Although routine review of the marker portfolio is scheduled at one-year intervals, substantial change in your personal situation may call for an earlier review.

2. Identify/Implement Your Index Fund Portfolio

Build your index fund portfolio plan to provide broad representation in both equities and fixed income securities. Don't count on the exceptional returns that the S&P 500 has achieved over the last few years to continue. Excessive concentration on any single index fund unnecessarily increases risk.

Development of the index fund portfolio plan follows from choice of the marker portfolio. As explained in Chapter 7, you select from the list of available index funds those that represent the three asset groups included in the marker portfolio. The goal is to diversify as completely as practical within each asset group. Because of fund limitations on minimum initial purchase, larger portfolios are able to include more individual index funds than are smaller portfolios.

Selecting from the list of available index funds is much simpler than choosing actively managed funds. The basic index fund portfolio may represent as few as five indexes. At year end 1996, the number of competing index funds was very small—71—compared with slightly more than 6000 actively managed funds. (Both figures refer to mutual funds available to the individual investor with minimum initial purchase of $5000 or less.) The designation of the index, since it identifies the approximate composition of the index fund, facilitates fund comparisons.

After identification of the leading index fund candidates, be sure to compare the information provided by the respective fund prospectuses. Expenses and other deductions from returns are extremely important, but other considerations, such as services and access to other funds provided by the same fund family, may also influence your choices.

Matching the Portfolio Plan.   Chapter 7 distinguishes between the index fund portfolio plan and the implementation of the plan in the actual portfolio. The portfolio plan consists entirely of index funds (or, if necessary, near-index funds) and a money market fund. The actual portfolio may differ to a degree for several reasons:

1. Implementation of the plan may phase in over varying periods. You may decide to extend the interval over several months, even as much as a year, to smooth fluctuations in market price. By way of example, suppose you begin with $30,000 in cash with the aim of investing as indicated by the intermediate portfolio plan. Instead of immediately buying $15,000 in equity funds, as called for by the plan, you might commit $9000 immediately to three equity funds (such as large-cap, m/s-cap, and foreign) and then switch $1000 each month from the money market fund to the equity funds. By the end of six months, the actual portfolio approximates the structure of the portfolio plan. Where capital gains taxes present an obstacle to restructuring (see next section), this process may require a longer period.

2. Once the plan has been implemented, differing returns for the component funds may result in a drift in asset allocation from that specified by the portfolio plan. Unless otherwise indicated, we assume that the mutual fund routinely reinvests dividends. As explained in Chapters 6 and 7, rebalancing of the portfolio plan automatically returns asset allocation to the targeted percentages at the beginning of each year. Corresponding adjustment of the actual portfolio requires investor initiative. You may decide to use the cash flows into or out of the fund over a period of months to correct the differences. Alternatively, you may delay correction because the overweighting or underweighting conforms to a currently desired strategy.

3. You may decide to make room for active investing within the index fund framework. Each of the portfolio plans (see Chapter 8) provides for at least 25% of portfolio assets to be invested actively.

3. Keep the Door Open for Active Investing

The guidelines for active investing make room for departure from the index fund portfolio plan. You don't have to invest actively, but, sooner or later, you will probably have reason to want to do so. As the occasion arises, the guidelines provide both the opportunity to implement your active judgments and the discipline necessary to control risk.

Active investing depends on your assessment of the opportunity. In the absence of a perceived opportunity, you shape the portfolio to conform as closely as practical to your index fund portfolio plan. When the appropriate opportunity becomes available, the guidelines provide flexibility to invest actively within specified limits. A continuing constraint is performance measurement. As illustrated in Chapter 9, performance measurement compares the returns from the active investments with those of the index fund benchmark that they have replaced.

4. Keep Track of Your Performance

Self-deception can rapidly turn into an expensive luxury. Even if you can't achieve perfect accuracy, use unbiased *approximations to monitor your investment performance.*

Although scheduled for the end of the measuring period, performance measurement occupies a central role from the beginning of the investment program. The benchmark portfolio, against which returns of your portfolio are measured, identifies the return target that you strive to exceed. At the same time, it imposes a discipline on active investing that requires an accounting for gains and losses relative to the portfolio plan. In the absence of a clearly defined performance benchmark, investment results are almost certain to reflect the underlying confusion concerning what the portfolio aims to accomplish.

Obstacles that Get in the Way

The last two items on the agenda relate to obstacles that, sooner or later, seem certain to get in the way of your investment program. Both agenda items point to the need for advance planning.

5. Don't Let Capital Gains Taxes Stop You

*Switching to an index fund portfolio, even if it results in significant lia-
bility for capital gains taxes, may still improve chances for higher returns
over the longer term. You need to assess the opportunities in your portfolio in light of your personal situation. But, if in doubt, move toward the
same goal over an extended time horizon through redirection of dividend
reinvestment.*

Other things equal, the likelihood that the switch from an actively managed fund to an index fund will prove advantageous depends on the balance between two opposing considerations:

- Deferral of liability for capital gains taxes argues in favor of retention of the actively managed fund.

- The index fund cost advantage provides the opposing argument
  in favor of the switch to the index fund.

Appendix 10-1 provides examples that show a series of switches
from actively managed mutual funds to index mutual funds. The
examples weigh the potential liability for capital gains taxes on redemption of a current portfolio holding against the index fund cost
advantage. Under a wide range of assumptions, the index fund
cost advantage significantly outweighs the liability for the capital
gains tax. We present the examples to encourage you to make calculations based on your own assumptions or, where more appropriate, to consult with your tax advisor.

Redirection of Dividend Reinvestment.   There may be several
reasons that you will not want to incur significant capital gains liability associated with portfolio restructuring.

- Perhaps the most compelling reason relates to the length of the
  anticipated holding period. If the anticipated holding period is
  only a few years, the projected advantage of the switch is, at best,
  small. Where you expect exemption from capital gains taxes at the
  time the shares are redeemed within a relatively few years, retention offers the likelihood of a better outcome than switching.

- No matter how clear the advantages of the switch appear under
  current assumptions, the assumptions themselves may require
  revision. Suppose, for example, individual circumstances

change, resulting in a reduction in the applicable tax rate within two or three years. Alternatively, legislation changing the tax schedules may bring about a similar result.

- Third, the assumptions concerning stock market returns may differ markedly, particularly over the short to intermediate term, from the assumptions used in our examples. If the stock market drops sharply over the next year, the switch could almost certainly be accomplished after the decline with a corresponding reduction in capital gains liability. (A further rise in stock prices, other things equal, works in the opposite direction.)

Finding the Middle Ground. If you are uncertain about the best course of action, redirecting dividend distributions provides a hedge between the two extremes. Up to this point, our illustrations have assumed reinvestment of all fund distributions, both income and capital gain dividends, in the shares of the same fund. As an alternative to redemption of the shares of the actively managed fund, you may direct that distributions from the actively managed fund be used to purchase shares of the index fund. Assuming both funds are part of the same family, you may request automatic transfer of the dividend from one fund to another on the payment date.

Appendix 10-2 provides examples of how the switch gradually takes place. If the subsequent unfolding of events favors the switch, you have secured at least a part of the benefits. If events work in the opposite direction, you are able to demonstrate an advantage relative to the switch.

6. Be Prepared for "This Time Is Different!"

This unsettling challenge to your carefully planned program of long-term investment will likely catch up with you when you least expect it. Prepare in advance by adhering to clear separation between indexing and active investing. Active investing allows you to adjust to your perception of changing opportunities and risks in the financial markets, while the index fund framework maintains the broad outlines of your long-term portfolio plan.

The message that *"This time is different!"* is almost certain, sooner or later, to challenge your investment decision making. This short phrase brings into question the fundamental principles that underlie investment planning. Mounting concern that the broad sweep of history no longer provides useful guidance raises formidable questions. If you have just begun restructuring, should you proceed according to plan? For an established portfolio, should you stay the course?

How Changing Market Conditions Reshape the Message.   *"This time is different!"* is a message that resurfaces in every bear market. During extended periods of rising stock prices, investors increasingly view market declines as temporary annoyances on the way to assured long-term rewards. So, rather than ride out the storm when the decline materializes, why do they continue to dump stocks even after the broad stock indexes have fallen 25%, 30%, or even more? The answer seems clear. Confidence *in the long term* deteriorates as the bear market gathers force. Visibility concerning the economy and the financial markets becomes increasingly clouded. The market action itself seems to confirm the bleak outlook. From the vantage point of sharply declining financial markets, investors no longer are sure the "fluctuation" will soon be reversed. They worry that this time *really* is different!

By way of example, we refer to the comment in early 1997 of Mark Holowesko, who manages more than $25 billion for Templeton Funds. Long before Templeton Funds became part of Franklin Resources, founder John Templeton had pioneered, with much success, investment in Japanese stocks. With the Nikkei index of Japanese stocks 50% below its 1989 peak, *The Wall Street Journal* quoted Holowesko's current assessment of Japanese stocks:

> I think the market is still tremendously overvalued. If it fell 50%, it wouldn't be a surprise, …
>
> Everyone is worried about [high] stock valuations in the U. S., but even if you adjust for accounting, in Japan they still are even higher, … So if you are nervous about the U. S., you should be frantic about Japan."[1]

Our purpose here is not to focus on the current outlook for the Japanese market, but rather to illustrate the unsettling views of the longer term that are likely to surface even after a prolonged period

---

[1]E. S. Browning, "Tokyo Stocks Look Cheap? Perhaps Not," *Wall Street Journal*, January 10, 1997, p. C-1. Reprinted by permission of *The Wall Street Journal*, © 1997 Dow Jones & Company, Inc. All Rights Reserved Worldwide.

of stock prices far below previous highs. Bear markets coincide with declining confidence. The widespread consensus concerning the favorable long-term outlook for stock prices that seemed so assured in the bull market becomes increasingly elusive as the bear market progresses.

Investors in bull markets, uplifted by a continuing flow of favorable news, may also become persuaded that *"This time is different!"* Whatever has worried investors in the past gives way, it seems, to happier prospects. At one time or another, enlightened fiscal policy, increasingly sophisticated monetary policy, or perhaps the shift to free markets and less regulation have received the credit for "permanently" improving the long-term business outlook. A combination of factors, such as the end of the Cold War and increasing competition from abroad as international trade grows, have spelled to some observers the end to troublesome inflation in the United States. Surging technology, according to another view, gives promise of both continuing improvement in productivity and unprecedented prosperity. Bolstered by the accumulation of good news, investment objectives selected earlier begin to appear far too cautious. Understandably, pressure mounts to abandon constraints initially developed to control risk. Staying on course may be just as difficult in bull markets as in bear markets.

Each of the two familiar responses to the argument that *"This time is different!"* represents a potential pitfall. The flexible response emphasizes timely reaction to the perception of changing prospects. Too much flexibility, however, can mean that risks are out of control. A contrasting response stresses staying the course, no matter what. But too much rigidity may also prove counterproductive.

Too Much Flexibility. The history of investing has produced numerous examples of the risks associated with too much flexibility. As discussed in Chapter 5, even highly qualified investment professionals demonstrate how difficult it is to achieve investment returns better than can be explained by chance. As an investor busy with your own career, you have even more reason to contain flexibility within a disciplined framework. You have fewer resources to develop and maintain the flow of up-to-date information. You have less time to dedicate to investing. Probably your background and experience emphasizes pursuits other than investing.

Paradoxically, investment flexibility may actually increase the risk that it seeks to avoid. Table 10-2, for purposes of illustration, provides an extreme example. The two investment alternatives consist of a stock fund and a money market fund. Over two years, the stock fund achieved a cumulative 12% return as the negative return in the second year largely offset the highly positive return for the first year. The money market fund, with the same return in both years, reported a two-year total return of 10%. Investors aiming to maximize their returns would have attempted to hold in each year the fund with the higher return. Assuming the strategy were entirely successful, Flexible Investor X could show a two-year return of 47%. To illustrate the results of completely unsuccessful strategy, we also show a two-year return of *negative* 16% for Flexible Investor Y. The costs of flexibility, meanwhile, add to investment risk. Switching from one mutual fund to another may entail payment of sales loads or transaction fees. For a taxable account, redemption of shares may trigger immediate liability for capital gains taxes. The resulting burden on net return not only limits upside potential but also adds to risks on the downside.

Too Much Rigidity. At the other extreme, rigid adherence to a long-term portfolio plan can also lead to unwelcome consequences. As presented in Chapters 6 and 7, the long-term portfolio plan occupies a central role in the investment program. Its development determines how you will shape the investment portfolio to meet your objectives. It provides a discipline that organizes the operation of the investment program into the long-range future. There's a difference, however, between useful disci-

Table 10-2: How investor flexibility increases risk.

	1st Year	*2nd Year*	*Total*
Investment Alternatives			
Stock Mutual Fund	+40%	−20%	+12%
Money Market Fund	+5	+5	+10
Investors			
Flexible Investor X	+40	+5	+47
Flexible Investor Y	+5	−20	−16

pline and paralyzing rigidity. Mechanical adherence to a portfolio plan—allowing no room to adjust to changing conditions—is unlikely to serve you well through the series of surprises that are almost certain to materialize as the years pass. Without appropriate balance between flexibility and rigidity, your investment program is likely to get into trouble.

Good intentions to adhere—no matter what—to a rigid portfolio plan are almost certain to crumble, probably sooner rather than later. One reason may be that the portfolio plan does not realistically reflect your objectives. Because it is either too aggressive or too conservative, the strain becomes unacceptable. Why does such a problem arise? Perhaps the plan was not carefully set up in the beginning. Perhaps your circumstances have changed in a material way, requiring substantial revision of the plan. At some point, moreover, you are likely to worry that the historical framework no longer serves as a useful guide to prospects for the financial markets. How can your investment portfolio stay on course when the targeted destination no longer appears even dimly visible? There is always the possibility that this time may *really* be different, at least over the time horizon that matters to you.

A brief review of the history of investing underscores the dangers of mechanically projecting current conventional wisdom into the long-range future.

- Prior to the 1950s, the widely accepted definition of investment centered on high-grade bonds. To the extent that stocks had a small place in an *investment* portfolio (in contrast to a *speculative* account), they were expected to provide well protected yields substantially higher than those generated by the bond market.

- By the end of the 1950s and into the 1960s, prospects for continued creeping inflation provided reason to shift a major part of long-term investments from bonds to stocks.

- From the early 1970s into the 1980s, the widespread acceptance of the inevitability of intense inflationary pressures greatly curtailed the attraction of both bonds and stocks. Long-term investors increasingly looked to real estate, oil-producing properties, precious metals, and short-maturity fixed income investments as hedges against the vulnerability of stocks and bonds in an inflationary world.

■ From the vantage point of the mid 1990s, in contrast, common stocks have again become the glistening centerpiece of long-term financial planning. Confidence in the assured returns from the stock market has mounted so high that prominent national leaders propose individual investments in the stock market as at least a partial substitute for the current Social Security retirement program. While we, too, look forward to favorable long-term prospects for the stock market, we also keep in mind how often the widely accepted consensus has undergone major revision.

Active Investing within an Index Fund Framework.   The investment approach described in this book presents a practical compromise between flexibility and rigidity. The index fund portfolio plan provides the framework solidly rooted in past experience. To establish the portfolio plan, you use history as a guide to select the mix of index funds that best serves your objectives. Although annual rebalancing routinely returns the portfolio plan to the targeted mix of index funds at the beginning of each year, either of two opportunities for flexibility may result in modification of the portfolio plan.

■ First, you review the structure of the portfolio plan at least annually to allow for changes in your individual circumstances. This review, taking into account the risks of investing as well as the prospective rewards, repeats the steps presented in Chapters 6 and 7. Since the portfolio plan assumes the absence of superior forecasting skill, such revisions aim at complete independence from current advice concerning the outlook for the financial markets.

■ Second, you adjust your portfolio, within prescribed limits, to allow for active investing. The process is opportunistic. It depends on access to a view of the investment outlook that you consider superior to that already incorporated in market prices.

By including active investing within an index fund framework, the investment program is designed *to bend rather than break*. The index fund portfolio plan serves as the core of your investment program, constraining flexibility within acceptable limits. Flexibility, as spelled out in our guidelines, guards against rigidity in the index fund framework. You may recognize a widening gap between objectives and the portfolio plan, or you may increasingly worry that *"This time is different!"* In either event, the program leaves the way open for timely response. If you are either smart enough or lucky enough, you may be able to bend your portfolio so that active investing adds incrementally to your returns. If it does not, at least the risks are under control and the long-term plan remains substantially intact.

Appendix 10-1: Weighing Capital Gains Tax Liability against the Index Fund Cost Advantage

Restructuring an investment portfolio often opens the way to immediate liability for capital gains taxes. Table 10-3 provides an example. Suppose that the current market value of Fund AM, an *actively managed* mutual fund holding large-cap stocks, is $10,000. To switch Fund AM to Fund IDX, an S&P 500 *index* fund, would entail realization of long-term capital gains of $2500. Assuming an applicable tax rate of 20%, the switch would result in a capital gains tax of $500. After deduction of payment for the capital gains tax, the proceeds from redemption of Fund AM would provide $9500 to be invested in Fund IDX. Even if the index fund benefits from a cost advantage of 2 or 3 percentage points per year, does it make sense for the investor to switch to the index fund?

Table 10-4 summarizes issues that bear on the decision to switch actively managed fund AM to index fund IDX. For each issue, an assumption follows. These are the same assumptions that we show for large-cap equity funds in Chapter 3.

Prospective Rate of Return.   The assumption for the overall annual rate of total investment return of 10% is very close to that achieved historically by large-cap stocks (represented by the record of the S&P 500 since 1926). While returns have averaged substantially higher in recent years, they have also averaged considerably lower in other periods.

Table 10-3: Potential capital gains taxes from redemption of actively managed fund AM.

Proceeds from redemption of fund AM	$10,000
Less cost of fund AM	(7,500)
Long-term capital gains	$ 2,500
Times applicable tax rate	× 20%
Capital gains tax	$ 500
Proceeds from fund AM *less* capital gains taxes	**$ 9,500**

Table 10-4: Assumptions relating to switch of fund AM to fund IDX.

Issue	*Assumption*
Prospective annual rate of return for the index	10% (7% appreciation, 3% div. yield)
Fund AM: Forecasting advantage	Uncertain
Fund IDX: Cost advantage	Reflects large-cap costs, Table 3-7
Current and future capital gains tax rate	20%
Current and future ordinary income tax rate	31%
Anticipated holding period	As indicated

Forecasting Advantage of Fund AM. Because of uncertainty concerning superior forecasting skill, let's assume that the stocks held by Fund AM will provide about the same returns *before costs and taxes* as those included in the S&P 500. This assumption provides a middle-of-the-range response to a lack of conviction concerning fund prospects. If, in contrast, you expect that fund AM will provide returns better than the competing index fund, you have reason to retain it. The index fund portfolio plan makes room, within limits, for active investing.

Cost Advantage of Fund IDX. As explained in Chapters 3 and 4, the index fund cost advantage for any specific holding period reflects comparison of average data for actively managed funds with that for the designated index fund benchmark. The large-cap, actively managed fund that serves here as example assumes the average data for expenses, cost per transaction, and portfolio turnover as shown in Table 3-7. For any specific fund, variations in the cost advantage depend in large measure on how the operating data for the actively managed fund differ from the average for its category. The cost advantage may also reflect choice of an index fund benchmark that differs from that used in our examples (see Chapters 3 and 4).

Current and Future Tax Rates. The tax rates shown in the table currently apply to many investors in mutual funds, but, clearly, not to everyone. Under current tax law (as revised in 1997), rates for individual readers may differ, and, as a result of future legislation, tax schedules may change. Even without revision of the tax schedules, investors may experience a change in applicable rates because of change in individual circumstances.

Holding Period. Other things equal, the attractiveness of the switch depends on the anticipated holding period—for fund IDX, if the switch takes place, or for fund AM, if it does not. Accordingly, let's examine the implications of variations in the time horizon.

Balancing Opposing Considerations

Let's examine the possibilities, using the assumptions listed in Table 10-4. A series of examples shows what would happen if the assumptions were to prove accurate. The actual outcomes are almost certain to be more or less advantageous, reflecting differences between the middle-of-the-range assumptions concerning an uncertain future and the actual unfolding of events. Moreover, these assumptions will differ at least in degree from those that apply to your situation.

Despite such limitations, we offer the examples because they demonstrate an important principle: *Under a wide range of assumptions, the prospective future savings related to the index fund cost advantage clearly outweigh the potential liability for capital gains taxes incurred in redeeming an actively managed fund.* Whatever your own situation, you may find it useful to apply a similar analysis to determine whether an immediate switch to an index fund is likely to be in your interest.

Allowing for Capital Gains Taxes at the End of the Holding Period

Panel A of Figure 10-1 traces the relative advantage of a switch from fund AM to fund IDX as the holding period lengthens. The middle (solid) line plots the index fund advantage when redemption of fund AM entails realization of a 25% capital gain, as assumed in Table 10-3. For comparison, we display the same data with the capital gains assumption increased to 50% (lower line, dotted) and reduced to zero (upper line, dashes[2]). Each of three lines traces the advantage of switching as the holding period extends from 1 year to 30 years.

---

[2]The upper line of Panel A, Figure 10-1, is identical to the upper line of Panel A, Figure 3-4.

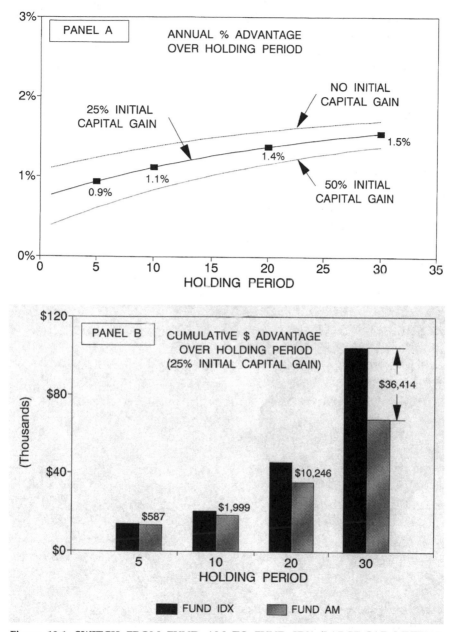

Figure 10-1: SWITCH FROM FUND AM TO FUND IDX (LARGE-CAP MUTUAL FUNDS). Advantage of switch with liability for capital gains taxes at end of holding period.

After allowing for potential capital gains liability, the incentive to switch increases with the expected holding period. The first point on each line graph (at the left of Panel A of Figure 10-1) represents a holding period of one year. (The one-year holding period means that, in the absence of a switch from fund AM to fund IDX, shares of fund AM would be redeemed at the end of the year. If the switch does take place, then the shares of fund IDX would be redeemed at the end of the year.) The net advantage of the switch with such a short holding period amounts to only a fraction of 1%—about 0.8% of ending market value. For a five-year holding period, the advantage amounts to 0.9% annually, or a cumulative five-year total of about 4% of the ending market value. For an expected holding period of ten years, the net advantage of the switch increases to 1.1% per year. For longer holding periods, it continues to increase (to 1.4% for 20 years and 1.5% for 30 years).

Panel B of Figure 10-1 compares the net contribution of the switch to investor wealth over four time horizons. If redeemed at the end of five years, the shares of fund AM, after allowance for capital gains taxes, would grow in value to $13,174. If the switch were made, the proceeds from redemption of the Fund IDX at the end of five years would amount to $13,761. The difference, although in favor of the switch to fund IDX, is only $587. For ten years, however, the net advantage of the switch increases to $1999. With a 20-year holding period, the market value of the investment in the fund IDX rises to $45,445. The comparable market value if the investor had retained fund AM until the end of 20 years would amount to $35,199. The net advantage of the switch therefore amounts to $10,246. With further lengthening of the holding period, the net advantage of the switch continues to expand rapidly. As projected by the set of bars at the far right, it exceeds $36,000 for a 30-year holding period.

No Capital Gains Taxes at End of Holding Period

Other things equal, the net advantage of switching changes substantially when you allow for exemption from capital gains taxes at the end of the holding period. Investments that pass into an estate upon the death of the investor qualify, as do certain investments donated to qualifying philanthropic organizations. As previously explained, panels A and B of Figure 10-1 trace the advantage of switching with allowance for capital gains taxes at the end of the

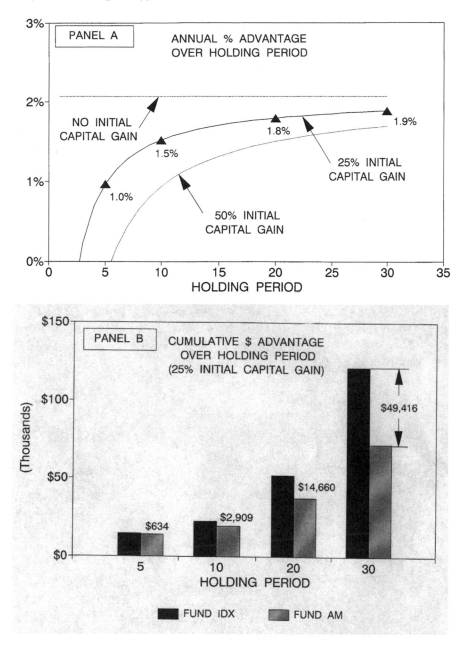

Figure 10-2: SWITCH FROM FUND AM TO FUND IDX (LARGE-CAP MUTUAL FUNDS, NO CAPITAL GAINS TAX AT END OF PERIOD). Advantage of switch with exemption from capital gains taxes at end of holding period.

holding period. The data plotted in panels A and B of Figure 10-2 differ only because of revision in the assumption concerning capital gains taxes to provide for exemption at the end of the holding period. Comparison of the corresponding panels of Figures 10-1 and 10-2 identifies how the change in assumption concerning capital gains taxes reshapes the advantage of switching.

To highlight these differences, Figure 10-3 brings together two line graphs, each of which assumes that redemption of fund AM at the beginning of the period would realize capital gains of 25%. The line with the square markers is the duplicate of the solid (middle) line shown in Panel A of Figure 10-1 (which allows for liability for capital gains taxes at the end of the holding period). The line with the triangular markers reproduces the path of the solid (middle) line shown on Panel A of Figure 10-2 (which anticipates tax exemption at the end of the holding period). Allowance for tax exemption at the end of the holding periods favors retention of fund AM for holding periods of up to about three years. Where the holding period extends beyond five years, however, the switch to fund IDX becomes even more advantageous than shown in Panel A of Figure 10-1. For a 20-year holding period, by way of example, the

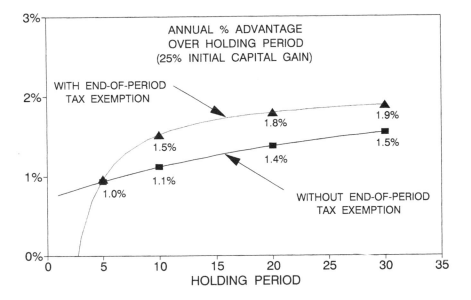

Figure 10-3: SWITCH FROM FUND AM TO FUND IDX (LARGE-CAP MUTUAL FUNDS). Advantages of switch (25% initial capital gain) with contrasting assumptions concerning capital gains taxes at end of holding period.

advantage of the switch increases to about 1.8% per year from about 1.4% in the absence of the tax exemption.

Restructuring the Portfolio with M/S-Cap Stocks

This final section of Appendix 10-1 substitutes data on m/s-cap stocks for the data on large-cap stocks discussed up to this point. As shown in Table 10-5, Figures 10-4 through 10-6 (m/s-cap stocks) correspond with Figures 10-1 through Figures 10-3 (large-cap stocks).

Table 10-5: Comparison of figures relating to large-cap stocks and m/s-cap stocks.

	Large-Cap	*M/S-Cap*
Capital gains tax liability at end of holding period	Figure 10-1	Figure 10-4
Exemption from capital gains taxes at end of holding period	Figure 10-2	Figure 10-5
Alternative tax status at end of holding period	Figure 10-3	Figure 10-6

Our assumptions on m/s-cap stocks, differ from those for large-cap stocks in several respects. Table 10-6, which follows the pattern of Table 10-3, identifies areas of difference in boldface type.

Table 10-6: Comparison of assumptions relating to large-cap stocks and m/s-cap stocks.

Issue	*Large-Cap Assumptions*	*M/S-Cap Assumptions*
Prospective annual rate of return for the index	10% **(7% appreciation, 3% dividend yield)**	10% **(8.5% appreciation, 1.5% dividend yield)**
Fund AM: Forecasting advantage	Uncertain (relative to **large-cap index**)	Uncertain (relative to **m/s-cap index**)
Fund IDX: Cost advantage	Reflects **average large-cap costs,** Table 3-7.	Reflects **average m/s-cap costs,** Table 3-7.
Current and future capital gains tax rate	20%	20%
Current and future income tax ordinary rate	31%	31%
Anticipated holding period	As indicated	As indicated

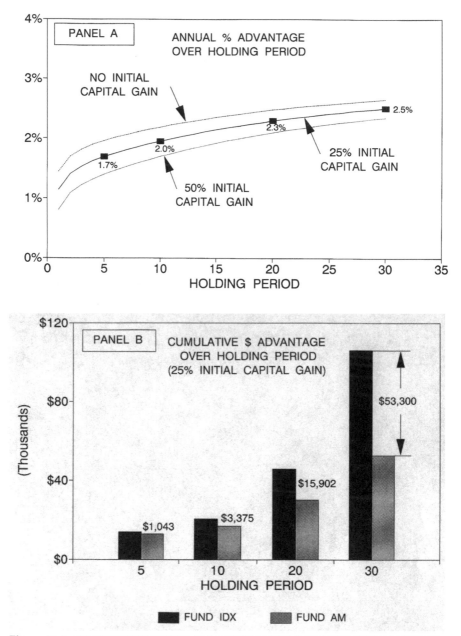

Figure 10-4: SWITCH FROM FUND AM TO FUND IDX (M/S-CAP MUTUAL FUNDS).
Advantage of switch with liability for capital gains taxes at end of holding period.

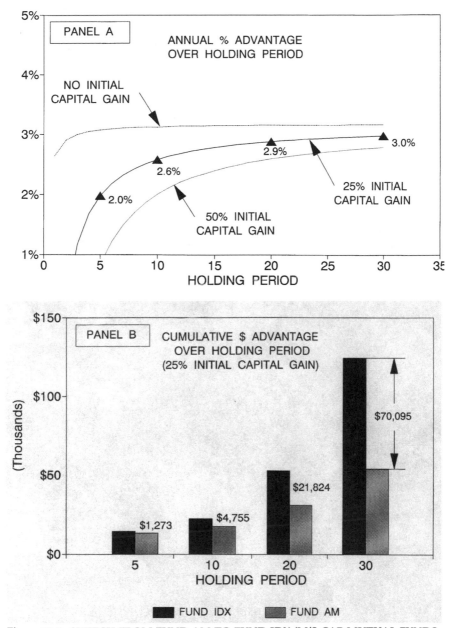

Figure 10-5: SWITCH FROM FUND AM TO FUND IDX (M/S-CAP MUTUAL FUNDS, NO CAPITAL GAINS AT END OF PERIOD). Advantage of switch with exemption for capital gains taxes at end of holding period.

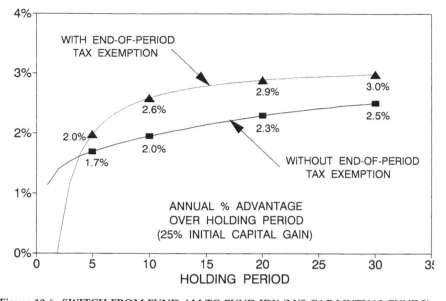

Figure 10-6: SWITCH FROM FUND AM TO FUND IDX (M/S-CAP MUTUAL FUNDS).
Advantage of switch (25% initial capital gain) with contrasting assumptions concerning capital gains taxes at end of holding period.

Appendix 10-2: Redirection of Dividend Reinvestment

Redirection of dividend reinvestment provides a method of gradually shifting assets from one fund to another. To illustrate, let's turn to the assumptions for large-cap actively managed equity mutual funds as explained in Chapter 3 and summarized in Table 10-4. The dividend payout of large-cap fund AM consists of two parts, as identified in Table 10-7. Distribution of income dividends, limited by the deduction of fund expenses, amounts to 1.8% of fund market value at the beginning of the year. Capital gains realized by the fund, reflecting allowance for transaction costs, translate into a dividend distribution of 4.6%. Total investment return, including unrealized capital gains of 1.9%, amount to 8.3% before taxes.

The redirection of dividend distributions permits gradual restructuring of the investment portfolio without redemption of the fund AM shares. Figure 10-7 provides comparisons over 5-, 10-, 20-, and 30-year time horizons. The first bar in each set represents the market value of fund AM with all dividends reinvested. The resulting growth compounds at an annual rate of 8.3%. The second bar, which assumes all dividends are redirected to another investment (such as fund IDX), shows growth at a much slower annual rate of 1.9%. By the end of five years, the redirection of dividend distributions has limited the market value of fund AM to about 75% of what it otherwise would have been. Comparable figures for 10, 20, and 30 years are 55%, 30%, and 15%, respectively. (The same analysis applied to m/s-cap stocks shows much the same results.)

Although redirection of dividend distributions, other things equal, gradually restructures the portfolio, additional opportuni-

Table 10-7: Total return for large-cap fund AM consists of dividends and unrealized capital gains.

	% Beg. Mkt. Val.	
Income Dividends	1.8%	
Capital Gains Dividends	4.6	
Total Dividends		6.4%
Unrealized Capital Gains		1.9
Total Return		8.3%

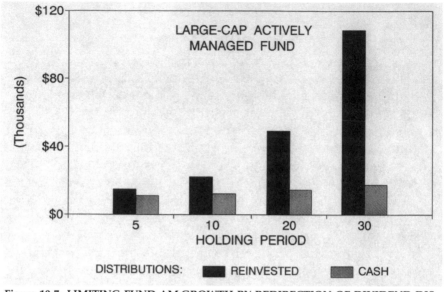

Figure 10-7: LIMITING FUND AM GROWTH BY REDIRECTION OF DIVIDEND DIS-TRIBUTIONS (LARGE-CAP). How redirection of dividend distributions limits growth of fund AM.

ties to accelerate the process often become available. You may direct additional cash contributions to other portfolio investments, more rapidly reducing the relative weight of fund AM. Unexpectedly, opportunities may develop to redeem shares of fund AM without incurring liability for capital gains taxes. Such opportunities could reflect realization of offsetting capital loss, change in the level of your personal income, revision in the tax laws or a substantial decline in stock prices.

chapter eleven

WHY INDEXING?

Two Contrasting Points of View

In the 1990s, two sharply contrasting approaches to investment, each representing a very different investment philosophy, compete for your attention. Since mutual funds increasingly provide the building blocks for portfolios of individual investors, they also serve as the format for our comparison of active investing and indexing:

- *Actively managed mutual funds*—representing the traditional approach to investing—confidently expect to achieve superior returns through superior forecasting.

- *Index mutual funds,* which have become practical in recent years as a result of advancing computer technology, look to a more predictable combination of advantages. The index fund advantage consists of lower costs, deferral of capital gains taxes, and control of risk through more complete diversification.

The investment approach presented in this book, although recognizing a role for active investing, places primary emphasis on indexing. Active investing serves as an option when you believe you are in a position to benefit from superior forecasting. In the event active investing fails, guidelines limit the risk. Indexing provides a significant advantage in the absence of superior forecasting. The growing use of indexing, first by institutional investors and now by individual investors, responds to the accumulating evidence concerning the performance of active investing. Even highly qualified active portfolio managers repeatedly demonstrate how difficult it is to produce returns better than can be explained by chance.

Revisiting the Record of Active Investing

Why is it that the investment professionals—who earn handsome compensation to anticipate returns in the financial markets—have not shown better results? Chapter 5 highlights the shortfall in returns reported by actively managed mutual funds in relation to broadly based stock market averages. As shown in Figure 11-1, actively managed portfolios serving tax-exempt pension funds report much the same shortfall in returns. Returns for the median manager in this large sample of equity portfolios exceeded those for the S&P 500 in only 4 of the past 15 years, with the average annual re-

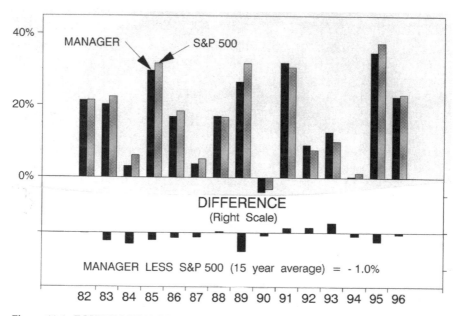

Figure 11-1: EQUITY MANAGER PERFORMANCE (15 YEARS, 1982-96). Performance of the median equity manager as measured against the S&P 500. (*Source:* Trust Universe Comparison Service (over 5000 institutional accounts at more than 300 plan sponsors with over $800 billion in total pension plan assets), Wilshire Associates, Inc., Santa Monica, CA, © 1997)

turn lagging the index by 1.0 percentage point. The shortfall would have been wider if, following the practice of mutual funds, portfolio returns had included allowance for management fees and other expenses.

Daunting Challenge

Active investing faces a daunting challenge for two reasons:

- Other investors with access to the same critical information available to you—or to your advisor—compete fiercely to gain advantage. As mispricings are discovered in the financial markets, intense competition rapidly moves market prices to narrow the opportunity. "Dumb" mistakes with the potential to result in mispricing, moreover, tend to offset each other, further limiting opportunities for you or other active investors to benefit.

- Forecasting skill for actively managed mutual funds not only has to be superior but sufficiently superior to more than offset the index fund cost advantage. In the absence of superior forecasting skill, such costs can account for startling differences in investor wealth over an extended period.

How Index Funds Gain Advantage

Index mutual funds, in comparison with actively managed mutual funds, depend on a combination of characteristics to gain advantage:

- Lower expense ratio
- Lower transaction costs, reflecting both lower turnover and lower cost per transaction
- Avoidance of sales loads
- Deferral of capital gains taxes
- Better control of risk through more complete diversification

Not all index funds qualify equally well by these standards. For example, expense ratios may vary widely, particularly where 12b-1 marketing expenses add to the total. In addition, a number of small index funds, although representing a tiny proportion of assets indexed by individuals, carry sales loads. Consulting the fund prospectuses will enable you to focus on the best-situated index fund candidates.

Ambitious Standard for Active Investing

While the index fund portfolio plan leaves room for active investing, it also presents an ambitious standard against which active investing is measured. Actively managed mutual funds must offset the index fund advantage just to equal the index fund returns. **The rule of 1-2-3,** reflecting a 20-year investment horizon as well as other assumptions spelled out in Chapter 5, addresses this issue. It shows that a representative actively managed large-cap stock fund, before allowance for expenses, transaction costs, and personal income taxes, would need to generate annual returns about 2 percentage points higher than the benchmark-index fund just to break even. The comparable figures are 1 percentage point for bond funds and 3 percentage points for small-cap stock funds.

How to Make Use of Indexing

Index funds serve not only as portfolio building blocks but also as tools for portfolio planning and as benchmarks for performance measurement. The six-item agenda presented in Chapter 10 outlines the steps. Through implementation of the agenda, you put together a combination of index funds that specifically meets your particular risk tolerance. Clearly defined guidelines allow for active investing—strategic departures from the index fund portfolio plan—within specified limits. Review of performance at least annually guards against wishful thinking and encourages timely portfolio adjustments.

"Do's and Don'ts"

Table 11-1 summarizes major points featured in previous chapters.

Table 11-1: Checklist for managing your portfolio.

What to Do	What Not to Do
Marker Portfolio	
Rely on history (summarized in Chapter 6) in developing the long-term plan for the asset mix that best meets your circumstances.	Don't let your choice of marker portfolio be influenced by current market forecasts, recent market experience or a choice by someone else (your circumstances are unlikely to coincide).
Index Fund Portfolio Plan	
Identify the combination of index funds that represents the asset mix of the marker portfolio, seeking to broaden diversification within each asset category.	Don't include taxable bond funds if comparable tax-exempt near-index fund offers a significantly better after-tax return.
Individual Index Funds	
Compare fund prospectuses, with particular emphasis on expense ratios, turnover and marketing costs.	Don't overlook other considerations, such as the strength of the fund family and services that may be particularly important to you.
S&P 500	
In anticipating future investment return, remember that the S&P 500 will lead m/s and foreign stocks in some years and lag one or both areas in other years.	Don't equate an S&P 500 index fund with a carefully planned, prudently diversified program of indexing over a long-term investment horizon.
Active Investing	
Evaluate actively managed alternatives in relation to the corresponding benchmark index fund.	Don't choose actively managed mutual funds that are overly burdened by high expense ratios, rapid turnover, or excessive marketing expenses (with special attention to sales loads).
Monitoring Performance	
Compute your performance at least annually, making use of unbiased short cuts where necessary.	Don't forget to make necessary allowances when comparing tax-exempt and taxable investments.
Agenda	
Establish an annual agenda that allows your investment program to bend rather than to break—and then stick to it.	Don't fall into either trap—paralyzing rigidity or undisciplined flexibility. Don't ignore necessary adjustments as circumstances change or let "This time is different!" disrupt your carefully planned investment program.

Future of Individual Indexing

Indexing by individual investors seems certain to account for an increasing share of individual investment portfolios over the longer term. There are three reasons:

- **Index Fund Advantage.** Individual investors, following the earlier pattern established by the large financial institutions, can be expected to make greater use of indexing as they better understand the index fund advantage. While in any year a portion of actively managed funds achieve higher returns than the corresponding index fund benchmark, a number of studies have shown how difficult it is to identify such funds in advance. More and more, this message is reaching individual investors. Consider the recent advice of Warren E. Buffett, Chairman of Berkshire Hathaway Inc. and widely recognized as among the most successful active managers. In his letter in the 1996 annual report of Berkshire Hathaway, Buffett includes the following counsel:

    > Let me add a few thoughts about your own investments. Most investors, both institutional and individual, will find that the best way to own common stocks is through an index fund that charges minimal fees. Those following this path are sure to beat the net results (after fees and expenses) delivered by the great majority of investment professionals.[1]

- **Opportunity to Invest in Index Funds.** The opportunity for individuals to invest in index mutual funds has widened dramatically in the last few years. As recently as 10 years ago, there were only 3 index mutual funds broadly available to individual investors. Now there are more than 70, with 4 of the 10 leading mutual fund families participating as well as over 30 other fund families. Moreover, a number of 401(k) plans and similar beneficiary-managed retirement plans offer plan participants additional index mutual funds.

- **Recognizing the Need.** In the last half of the 1990s, individuals increasingly recognize the need to take charge of investing for

---

[1]1996 Annual Report, Chairman's Letter, Berkshire Hathaway Inc., © 1997 by Warren E. Buffett.

their own retirement. Prospects for the Social Security retirement income and Medicare hospital and doctor insurance, which also provides financial support for retirees, are clouded by pressures to control future budget deficits of the Federal government. Defined-benefit pension plans, where the employer takes full responsibility for investment management, have been losing ground to 401(k) and other defined-contribution retirement plans that turn key investment decisions back to the beneficiary. Meanwhile, retirees are looking forward to living longer, while widespread downsizing in the corporate work force means early retirement (or fear of early retirement) for many employees.

Changing Patterns in the Financial Markets

Despite the promising long-term prospects for growth of individual indexing, changing patterns in the financial markets may temporarily delay—or even interrupt—the rate of progress. Over the three years ended 1996, two factors have created an unusually favorable environment for index funds.

- **Unusual Performance Gap.** Returns for a more-than-usual number of actively managed equity mutual funds have lagged those of the S&P 500. This extreme pattern reflects temporarily higher returns for large-cap stocks, heavily concentrated in the S&P 500, than for medium- and small-cap stocks, more heavily represented in actively managed mutual funds. Such temporary variations in return do not address the merits of indexing, which are more reliably supported by longer term comparisons over a wide range of market conditions. The recent shortfall of actively managed returns, nevertheless, has focused favorable attention on indexing, particularly since the S&P 500 serves as the target for more than half the assets in index funds.

- **Exceptional Equity Returns.** The stock market, as measured by the S&P 500, has reported a compound annual rate of return almost twice the long-term average over the same three years ended 1996. The dynamic upward trend in stock prices has clearly accelerated the net flow of cash into index mutual funds (as well as into mutual funds generally).

Maintaining Historical Perspective

Although either of these factors may account for substantial variations from year to year in the net cash flow into index funds, history shows that extremes in either direction largely offset each other
over an extended period. The extraordinary gains for indexing—
and particularly for S&P 500 index funds—in the last several years
are not a fair indication of future trends. In a similar way, a down-
turn in the stock market or a reversal of the pattern of returns relating to market capitalization would not provide reason for a different view of indexing. Whatever the shorter term pattern, we
would still expect that individual investors—in their own self-interest—would make greater use of indexing over the longer term.

Following the Institutional Pattern?

Institutional investors hold a smaller proportion of publicly traded
securities than do individual investors, but their investments in
index funds are much larger. Institutions have led the way in the
use of index funds for a number of reasons. In the early days of indexing, it was much easier to market the concept to a few large institutions than attempt to set up index mutual funds to attract
small investments from thousands of individual investors. The
professional investors in charge of large institutional funds, moreover, were often in a better position than individual investors to explore and evaluate what was then a radical innovation. Perhaps
most important have been differences in accountability. The fund
manager for a large retirement or endowment fund, facing quarterly performance measurement by outside consultants, must routinely defend the results. If an actively managed portfolio does not
perform as well as its index fund benchmark, the pressure is strong
to consider the index fund alternative. Individual investors, often
lacking an objective program of performance measurement as well
as outside pressure to account for results, understandably have
taken longer to recognize the merits of indexing.

So far, growth of indexing by individuals appears to have followed the pattern of institutional indexing with about a 10-year
lag. In Figure 11-2, the lower line of Panel A traces the dollar value
of equity index funds held by individuals at the end of each year
1990-96. The upper line in Panel A shows the comparable figure for

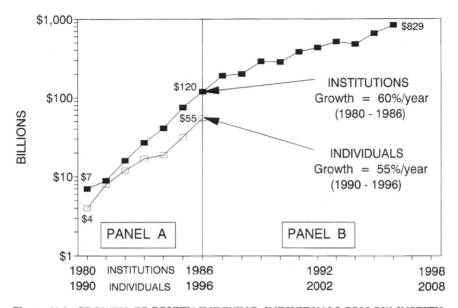

Figure 11-2: GROWTH OF EQUITY INDEXING, INDIVIDUALS FOLLOW INSTITU-TIONS? Recent growth of equity indexing for individual investors parallels that for institutional investors 10 years earlier. (*Sources: Pension & Investments,* Crain Communications, Inc., New York, NY, © 1997; *Morningstar Principia for Mutual Funds, January 1997,* Morningstar, Inc., Chicago, IL, © 1997; The Vanguard Group of Investment Companies, Valley Forge, PA)

equity indexing by institutions at the end of each year 1980-86—the same 6-year time interval but 10 years earlier. Over the indicated 6-year periods, the two series have traced similarly dramatic rates of compound annual growth, 55% and 60%, respectively. By way of perspective, Panel B displays the further growth of institutional indexing subsequent to year end 1986. Although the growth rate has tapered off over the past decade (to about 20% per year), index funds have continued to account for an increasing share of institutional portfolios during this period.

If the growth of individual indexing were to continue to follow the institutional pattern with a 10-year lag, holdings of equity index funds in individual portfolios would increase sevenfold to almost $400 billion over the next decade. While the history of institutional investing may not provide a reliable guide to the future of individual indexing, this projection serves as an illustration of the possible 10-year potential. What is important to you, however, is not what others do but, rather, your own investment portfolio. By starting to build your own index fund portfolio now, you can benefit over your investment horizon from (1) the index fund cost advantage, (2) deferral of capital gains taxes associated with low index fund turnover and (3) the improvement in risk control made possible by more complete index fund diversification.

INDEX